Census Regions and Divisions of the United States

MIDWEST

NORTHEAST

MN
WI
MI
IA
IL
IN
OH
MO
EAST NORTH CENTRAL

ME
NEW ENGLAND
VT
NH
MA
CT
RI
NY
MIDDLE ATLANTIC
PA
NJ

MD
DE
DC
WV
VA
KY
NC
TN
SOUTH ATLANTIC
SC
GA
FL
EAST SOUTH CENTRAL
AR
MS
AL
LA

SOUTH

LEGEND
REGION
DIVISION
STATE

Census Regions from www2.census.gov.

Children's
ATLAS
of the
U.S.A.
WASHINGTON
OREGON
WYOMING
NEVADA
COLORADO
KANSAS
IOWA
ILLINOIS
ARIZONA
NEW MEXICO
TEXAS
LOUISIANA
MISSISSIPPI
ALABAMA
GEORGIA
SOUTH CAROLINA
FLORIDA
MAINE
NH
MASS
CONN
Craig Froman

INTRODUCTION

First printing: July 2020
Fourth printing: August 2024

For information write:
Master Books, P.O. Box 726,
Green Forest, AR 72638

Master Books® is a division of the New Leaf Publishing Group, LLC

ISBN: 978-1-68344-194-6
ISBN: 978-1-61458-750-7 (digital)
Library of Congress Number: 2020935298

Cover & Interior by
Diana Bogardus

Unless otherwise noted, Scripture is from the English Standard Version (ESV) of the Bible.

Printed in China

Please visit our website for other great titles:

www.masterbooks.com

Craig Froman was born in California (in the West), then moved to Missouri (in the Midwest), and now he lives with his precious wife and kids in Arkansas (in the South). The year before he started 6th grade, his family loaded up in a camper and drove for six weeks around the United States, traveling through 31 states and exploring so many wonders of God's world. He's since traveled to 40 of the 50 states, including Hawaii, and loves all the places he's been able to see with his own eyes. Now he is the assistant editor at New Leaf Publishing Group and author of *Passport to the World* and *Children's Atlas of God's World*. He has a Bachelor of Arts in business administration and a master's degree in education.

AMERICA BEGINS! There are just about 200 countries in the world today. Each has wondrous people, whom God made in His image, and beautiful natural wonders, including some with mountains, rivers, and vast, grassy plains. Countries are recognized areas of land all over the earth with people who rule their own territory and have no other country that rules over them. This book's focus is on one particular country, the United States of America. While some countries in the world have been around for thousands of years, like Egypt and China, and others no longer exist, like the Roman Empire and Persia, America is fairly young. The birthdate, or independence date, of America is July 4, 1776, so it is a little less than 250 years old!

The first people who settled and lived in the area that has become the United States were the Native American people, sometimes called indigenous people or first peoples. Several thousand years ago, they walked across an area called the Bering Land Bridge or Bering Strait, which was created during the Ice Age. This bridge of ice connected the continent of Asia with the North American continent.

The first European settlers of the United States came primarily from Spain and Great Britain. The first 13 states were once colonies of Great Britain. These 13 original states have grown to 50 states, with additional territories as well. There are now people living here from all over the world!

GOVERNMENT SYSTEM The government system of the United States is called a constitutional federal republic. This means that there is a document, called a constitution, that guides the representatives who help make laws and interpret the laws, and these representatives are voted for by the people of the country. The head of the government, called the president, is elected for four-year terms. The people who govern the country, which includes the president, the Senate (100 people), the House of Representatives (435 people), and the U.S. Supreme Court (9 justices), meet in Washington, D.C.

THE AMERICAN LANDSCAPE At 3.8 million square miles, the United States is the third-largest country by size (after Russia and Canada), with the third-largest population (after China and India). The country has nearly every kind of biome that is found throughout the world, including vast plains, high mountain regions, frozen tundra, broad river valleys, and volcanic islands. These very different areas obviously have very different kinds of weather too, including arctic areas in Alaska, tropical areas in Hawaii and Florida, plains with semiarid weather, and arid weather in the southwest.

The natural resources found in the country reflect the wonderful diversity of the biomes above ground and the minerals within the earth. This includes coal, copper, gold, mercury, natural gas, petroleum, timber, and uranium. And the United States exports or sends out more food products around the world than any other country. This includes chicken, corn, milk, soybeans, sugar cane, and wheat.

The economy of the United States remains one of the strongest in the world. It is considered the most powerful in the areas of aerospace and military, computers, and pharmaceuticals.

THE ROAD AHEAD The name "America" comes from an Italian explorer and mapmaker, Amerigo Vespucci (1454–1512). Soon after he first sailed to what is now known as South America, there were people making their way to the New World to make a new home for themselves. Soon, people would come from all parts of the world. Some came for religious freedom or freedom to express their own beliefs openly, others were escaping violent oppression and war, while others came for economic or educational opportunities. Even now there are people wanting to come to this land of opportunity.

A sonnet called "The New Colossus" by Emma Lazarus was written in 1883 and was used to raise money to help build the base of the Statue of Liberty. This poem was eventually put on an interior wall of the base, or pedestal, of the statue. It speaks of all those who have come to this country to seek a better life, the Statue of Liberty and America becoming for them a Mother of Exiles:

Not like the brazen giant of Greek fame,
With conquering limbs astride from land to land;
Here at our sea-washed, sunset gates shall stand
A mighty woman with a torch, whose flame
Is the imprisoned lightning, and her name
Mother of Exiles. From her beacon-hand
Glows world-wide welcome; her mild eyes command
The air-bridged harbor that twin cities frame.
"Keep, ancient lands, your storied pomp!" cries she
With silent lips. "Give me your tired, your poor,
Your huddled masses yearning to breathe free,
The wretched refuse of your teeming shore.
Send these, the homeless, tempest-tost to me,
I lift my lamp beside the golden door!"

GOD'S DESIRE FOR THE NATIONS Speaking some two thousand years ago of people and nations, the apostle Paul said in Acts 17:24–26:

> The God who made the world and everything in it, being Lord of heaven and earth, does not live in temples made by man, nor is he served by human hands, as though he needed anything, since he himself gives to all mankind life and breath and everything. And he made from one man every nation of mankind to live on all the face of the earth, having determined allotted periods and the boundaries of their dwelling place.

So, all of us came from Adam and Eve. There are not races of people, but only the human race. And though we live in different countries and often see more differences than similarities between us, it's God's desire that all would be saved (1 Timothy 2:4).

Jesus shared this desire that His truth would be taken to all nations. He said, "Go therefore and make disciples of all nations, baptizing them in the name of the Father and of the Son and of the Holy Spirit, teaching them to observe all that I have commanded you. And behold, I am with you always, to the end of the age" (Matthew 28:19–20).

TABLE OF CONTENTS

THE KEY TO YOUR CHILDREN'S ATLAS OF THE U.S.

Welcome to your wondrous journey of the United States! Here's what to watch for along the way to help you get the most out of each step.

CHRISTIAN FOUNDATIONS

Each state's preamble shows the ***godly beginnings*** of its constitutions.

BLUE PINS

When you see a blue pin in the book, you'll find that numbered pin on the map to designate a geographic location.

Note: State regions are based on the U.S. Census Bureau.

INNESOTA
50
MICHIGAN
WISCONSIN
102
MICHIGAN
48
IOWA
34
ILLINOIS
30
INDIANA
32
OHIO
74
MISSOURI
54
KENTUCKY
38
WEST VIRGINIA
100
VIRGINIA
96
D.C.
106
MD
44
DE
20
NJ
64
PENNSYLVANIA
80
NEW YORK
68
CONN
18
RI
82
MASS
46
VT
94
NH
62
MAINE
42
NORTH CAROLINA
70
SOUTH CAROLINA
84
TENNESSEE
88
ARKANSAS
12
MISSISSIPPI
52
ALABAMA
6
GEORGIA
24
LOUISIANA
40
FLORIDA
22
N
S
E
W
A
WONDERS IN GOD'S WORLD
The lettered red flags denote special sites that have been preserved as national or state parks or monuments within each state.

ALABAMA

ALABAMA PREAMBLE

We the people of the State of Alabama, in order to establish justice, insure domestic tranquility, and secure the blessings of liberty to ourselves and our posterity, invoking the favor and guidance of ***Almighty God***, do ordain and establish the following Constitution and form of government for the State of Alabama.

Statehood	1819 (22nd state)
Population ranking	24th
Capital	Montgomery
State flower	Camellia
State bird	Yellowhammer
Nickname	The Yellowhammer State / The Heart of Dixie
Highest point	Cheaha Mountain, 2,413 feet

911
Emergency Call
calling...

Most people have learned the three-digit number used to call for help in an emergency. Alabama was the first state to use 911 for emergencies back in 1968.

Alabama is a state in the American South. It became the 22nd state in 1819 and has an official state song appropriately called "Alabama." And the state fossil? The *Basilosaurus cetoides*, of course!

1 Spanish explorers sailed around the Mobile Bay area as early as 1500. They marked it on their maps as Bahia del Espiritu Sancto, or the Bay of the Holy Spirit. The first European to sail into the bay was Admiral Alvarez de Pineda of Spain in 1519.

We should all know the name of Dr. Luther Leonidas Hill. He performed the first open-heart surgery in the Western Hemisphere in 1902. He was able to suture a stab wound that pierced a young boy's heart.

2 Welcome to the Space Camp in Huntsville. Trainees come here from all 50 states, as well as more than 120 nations around the world. It's considered the second-largest research park in the United States.

A **Freedom Riders National Monument**

In 1961, a group of "Freedom Riders" set out on a bus to challenge laws that were discriminatory. At that time, blacks and whites had to be separated on buses, in waiting areas, at lunch counters, and in restrooms. Here in Anniston, you can explore this story of the Civil Rights movement.

B **Russell Cave National Monument**

This cave is also an archaeological site. It has information on the early native cultures who lived in this area. Several thousand years ago, part of the entrance to the cave collapsed, creating a sheltered area for the people who lived here.

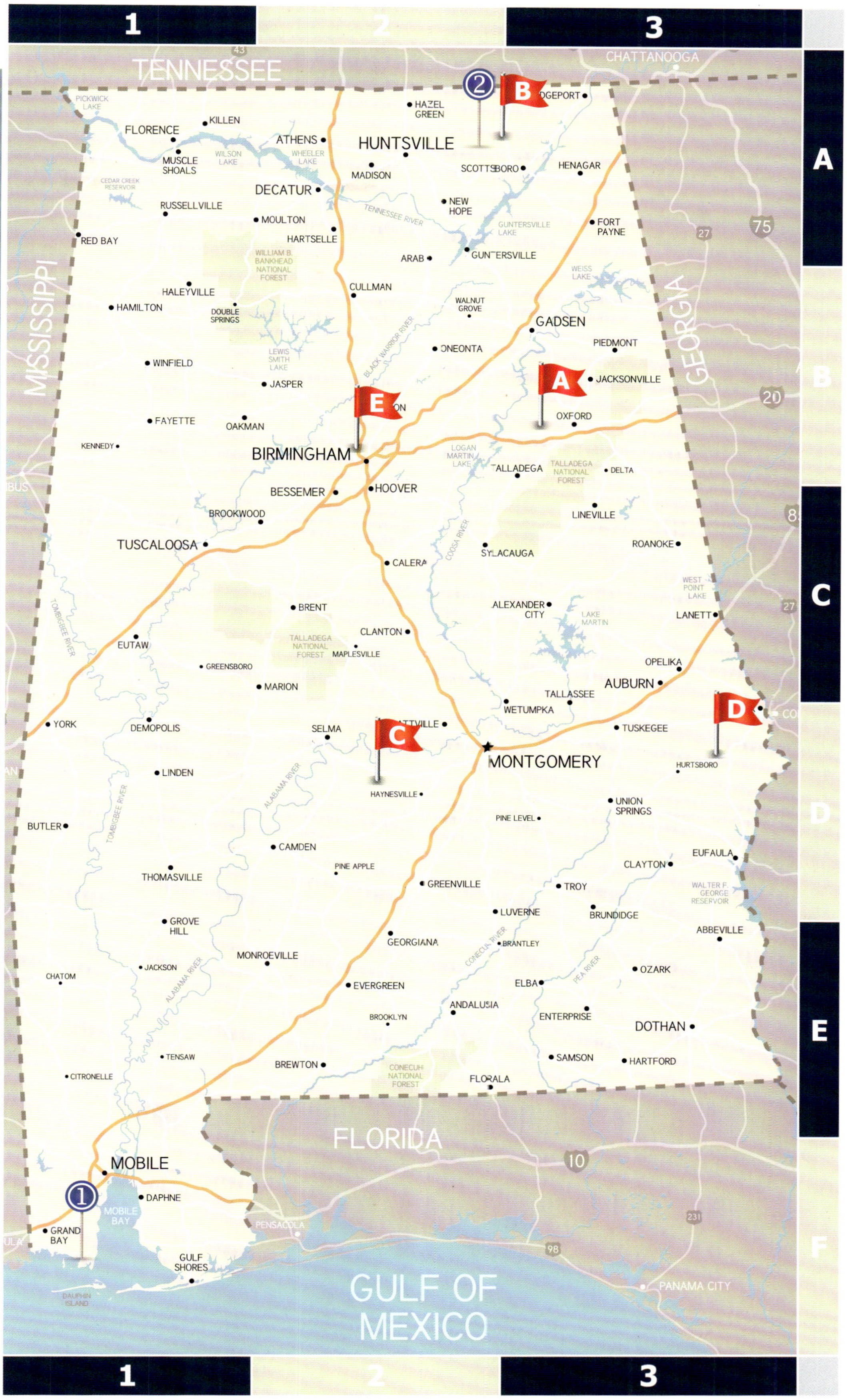

C **Selma to Montgomery National Historic Trail**

On August 6, 1965, President Lyndon Johnson signed the Voting Rights Act of 1965. This gave equal voting rights to African Americans. Trace the 54-mile trail of those who marched for freedom and see their stories at various Interpretive Centers.

D **Tuskegee Airmen National Historic Site**

Come share the adventure here of the first African American military pilots who came to be called the "Red Tails." Their story started at Moton Field in Tuskegee, Alabama.

1 2 3

TENNESSEE
MISSISSIPPI
GEORGIA
FLORIDA
GULF OF MEXICO
HUNTSVILLE
BIRMINGHAM
MONTGOMERY
MOBILE
TUSCALOOSA
GADSDEN
DECATUR
FLORENCE
SELMA
AUBURN
DOTHAN
A B C D E F

E **Birmingham Civil Rights National Monument**

In 1963, Birmingham, Alabama, was filled with scenes of violent aggression toward non-violent protestors seeking civil rights for all. Now, the Gaston Motel where Dr. King and others stayed has been set aside as a National Monument to peace.

ALASKA

ALASKA PREAMBLE

We the people of Alaska, grateful to ***God*** and to those who founded our nation and pioneered this great land, in order to secure and transmit to succeeding generations our heritage of political, civil, and religious liberty within the Union of States, do ordain and establish this constitution for the State of Alaska.

Statehood	1959 (49th state)
Population ranking	48th
Capital	Juneau
State flower	Forget-me-not
State bird	Willow ptarmigan
Nickname	The Last Frontier
Highest point	Denali, or Mount McKinley, 20,310 feet

Alaska is considered part of the West Region, the largest region of the country. In 1959 it became the 49th state. The official song of the state is called "Alaska's Flag." And the state dog? The Alaskan Malamute!

CANADA

In 1784, Russian whalers and fur traders like these white fox traders established the first settlements in Alaska. It stayed a part of Russia for nearly 100 years.

1 2 3 4

In 1867, William H. Seward, who was the U.S. Secretary of State, offered Russia two cents per acre for Alaska, which included the Aleutian Islands. The total cost was $7,200,000, and so on October 18, 1867, the area became the property of the United States. At the time, many thought that this was a bad deal, so they called it "Seward's Folly."

Eyak, Iñupiat (eh-NEW-pea-ack), and Yupik are the names of some of the native peoples of Alaska. Their ancestors would have left the Tower of Babel then traveled to Alaska thousands of years ago.

A Denali National Park

This national park is 6 million acres of mostly native landscape. Denali, the tallest mountain in North America, rises here, while wild animals wander this beautiful wilderness of God's making.

B Gates of the Arctic National Park

You won't find roads getting in your way as you walk through this wilderness. Look out at the valleys carved by glaciers, the caribou walking the unfenced land, the beautiful rivers, and so much more.

C Tongass National Forest

At 16.7 million acres, the Tongass National Forest is the largest national forest in the United States.

D Glacier Bay National Park

Here in Glacier Bay, you can experience the cold wonder of glaciers remaining from the Ice Age that occurred after the Flood. These 3.3 million acres also have rocky mountains, beautiful fjords, and even temperate rainforests.

E Kenai Fjords National Park

You can discover more of the lingering Ice Age here, where nearly 40 glaciers flow out of the Harding Icefield. There is also plenty of wildlife roaming these chilly lands.

F Wrangell-St. Elias National Park

This park is vast, stretching from the sea all the way up to 18,008 feet. At 13.2 million acres, the National Park Service declares that it is the size of Yellowstone National Park, Yosemite National Park, and the country of Switzerland combined!

ARIZONA

ARIZONA PREAMBLE

We the people of the State of Arizona, grateful to ***Almighty God*** for our liberties, do ordain this Constitution.

Statehood	1912 (48th state)
Population ranking	14th
Capital	Phoenix
State flower	Blossom of the Saguaro Cactus
State bird	Cactus wren
Nickname	The Grand Canyon State
Highest point	Humphreys Peak, 12,637 feet

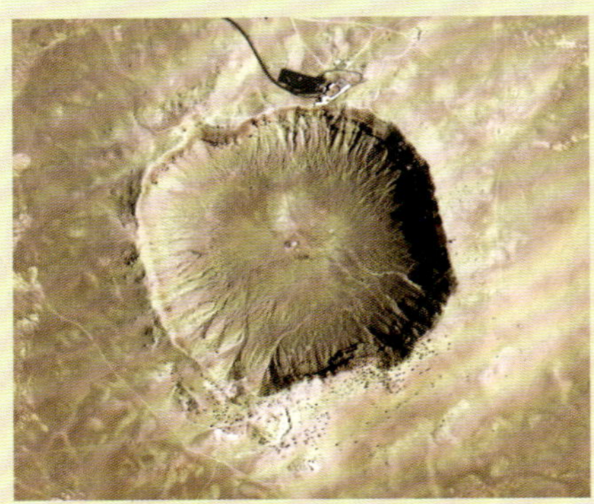

Meteor Crater is a cavity in the Earth that is 4,200 feet wide and 570 feet deep. It is what remains of a meteorite impact.

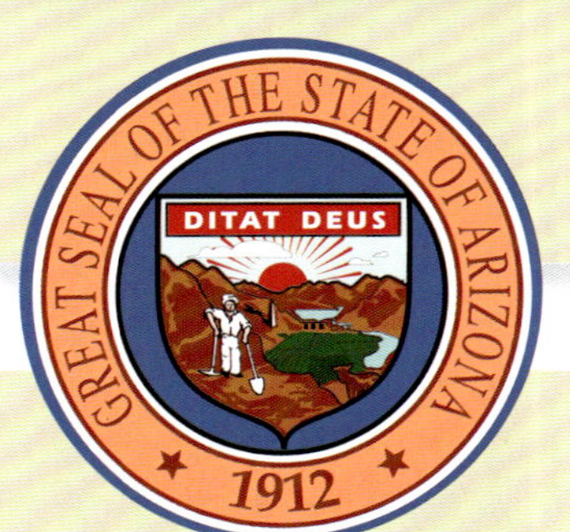

Arizona is a part of the West Region. It became the 48th state in 1912, and "Arizona" is their state song. And the state reptile? The Arizona Ridge-Nosed Rattlesnake!

The Spanish were the first Europeans to find the area we now know as Arizona. This was back in the 1500s. They encountered a vibrant population of native peoples here at that time.

① Come to Kitt Peak National Observatory when you get a chance. It has the world's largest solar telescope for use in their daytime studies of the sun and many other astronomical programs.

At one time, the U.S. Army talked about having a Camel Corps, especially out in the Southwestern United States, including Arizona. The military found that they were very hardy in the desert areas, but they eventually decided against them. The last camels were seen roaming in Arizona in 1891.

(Hi Jolly Camel Driver's Tomb Quartzsite Arizona, USA)

② The Arizona capitol building has a copper roof. It is enough copper to make 4,800,000 pennies.

A Grand Canyon National Park

Come see this massive canyon carved by the receding waters of the Great Flood. The Grand Canyon is 277 river miles long, up to 18 miles wide in parts, and a mile deep. It's one of the oldest national parks in the United States.

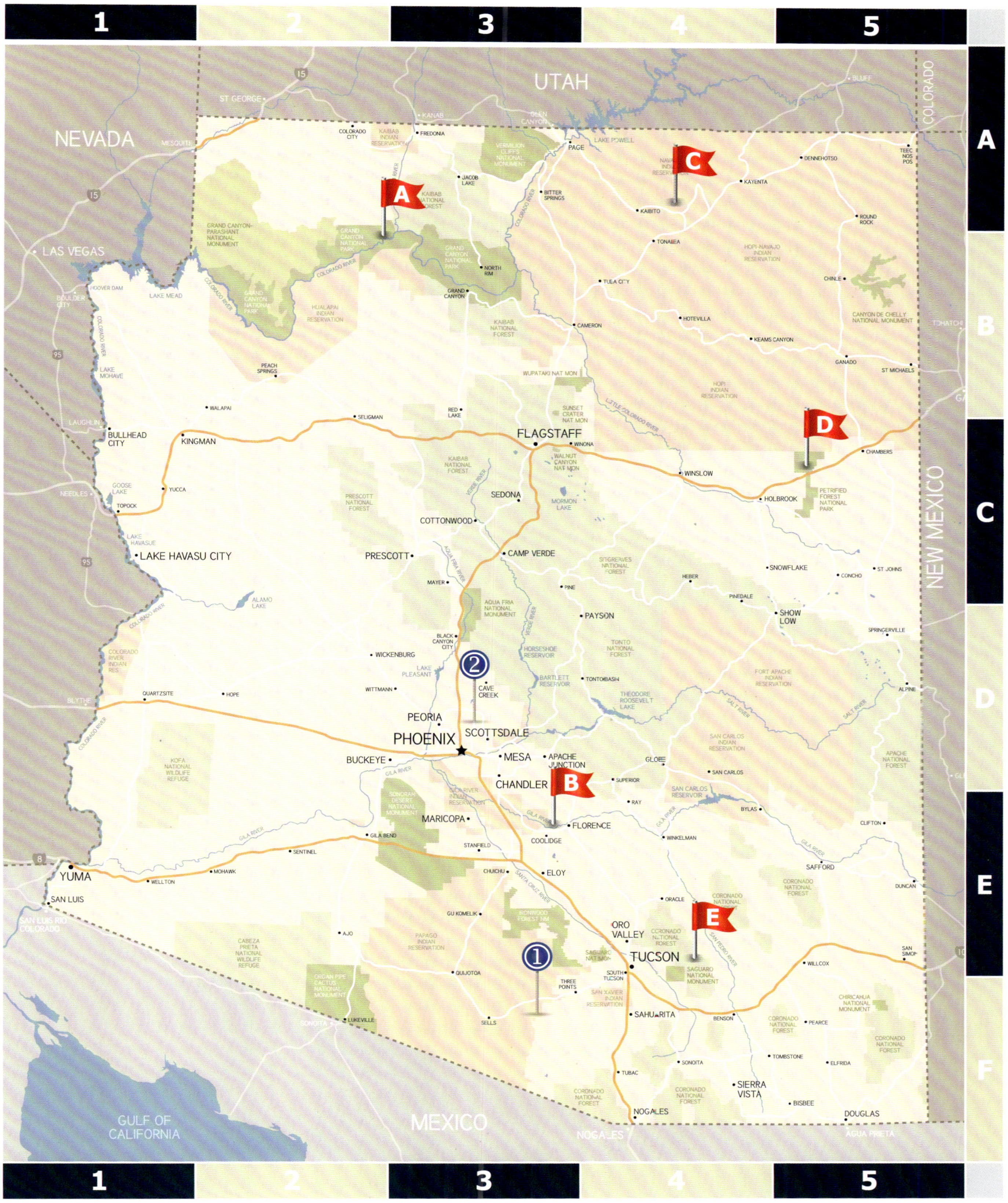

B Casa Grande Ruins National Monument

Casa Grande, or Great House, is a historical site that gives us a glimpse into the life of the Sonoran Desert people who once lived here. There is even evidence of wide-scale irrigation that helped make the desert thrive until the area was abandoned around A.D. 1450.

C Navajo National Monument

This monument to honor and preserve the cultural heritage of the Pueblo people was established in 1909. You can see the cliff dwellings of the Navajo (NAH-veh-hoe) people who lived in this area from A.D. 1250 to A.D. 1300.

D Petrified Forest National Park

Named as such because it is one of the world's largest areas covered in petrified wood, this wondrous park is 230 square miles. Portions of it are covered in painted desert lands, some of which are colorful badlands, but everything is amazing.

E Saguaro National Park

Here near the Tucson area, you'll find one of the nation's largest cactus species. It's called the giant saguaro (sah-GWAR-oh), and it is known as a symbol of the American West. The beauty of these cacti contrasts with the harsh desert to make a wondrous display of God's glory in His creation.

ARKANSAS

ARKANSAS PREAMBLE

We, the People of the State of Arkansas, grateful to ***Almighty God*** for the privilege of choosing our own form of government; for our civil and religious liberty; and desiring to perpetuate its blessings, and secure the same to our selves and posterity; do ordain and establish this Constitution.

Statehood	1836 (25th state)
Population ranking	33rd
Capital	Little Rock
State flower	Apple blossom
State bird	Mockingbird
Nickname	The Natural State
Highest point	Mount Magazine, 2,753 feet

The Great Passion Play in Eureka Springs is set in an outdoor amphitheater with live animals and a cast of 150 actors in period costume. They recreate Christ's last days on Earth.

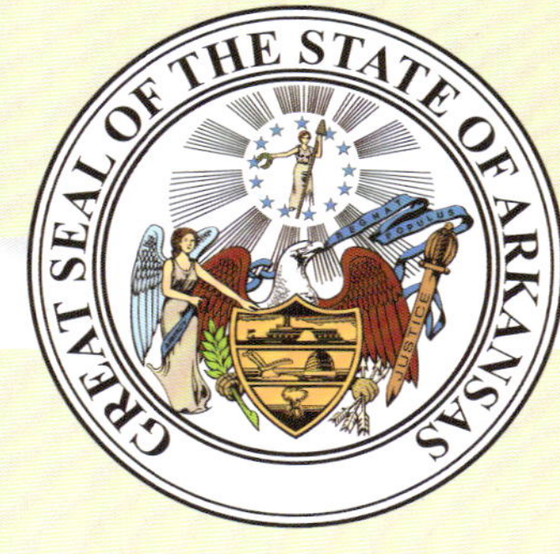

Arkansas is a state in the South. In 1836 it became the 25th state. "Arkansas" is the state anthem. And the state musical instrument? The fiddle!

① President William Jefferson Clinton Birthplace Home National Historic Site — See the birthplace of the 42nd president of the United States, where he was born on August 19, 1946.

② Texarkana is the mash-up name of the town that borders both Texas and Arkansas. The post office and the courthouse were built on the state line, with the main entrance in both states.

③ Come see why the community of Mountain View is sometimes called the Folk Capital of America. They are not only home to one of the largest producers of handmade dulcimers in the world, but the town preserves the pioneer way of life in other ways too. See it all at the Ozark Folk Center State Park from March through October.

Rice has replaced cotton as the primary crop of the state. At times, Arkansas has grown nearly half of the rice produced in the United States.

The first Europeans to visit this area were the Spanish in 1541. The first of these Europeans was Spanish explorer Hernando de Soto, who crossed the Mississippi and marched across central Arkansas and the Ozark Mountains. It became a part of the United States after the Louisiana Purchase in 1803.

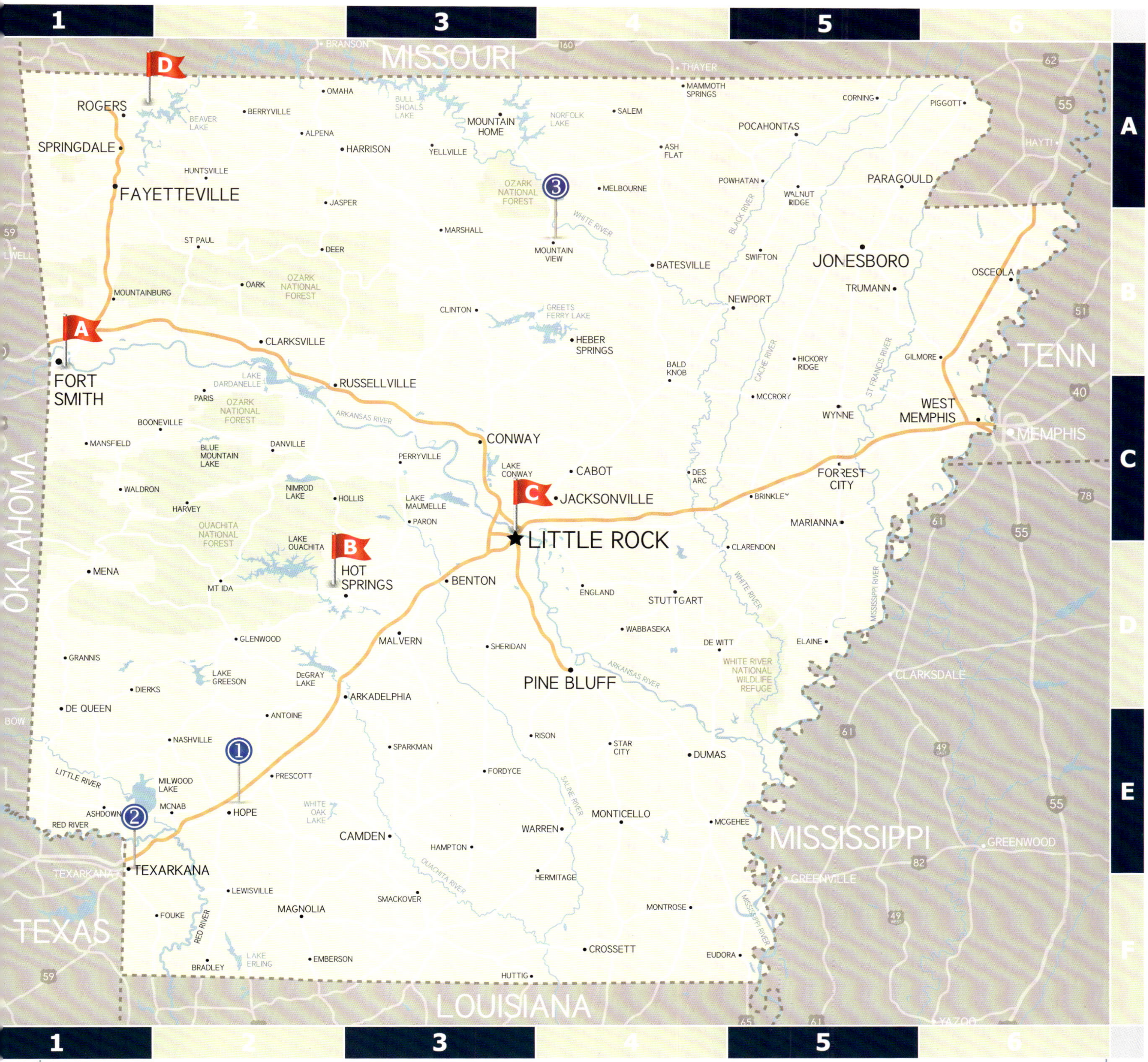

1 2 3 4 5 6

A B C D E F

MISSOURI
BRANSON
THAYER
MAMMOTH SPRINGS
CORNING
PIGGOTT
HAYTI
ROGERS
SPRINGDALE
BEAVER LAKE
BERRYVILLE
OMAHA
BULL SHOALS LAKE
MOUNTAIN HOME
NORFOLK LAKE
SALEM
POCAHONTAS
ALPENA
HARRISON
YELLVILLE
ASH FLAT
HUNTSVILLE
FAYETTEVILLE
JASPER
OZARK NATIONAL FOREST
MELBOURNE
POWHATAN
WALNUT RIDGE
PARAGOULD
BLACK RIVER
WHITE RIVER
MARSHALL
MOUNTAIN VIEW
ST PAUL
DEER
BATESVILLE
SWIFTON
JONESBORO
OSCEOLA
TRUMANN
MOUNTAINBURG
OARK
CLINTON
GREERS FERRY LAKE
NEWPORT
FORT SMITH
CLARKSVILLE
HEBER SPRINGS
BALD KNOB
CACHE RIVER
HICKORY RIDGE
ST FRANCIS RIVER
GILMORE
TENN
LAKE DARDANELLE
PARIS
RUSSELLVILLE
MCCRORY
WYNNE
WEST MEMPHIS
MEMPHIS
BOONEVILLE
ARKANSAS RIVER
MANSFIELD
BLUE MOUNTAIN LAKE
DANVILLE
CONWAY
PERRYVILLE
LAKE CONWAY
CABOT
DES ARC
FORREST CITY
WALDRON
NIMROD LAKE
HOLLIS
LAKE MAUMELLE
JACKSONVILLE
BRINKLEY
HARVEY
PARON
MARIANNA
OKLAHOMA
OUACHITA NATIONAL FOREST
LAKE OUACHITA
HOT SPRINGS
LITTLE ROCK
CLARENDON
MENA
MT IDA
BENTON
ENGLAND
STUTTGART
MISSISSIPPI RIVER
GLENWOOD
MALVERN
SHERIDAN
WABBASEKA
DE WITT
ELAINE
GRANNIS
LAKE GREESON
DEGRAY LAKE
PINE BLUFF
WHITE RIVER NATIONAL WILDLIFE REFUGE
CLARKSDALE
DIERKS
ARKADELPHIA
DE QUEEN
ANTOINE
NASHVILLE
SPARKMAN
RISON
STAR CITY
DUMAS
LITTLE RIVER
MILWOOD LAKE
PRESCOTT
FORDYCE
SALINE RIVER
ASHDOWN
MCNAB
HOPE
WHITE OAK LAKE
MONTICELLO
MCGEHEE
RED RIVER
CAMDEN
WARREN
MISSISSIPPI
GREENWOOD
HAMPTON
TEXARKANA
OUACHITA RIVER
HERMITAGE
GREENVILLE
LEWISVILLE
SMACKOVER
MAGNOLIA
MONTROSE
FOUKE
TEXAS
LAKE ERLING
EMBERSON
CROSSETT
EUDORA
BRADLEY
HUTTIG
LOUISIANA
YAZOO

WONDERS IN GOD'S WORLD

A Fort Smith National Historic Site

Fort Smith was first established on December 25, 1817. The historic site details the history of the fort through 1896, when it was considered a part of Indian Territory. See stories of soldiers, the native people, outlaws of the territory, and lawmen keeping the peace.

B Hot Springs National Park

People have known of these God-created hot and cold springs for several thousand years. In the early 1800s, the first Europeans started coming to soak in the geothermal waters that were thought to bring healing.

C Little Rock Central High School National Historic Site

This is the only operating high school in America that is designated as a National Historic Site. Come learn of the nine black teens during the Civil Rights era who struggled to help bring equality to the school system and beyond.

D Pea Ridge National Military Park

This former battlefield recalls what happened on March 7–8, 1862. This was the most significant battle of the Civil War west of the Mississippi River, where 23,000 soldiers fought for the future of the union in the Midwest.

CALIFORNIA

CALIFORNIA PREAMBLE

We, the People of the State of California, grateful to ***Almighty God*** for our freedom, in order to secure and perpetuate its blessings, do establish this Constitution.

Statehood	1850 (31st state)
Population ranking	1st
Capital	Sacramento
State flower	Golden poppy
State bird	California valley quail
Nickname	The Golden State
Highest point	Mount Whitney, 14,505 feet

When it first opened in 1937, the Golden Gate Bridge was the longest (4,200 feet) and the tallest (746 feet) suspension bridge in the world.

California is in the West Region of the U.S., and Los Angeles is the largest city in this region. It became the 31st state in 1850, and "I Love You, California" is the state song. And the state fabric? That would be denim!

1. Death Valley is known as the hottest and the driest place in the United States. Sometimes the summer temperatures reach as high as 115ºF or more!

2. One of the world's most productive agricultural areas is the San Joaquin Valley. They are a major exporter of fruits, nuts, and vegetables to places all around the world.

The first Spanish and English explorers saw California in the 1500s. The first Spanish missions here began in 1769.

3. Want to see the tallest trees on earth? Come to California! Here you'll find the giant redwoods, which can easily grow as tall as 300 feet. And the largest of the redwoods? Well, that would be Hyperion, a tree that is right around 380 feet tall! The giant sequoias here are big too, like the General Sherman, the largest single stem tree in the world.

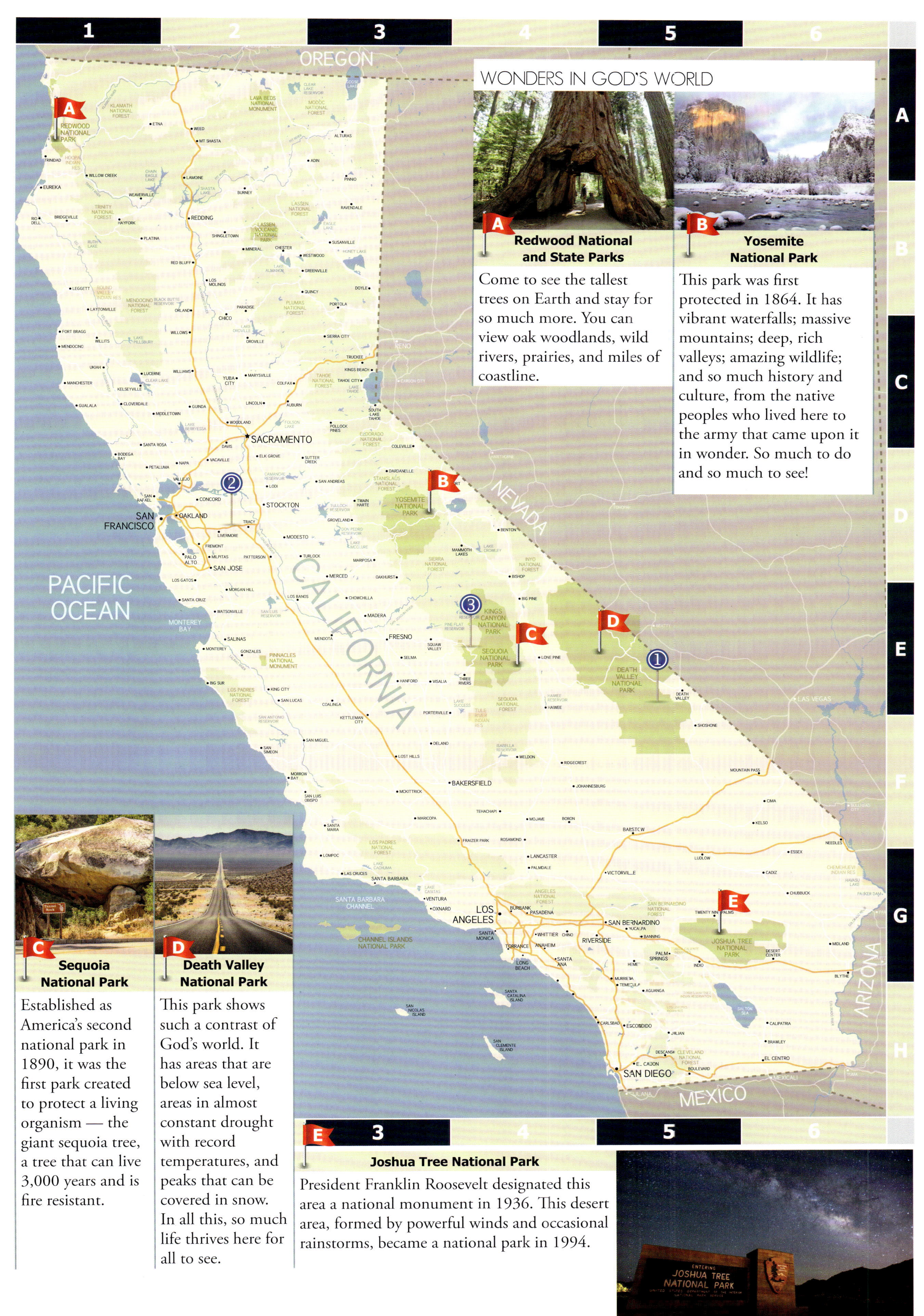
WONDERS IN GOD'S WORLD
A Redwood National and State Parks
Come to see the tallest trees on Earth and stay for so much more. You can view oak woodlands, wild rivers, prairies, and miles of coastline.
B Yosemite National Park
This park was first protected in 1864. It has vibrant waterfalls; massive mountains; deep, rich valleys; amazing wildlife; and so much history and culture, from the native peoples who lived here to the army that came upon it in wonder. So much to do and so much to see!
C Sequoia National Park
Established as America's second national park in 1890, it was the first park created to protect a living organism — the giant sequoia tree, a tree that can live 3,000 years and is fire resistant.
D Death Valley National Park
This park shows such a contrast of God's world. It has areas that are below sea level, areas in almost constant drought with record temperatures, and peaks that can be covered in snow. In all this, so much life thrives here for all to see.
E Joshua Tree National Park
President Franklin Roosevelt designated this area a national monument in 1936. This desert area, formed by powerful winds and occasional rainstorms, became a national park in 1994.
ENTERING JOSHUA TREE NATIONAL PARK
1 2 3 4 5 6
A B C D E F G H
OREGON
NEVADA
ARIZONA
MEXICO
CALIFORNIA
PACIFIC OCEAN
SACRAMENTO
SAN FRANCISCO
OAKLAND
SAN JOSE
STOCKTON
FRESNO
BAKERSFIELD
LOS ANGELES
SAN BERNARDINO
RIVERSIDE
SAN DIEGO
REDWOOD NATIONAL PARK
YOSEMITE NATIONAL PARK
KINGS CANYON NATIONAL PARK
SEQUOIA NATIONAL PARK
DEATH VALLEY NATIONAL PARK
JOSHUA TREE NATIONAL PARK
CHANNEL ISLANDS NATIONAL PARK
SANTA BARBARA CHANNEL

COLORADO

COLORADO PREAMBLE

We, the people of Colorado, with profound reverence for the ***Supreme Ruler of the Universe***, in order to form a more independent and perfect government; establish justice; insure tranquility; provide for the common defense; promote the general welfare and secure the blessings of liberty to ourselves and our posterity, do ordain and establish this constitution for the "State of Colorado."

Statehood	1876 (38th state)
Population ranking	21st
Capital	Denver
State flower	Rocky mountain columbine
State bird	Lark bunting
Nickname	The Centennial State
Highest point	Mount Elbert, 14,440 feet

Historic gold specimen from Telluride, Colorado

Colorado is a part of the West Region. In 1876, Colorado became the 38th state. They have two state songs, which are "Where the Columbines Grow" and "Rocky Mountain High." And the state pets? Rescue dogs and cats.

The Pueblo (PWEB-low) people lived here from around A.D. 600 to A.D. 1300. It wasn't until 1541 that the first Europeans saw the area.

1. Denver hosts one of the world's largest rodeos every year. It's called the Western Stock Show. The very first rodeo in Colorado was on July 4, 1869 in Deer Trail.

2. Katherine Lee Bates wrote "America the Beautiful" back in 1893 after being inspired by a visit to Pikes Peak in Colorado. The first verse of the song shares the joy of God's world:

O beautiful for spacious skies
For amber waves of grain
For purple mountain majesties
Above the fruited plain!
America! America!
God shed his grace on thee
And crown thy good with brotherhood
From sea to shining sea.

3. Want to know the highest incorporated city in the whole United States? That would be Leadville, Colorado, at an altitude of 10,152 feet.

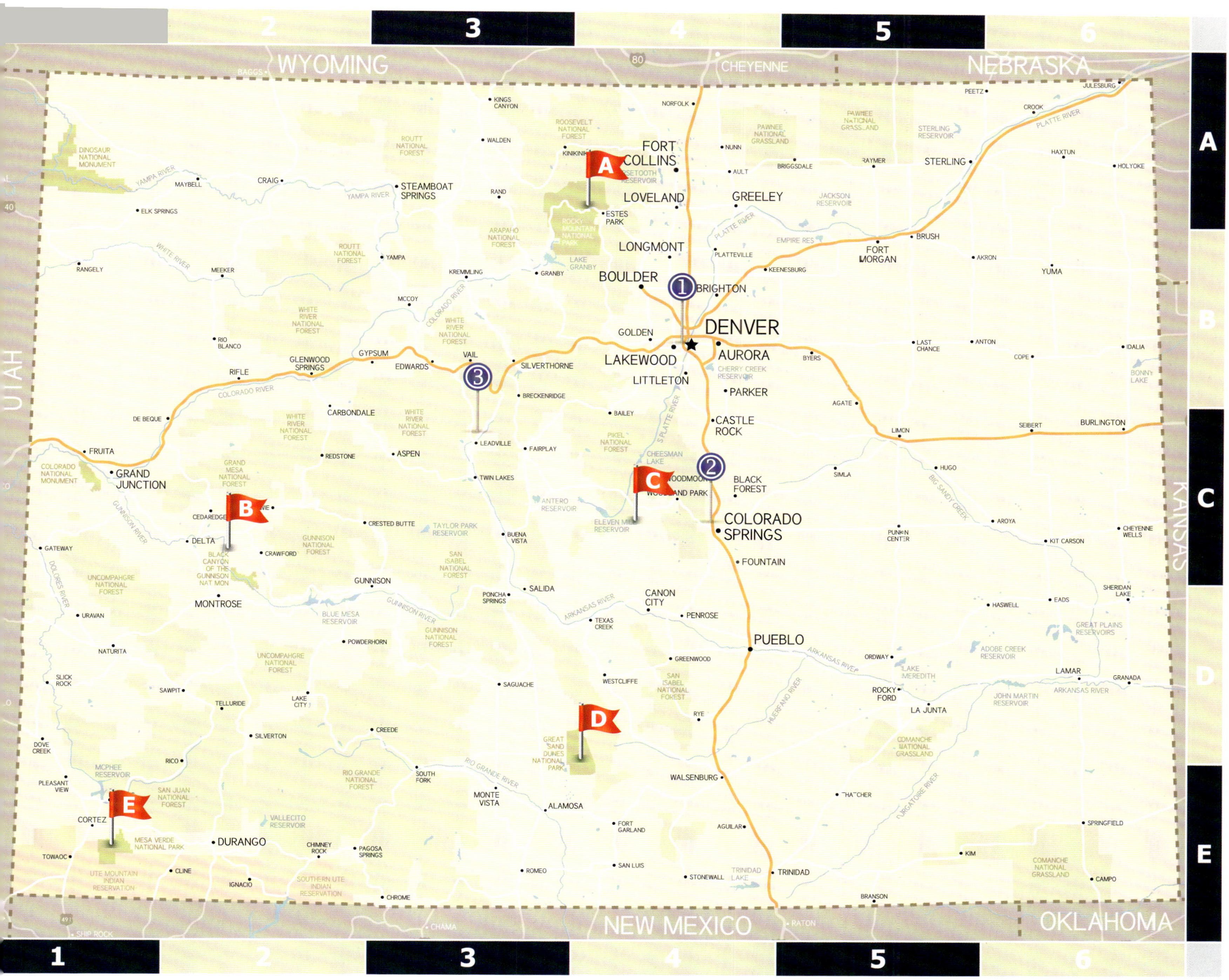

WONDERS IN GOD'S WORLD

A Rocky Mountain National Park

There are 415 square miles to explore here, with over 300 miles of hiking trails filled with seemingly endless mountains and valleys. If you drive on the Trail Ridge Road, you will rise up to 12,000 feet and can park and look out over the vast land.

B Black Canyon of the Gunnison National Park

The name comes from the fact that the deep gorge only receives about 33 minutes of sunlight a day. It was first established as a national monument in 1933 and as a national park in 1999.

C Florissant Fossil Beds National Monument

This monument was created in 1969 to protect some of the world's most amazing fossil beds. You can see fossils formed during the Flood and read the histories of the peoples who first lived here.

D Great Sand Dunes National Park

Surf the tallest dunes in North America surrounded by mountains covered in snow. Also see the diverse creation of God, including wetlands, forests, tundra, and grasslands.

E Mesa Verde National Park

Established in 1906, the park was created to protect and preserve the culture of the Ancestral Pueblo people who lived in this area for over 700 years. There are 600 protected cliff dwellings alone!

CONNECTICUT

CONNECTICUT PREAMBLE

The People of Connecticut acknowledging with gratitude, the good providence of ***God***, in having permitted them to enjoy a free government; do, in order more effectually to define, secure, and perpetuate the liberties, rights and privileges which they have derived from their ancestors; hereby, after a careful consideration and revision, ordain and establish the following constitution and form of civil government.

Statehood	1788 (5th state)
Population ranking	29th
Capital	Hartford
State flower	Mountain laurel
State bird	American robin
Nickname	The Constitution State
Highest point	Mount Frissell, 2,380 feet

Battell Chapel is the largest chapel at Yale in New Haven. It is a part of the Connecticut Freedom Trail.

Connecticut is in the Northeast. It became the 5th state in 1788, and the state song is "Yankee Doodle." And the state dinosaur? The *Dilophosaurus*!

1. Mystic Seaport is the largest maritime museum in the United States. That means its displays speak of the sea and those who sailed on the sea. This 19-acre site has more than 60 historic buildings and recreates a seafaring village from the 1800s.

The first Europeans settled here in 1635. These were the English puritans. The fundamental orders of 1639 helped establish a democratic government for Connecticut and were a model for the Constitution of the United States.

2. The Library of Congress gives credit to Danish immigrant Louis Lassen of New Haven for selling the first hamburger in the U.S. in 1895.

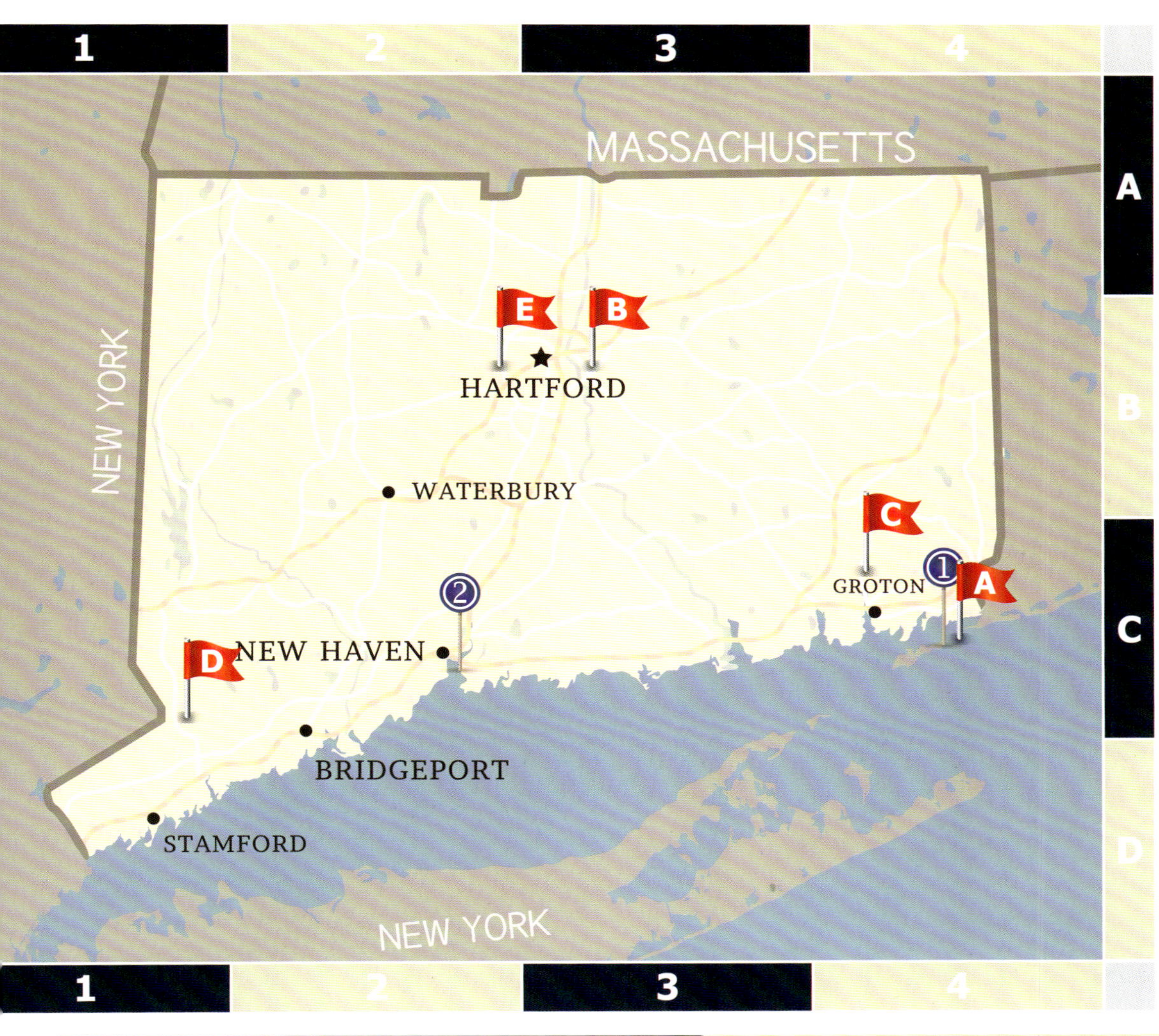

B Connecticut State Capital National Historic Landmark

This landmark located in Hartford was built between 1872 and 1878. It still fully functions as the capital of Connecticut and is the third capitol building for the state since the American Revolution.

A Charles W. Morgan (Bark) National Historic Landmark

The *Charles W. Morgan* is actually an American whaling ship that was built in 1841. It has been a museum since the 1940s and a national landmark since 1966. This is the world's oldest surviving merchant vessel.

C USS Nautilus (nuclear submarine) National Historic Landmark

This was the world's first operational nuclear-powered submarine, launching in 1954. It got its name from the science fiction book *Twenty Thousand Leagues Under the Sea* by Jules Verne.

D Weir Farm National Historic Site

This is the home and studio of the American artist J. Alden Weir. The farm celebrates the Impressionistic art of Weir and the beauty of the surrounding fields, waterways, and woods.

E Noah Webster Birthplace

This historic house museum is in West Hartford. It honors the legacy of Noah Webster, who helped to lay the foundation of the "American language" with various books on the subject, including his famous dictionary. He was born in West Hartford, and his first dictionary was published in 1807.

DELAWARE

DELAWARE PREAMBLE

Through Divine goodness, all people have by nature the rights of worshiping and serving their ***Creator*** according to the dictates of their consciences, of enjoying and defending life and liberty, of acquiring and protecting reputation and property, and in general of obtaining objects suitable to their condition, without injury by one to another; and as these rights are essential to their welfare, for due exercise thereof, power is inherent in them; and therefore all just authority in the institutions of political society is derived from the people, and established with their consent, to advance their happiness; and they may for this end, as circumstances require, from time to time, alter their Constitution of government.

Statehood	1787 (1st state)
Population ranking	45th
Capital	Dover
State flower	Peach blossom
State bird	Blue hen chicken
Nickname	The First State
Highest point	Ebright Azimuth, 447 feet

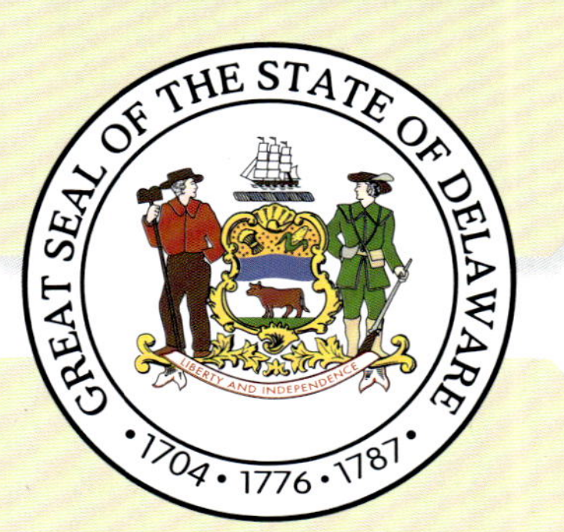

Delaware is a state in the American South. In 1787 it became the very first state. The state song is called "Our Delaware." And the state sport? It's bicycling!

① Barratt's Chapel, built in 1780, came to be known as the Cradle of Methodism, a Christian denomination that rose in the 1700s. Located in Kent County, Delaware, it is the oldest surviving church that was built by and for Methodists in America.

② It is supposed that the first log cabins originated in Finland and Sweden. The Finnish settlers who came to Delaware in the mid-1600s brought the designs for them to America. This became a symbol of the American pioneer. The Delaware Agricultural Museum in Dover has a preserved cabin on display.

Delaware was the very first state to ratify, or approve, the United States Constitution. This was on December 7, 1787.

A Captain John Smith Chesapeake National Historic Trail

The Englishman John Smith explored the area of Chesapeake Bay between 1607 and 1609. This is the man who encountered Pocahontas and her people. Maps and journals of this time are on display here.

B Fort Delaware State Park

Located on Pea Patch Island, this Civil War-era fort can be reached by a fun ferry ride. The park offers living history events, making it a fascinating and educational day out for the whole family.

C First State National Historical Park

Delaware, celebrated as the first state, has a unique park that honors these early steps to independence. The park is made up of seven sites found around the entire state. Each site shares a bit about Delaware's role in our new nation.

D Washington-Rochambeau National Historic Trail

Back in 1781, General Rochambeau's French army joined with the forces of General Washington to fight against the British army in Yorktown, Virginia. Trace part of this historic trail that passed through Delaware on the way to victory.

E Chesapeake Bay Watershed

This is the largest estuary on the continent, containing some 150 rivers and streams in the watershed. You will find over 300 types of fish, shellfish, and crabs here, as well as many other kinds of wildlife that live in and around the bay.

FLORIDA

FLORIDA PREAMBLE

We, the people of the State of Florida, being grateful to ***Almighty God*** for our constitutional liberty, in order to secure its benefits, perfect our government, insure domestic tranquility, maintain public order, and guarantee equal civil and political rights to all, do ordain and establish this constitution.

Statehood	1845 (27th state)
Population ranking	3rd
Capital	Tallahassee
State flower	Orange blossom
State bird	Mockingbird
Nickname	The Sunshine State
Highest point	Britton Hill, 345 feet

Florida is the leading producer of citrus in the United States, which includes oranges and grapefruit.

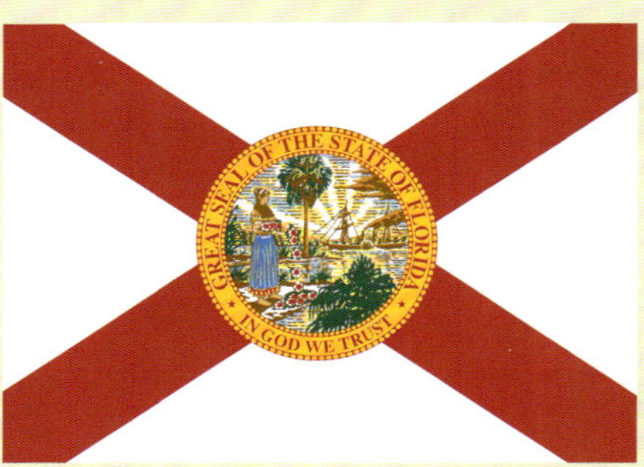

Florida is a part of the South. It became the 27th state in 1845. The official state song is called "Old Folks at Home." And the state beverage? That would be orange juice!

1. The St. Augustine alligator farm has alligator wrestling and lots of other amazing creatures to view. Did you know that alligators are the largest reptiles in North America, and they can sometimes reach up to 15 feet in length?

2. Come visit the museum and gardens of Vizcaya, built in Miami between 1914 and 1922 by local workers, as well as European and Bahamian craftsmen. It has a beautiful Mediterranean-style architecture and has museum collections dating from ancient Pompeii through the early 20th century.

3. Fort Lauderdale is known as the Venice of America. Why? Because the city has some 165 miles of local waterways!

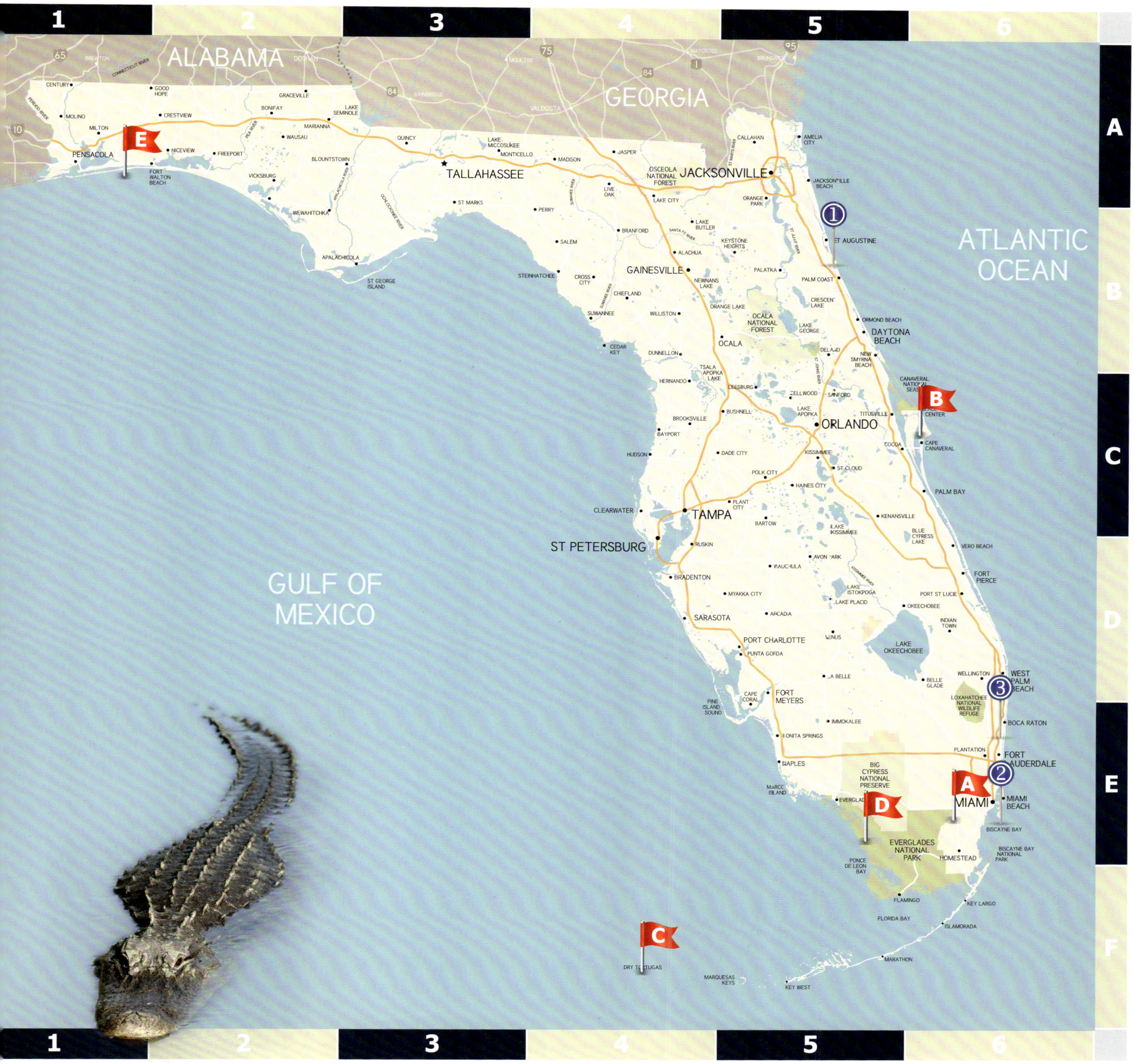
1
2
3
4
5
6
A
B
C
D
E
F
ALABAMA
GEORGIA
ATLANTIC OCEAN
GULF OF MEXICO
PENSACOLA
TALLAHASSEE
JACKSONVILLE
ST AUGUSTINE
GAINESVILLE
OCALA
DAYTONA BEACH
ORLANDO
TAMPA
ST PETERSBURG
SARASOTA
PORT CHARLOTTE
FORT MEYERS
LAKE OKEECHOBEE
WEST PALM BEACH
BOCA RATON
FORT LAUDERDALE
MIAMI
MIAMI BEACH
EVERGLADES NATIONAL PARK
BIG CYPRESS NATIONAL PRESERVE
NAPLES
HOMESTEAD
KEY LARGO
MARATHON
KEY WEST
DRY TORTUGAS
MARQUESAS KEYS
CAPE CANAVERAL
PALM BAY
FORT PIERCE
OCALA NATIONAL FOREST
OSCEOLA NATIONAL FOREST
ST GEORGE ISLAND
APALACHICOLA
BRADENTON
CLEARWATER
BISCAYNE BAY
FLORIDA BAY
ISLAMORADA
1
2
3
A
B
C
D
E

WONDERS IN GOD'S WORLD

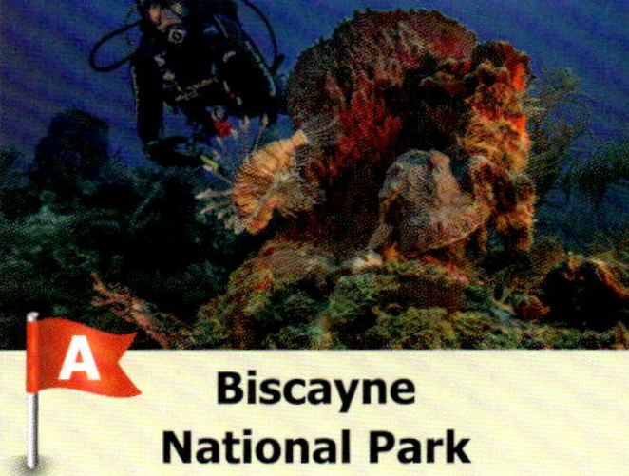

A Biscayne National Park

Located just south of Miami, the park helps protect Biscayne Bay and the offshore barrier reefs in the area. You can boat, snorkel, camp, explore pirate history, and more. But know that 95 percent of the park is water!

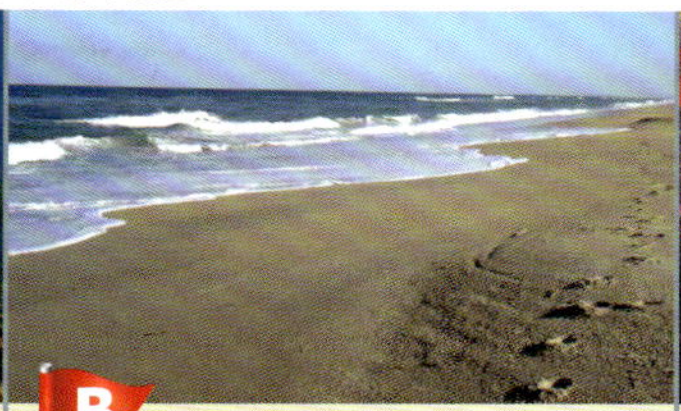

B Canaveral National Seashore

Created as a national seashore in 1975, this barrier island area has been a refuge for both people and wildlife for centuries. You can walk the beautiful shores, but make sure you stay clear of sea turtles and other creatures that thrive here.

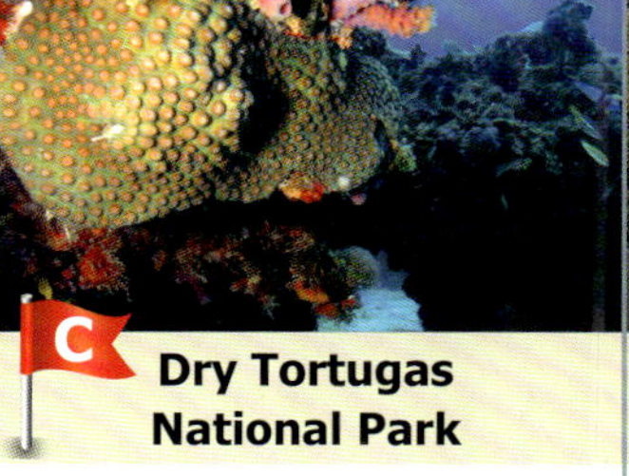

C Dry Tortugas National Park

Come and explore this 19th century fort or swim in the beautiful, clear waters surrounding it. This is a 100-square-mile park that includes seven small islands. God's wondrous sea creatures and birds are everywhere to be seen!

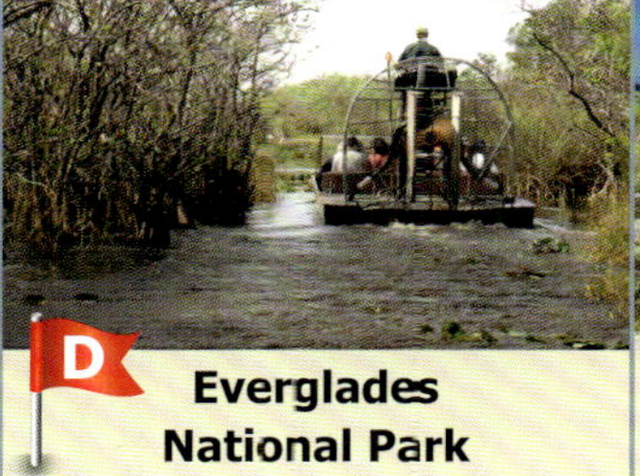

D Everglades National Park

The Everglades is considered the largest subtropical wilderness in the United States. Note that many rare and endangered creatures live here, including the Florida panther, the manatee, and the American crocodile. Help keep them safe!

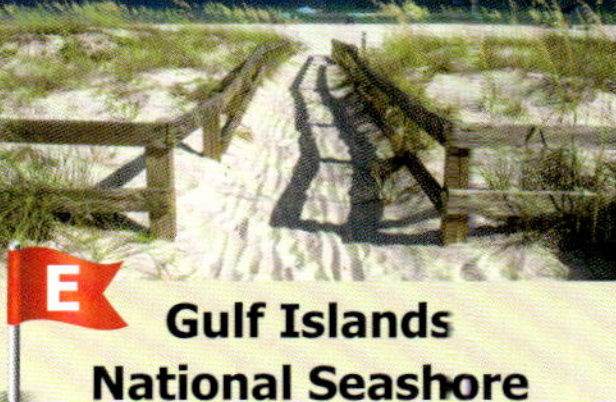

E Gulf Islands National Seashore

You can find both beauty here and lots of fun things to do. There is the mainland area and seven islands connected to the national seashore and history that extends back hundreds of years

GEORGIA

GEORGIA PREAMBLE

To perpetuate the principles of free government, insure justice to all, preserve peace, promote the interest and happiness of the citizen and of the family, and transmit to posterity the enjoyment of liberty, we the people of Georgia, relying upon the protection and guidance of ***Almighty God***, do ordain and establish this Constitution.

Statehood	1788 (4th state)
Population ranking	8th
Capital	Atlanta
State flower	Cherokee rose
State bird	Brown thrasher
Nickname	The Peach State
Highest point	Brasstown Bald, 4,784 feet

Georgia is known for its delicious peaches. Peaches were first grown in China thousands of years ago. They made their way to Persia (present-day Iran), then to Europe, and finally South America by Spanish explorers in the 16th century. It is said that they were brought to the American colonies in the early 17th century, and in the 19th century they became a commercial crop in Georgia and other states.

Georgia is in the South. It became a state in 1788, which made it the 4th state. Their song is "Georgia on My Mind." And the state BBQ cookoff for pork? That's the Slosheye Trail Big Pig Jig!

1 Like aquariums? The Georgia Aquarium is the largest one in the Western Hemisphere! The blue exterior is made of metal and glass and is supposed to look like a giant ark coming through a wave. The exhibits hold an amazing 8,000,000 gallons of fresh and saltwater.

2 The busiest airport in the United States is Atlanta's Hartsfield-Jackson international airport. It has 192 total gates, with 152 set aside for U.S. flights and 40 for international flights.

3 Okefenokee Swamp covers over 400,000 acres of canals, moss-covered cypress trees, and prairies. These areas provide a sanctuary for hundreds of different types of birds and other wildlife, some of which are endangered. There are also meat-eating plants!

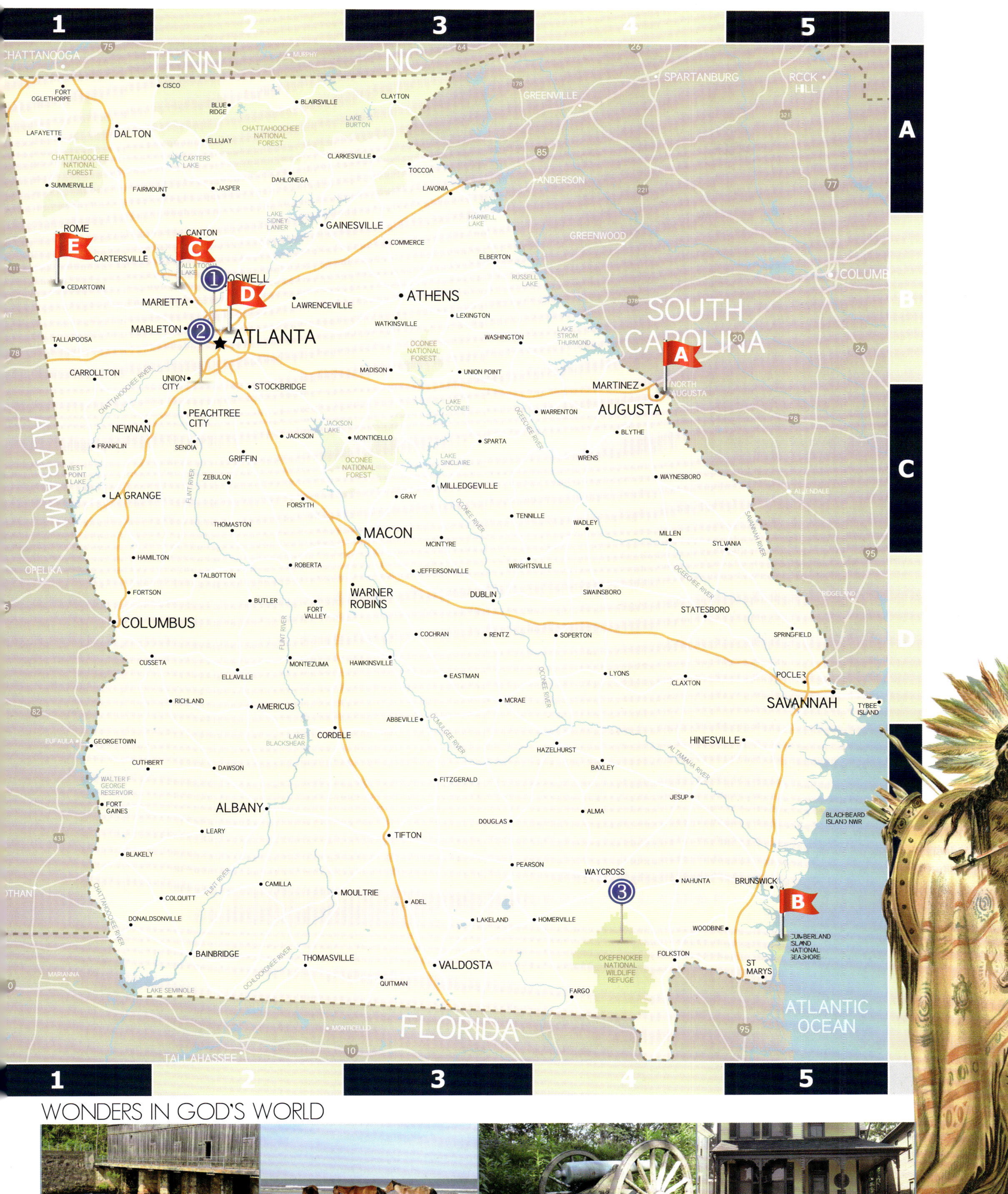

WONDERS IN GOD'S WORLD

A — Augusta Canal National Heritage Area

First built in 1845, the canal was created to provide a source of power, transportation, and water. It's the only intact American industrial canal that is still in continuous operation.

B — Cumberland Island National Seashore

Established in 1972, the area is home to Georgia's largest barrier island. You can see maritime forest, beautiful beaches, and wondrous marshes. The island has over 9,800 acres of protected wilderness.

C — Kennesaw Mountain National Battlefield Park

This 2,965-acre park protects and preserves a Civil War battleground. The battle raged between June 19, 1864 and July 2, 1864. Kennesaw Mountain is a beautiful area where you can hike and explore as well.

D — Martin Luther King Jr. National Historical Park

This area honors the legacy of Martin Luther King Jr. and his struggle during the Civil Rights Era of the 1950s and 1960s. The tour here includes his birth home, the Ebenezer Baptist Church where he was a pastor, and his gravesite.

E — Trail of Tears National Historic Trail

This commemorates the survival of the Cherokee people who were forcefully removed in 1838 through 1839 from their homelands in Alabama, Georgia, and Tennessee to live in Indian Territory, what is now Oklahoma.

HAWAII

HAWAII PREAMBLE

We, the people of Hawaii, grateful for ***Divine Guidance***, and mindful of our Hawaiian heritage and uniqueness as an island State, dedicate our efforts to fulfill the philosophy decreed by the Hawaii State motto, "Ua mau ke ea o ka aina i ka pono." We reserve the right to control our destiny, to nurture the integrity of our people and culture, and to preserve the quality of life that we desire. We reaffirm our belief in a government of the people, by the people and for the people, and with an understanding and compassionate heart toward all the peoples of the earth, do hereby ordain and establish this constitution for the State of Hawaii.

Statehood	1959 (50th state)
Population ranking	40th
Capital	Honolulu
State flower	Yellow hibiscus
State bird	Nene (Hawaiian goose)
Nickname	The Aloha State
Highest point	Mauna Kea, 13,803 feet

There are only 12 letters in the Hawaiian alphabet. This would be the five vowels (A, E, I, O, and U) and seven consonants (H, K, L, M, N, P, and W).

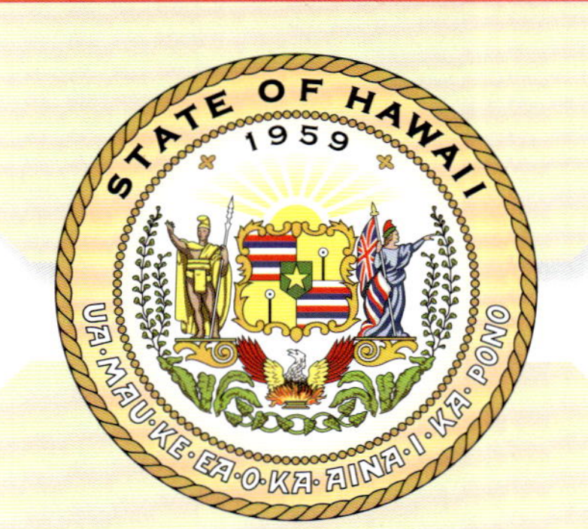

Hawaii is considered part of the West Region. In 1959 it became the last state to become a part of the U.S. The state anthem is called "Hawaii Pono`ī," a phrase that means "Hawaii's own true sons." And the state dance? The hula! Hawaii is a string of 137 islands spread out across 1,500 miles of the Pacific Ocean. This is about halfway across the 48 contiguous states!

What is the southernmost state? Well, yes, that would be Hawaii. And the southernmost point is Ka Lae (South Cape).

1 Haleakalā Crater (Ha-lay-ah-ka-law) is the world's largest dormant, or non-active, volcano. Many go up the steep road to watch the sunrise from the rim.

The Hawaiian people have been surfing for hundreds of years. They called it he'e nalu, which means "wave sliding."

2 Mauna Kea is considered the tallest mountain in the world if you are measuring from its base at the ocean floor. On the top of Mauna Kea you will find observatories and research facilities for astronomical research.

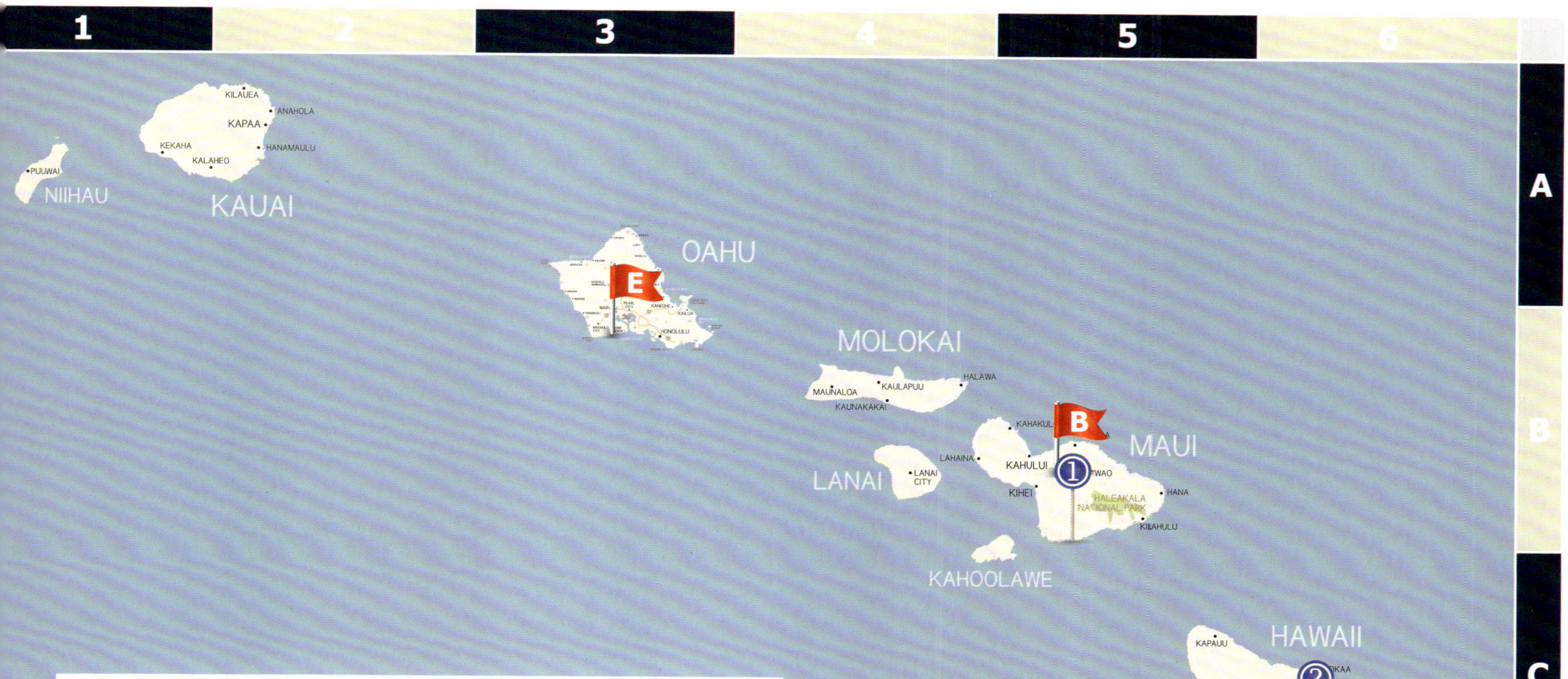

1 2 3 4 5 6

A B C D

NIIHAU
PUUWAI
KAUAI
KILAUEA
ANAHOLA
KAPAA
KEKAHA
HANAMAULU
KALAHEO
OAHU
HONOLULU
MOLOKAI
MAUNALOA
KAULAPUU
KAUNAKAKAI
HALAWA
LANAI
LANAI CITY
LAHAINA
KAHAKULOA
KAHULUI
WAILUKU
KIHEI
MAUI
HALEAKALA NATIONAL PARK
HANA
KIPAHULU
KAHOOLAWE
HAWAII
KAPAAU
WAIMEA
PUAKO
KAILUA KONA
PEPEEKEO
HILO
KEAAU
PAHOA
HAWAII VOLCANOES NATIONAL PARK
KALAPANA
MILOLII
PAHALA
NAALEHU

WONDERS IN GOD'S WORLD

A Ala Kahakai National Historic Trail

The trail was set aside in the year 2000 for the preservation and protection of traditional Native Hawaiian culture. This 175-mile network of trails crosses ancient Hawaiian settlements and God's beautiful creation here.

B Haleakalā National Park

Set aside as a protected area in 1976 and expanded in 2005, Haleakalā, a dormant volcano, and the park around it covers some 33,265 acres of wilderness area. There are endangered species that are only found here on the island of Maui.

C Hawaii Volcanoes National Park

The park was set up to protect unique geological and biological areas of Hawaii, and it stretches all the way from the sea to the summit of Mauna Loa, which is 13,677 feet up. Two of the world's most active volcanoes are here.

D Pu'uhonua O Hōnaunau National Historical Park

This park preserves the culture of the islands. The area was used as a safe place up until the early 19th century. People could flee here and find refuge and forgiveness.

E Pearl Harbor National Memorial

Located on the island of Oahu, the memorial lays over the Battleship USS *Arizona.* This ship was bombed and sank here on December 7, 1941 during the Japanese attack on Pearl Harbor.

IDAHO

IDAHO PREAMBLE

We, the people of the State of Idaho, grateful to ***Almighty God*** for our freedom, to secure its blessings and promote our common welfare do establish this Constitution.

Statehood	1890 (43rd state)
Population ranking	38th
Capital	Boise
State flower	Syringa
State bird	Mountain bluebird
Nickname	The Gem State
Highest point	Borah Peak, 12,668 feet

The Rev. Henry Spalding came to Idaho back in 1836 to establish a mission outreach to the Nez Perce. He started the first school here, grew the area's first potatoes, and translated portions of the Bible into the native language.

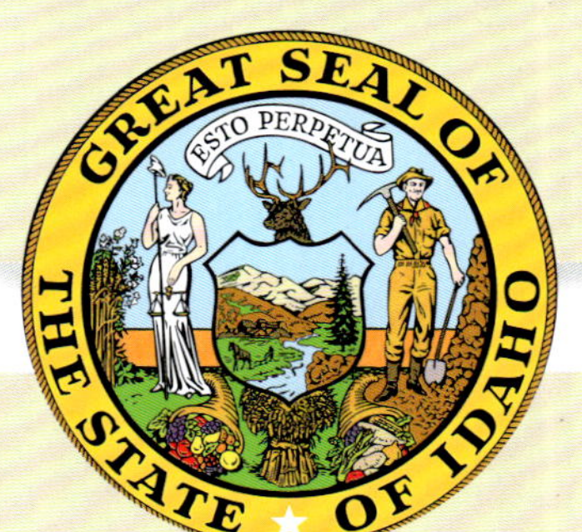

Idaho is in the West Region of the U.S. It became the 43rd state in 1890. The state song is called "Here We Have Idaho." And the state fossil? The Hagerman Horse Fossil!

1 There is a place called Seven Devils Mountains in Idaho, and this includes Heaven's Gate Lookout. From that spot, you can look out into four states.

Farmers of Idaho grow over 30 kinds of potatoes. They were originally grown by South American natives. In fact, nearly 40 percent of the land is used for farming — growing potatoes, barley, and wheat — and over 50 percent of the land is forest.

The mountains of Idaho are filled with many rare minerals, including gold, silver, and copper. There are various gemstones too, including jasper, jade, and opal. That's one good reason to be known as "the gem state."

Herd of Bison walking freely in Yellowstone National Park

City of Rocks National Reserve

This protected area is also known as the Silent City of Rocks, which draws many hikers and climbers. Wagons on the way to California in the 1840s and 1850s often passed through here, and you can still see ruts from the wagon wheels in the rock.

Nez Perce National Historical Park

This historic park is connected through 38 various sites across Idaho, Montana, Oregon, and Washington. The Nez Perce people are often known historically through their fight to keep their freedom, as led by Chief Joseph.

Hagerman Fossil Beds National Monument

The area has the largest grouping of Hagerman horse fossils in North America. The fossil beds were set aside as a national landmark in 1975.

Craters of the Moon National Monument & Preserve

The monument was established back in 1924 and expanded in 2000 and 2002. In the 400-square-mile area, there are three lava fields, including the deepest known open rift crack in the world at 800 feet.

Yellowstone National Park

Yellowstone became the very first national park on March 1, 1872. There is so much to explore in this vast parkland, including the diverse wildlife, geysers, hot springs, waterfalls, rushing rivers, and much more.

ILLINOIS

ILLINOIS PREAMBLE

We, the People of the State of Illinois - grateful to ***Almighty God*** for the civil, political and religious liberty which He has permitted us to enjoy and seeking His blessing upon our endeavors - in order to provide for the health, safety and welfare of the people; maintain a representative and orderly government; eliminate poverty and inequality; assure legal, social and economic justice; provide opportunity for the fullest development of the individual; insure domestic tranquility; provide for the common defense; and secure the blessings of freedom and liberty to ourselves and our posterity - do ordain and establish this Constitution for the State of Illinois.

Statehood	1818 (21st state)
Population ranking	6th
Capital	Springfield
State flower	Native violet
State bird	Cardinal
Nickname	The Prairie State / Land of Lincoln
Highest point	Charles Mound, 1,235 feet

Illinois can be found in the Midwest, and Chicago is the largest city in this region. Illinois became the 21st state in 1818. Their state song is simply called "Illinois." And the state pie? The pumpkin pie!

1. Do you like libraries? Well, the Chicago Public Library is connected through 80 locations across the city with almost 6 million volumes you can check out!

2. The earliest Europeans came through the Illinois area as early as 1673. Before that, the native people created Cahokia Mounds, which is now a historic site. It highlights what is perhaps the most sophisticated native civilization that is found north of Mexico.

3. If you go to the top of the Chicago Sears Tower — now known as the Willis Tower —on a clear day, you can look out and see four states, which includes Illinois, Michigan, Indiana, and Wisconsin. It's a 110-story, 1,450-foot-tall skyscraper that was completed in 1973 and was the tallest building in the world for almost 25 years.

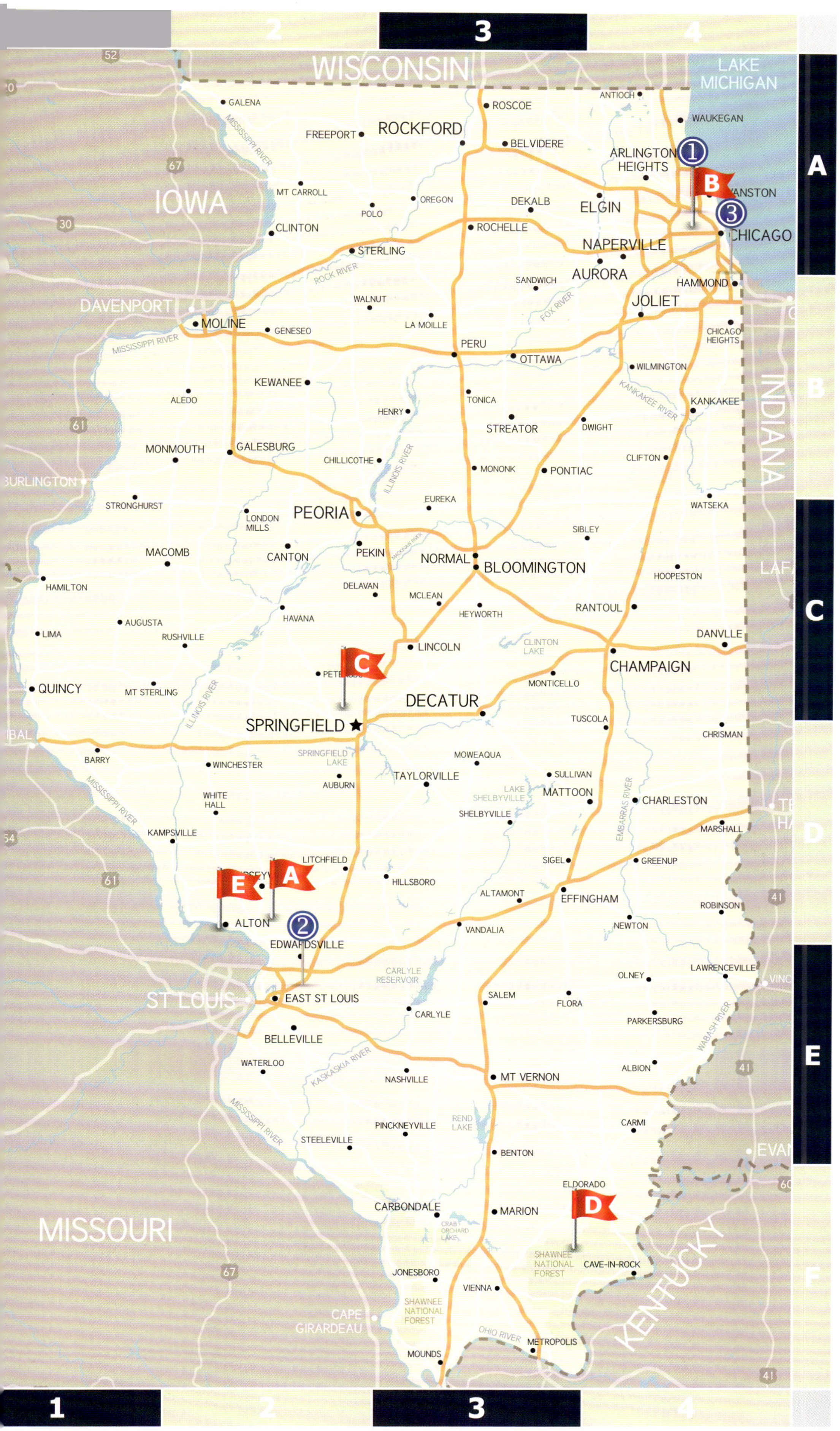

A

Lewis & Clark National Historic Trail

This trail covers 16 states, over 4,900 miles! It starts in Pittsburgh, Pennsylvania, and goes to the mouth of the Columbia River, near Astoria, Oregon. The famed Lewis and Clark expedition passed this way from 1804 to 1806. This is Camp Dubois on this trail.

B

Pullman National Monument

The Pullman Historic District is in Chicago. It is known for being the first model, planned industrial community in the U.S. George Pullman created this area as a place to produce his famous Pullman sleeping train cars.

E

Trail of Tears National Historic Trail

The trail of suffering is over 5,043 miles long, over nine states, including southern Illinois. This replica of a Piasa Bird image by the Illini Tribe was discovered in 1673 near Alton, IL on the bluffs of the Mississippi River. The Illini also faced forced removal like the Cherokee.

C

Lincoln Home National Historic Site

Before becoming the 16th president of the United States, he lived here from 1844 to 1861. Both the home of Abraham Lincoln and the area around it are a part of this historic site.

D

Shawnee National Forest

Located in southern Illinois, the Shawnee National Forest offers hiking trails, horseback riding, and camping. There are over 146 miles of rivers and streams and more than 200 lakes and ponds.

INDIANA

INDIANA PREAMBLE

TO THE END, that justice be established, public order maintained, and liberty perpetuated; WE, the People of the State of Indiana, grateful to ***ALMIGHTY GOD*** for the free exercise of the right to choose our own form of government, do ordain this Constitution.

Statehood	1816 (19th state)
Population ranking	17th
Capital	Indianapolis
State flower	Peony
State bird	Cardinal
Nickname	The Hoosier State
Highest point	Hoosier Hill, 1,257 feet

Bluespring Caverns near Bedford is the longest underground river in the U.S. that we know of. Within this 21-mile long system of caves you can see countless blind and albino creatures, like spiders, frogs, and crayfish. Underground boat tours are available.

Indiana is considered part of the Midwest Region. In 1816 it became the 19th state. Indiana's song is called "On the Banks of the Wabash, Far Away." And the state languages? English and American Sign Language!

1 If you dig down deep in southern Indiana, you will find one of the richest deposits of top-quality limestone found anywhere in the world. In fact, New York City's Empire State Building, the Pentagon, and 35 of the 50 state capitol buildings in the U.S. are made of the Indiana limestone.

The city of Vincennes is the oldest city in Indiana. It was started in 1732 by Francois Marie Bissot-sieur de Vincennes, who was a French officer. It was both a military post and a fur trading area.

2 If you visit the Children's Museum of Indianapolis, you'll be in the largest children's museum in the world. It has over 472,000 square feet of space, with 29 acres dedicated to educational fun.

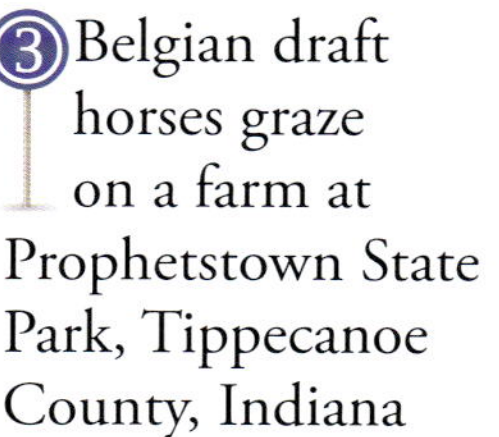

3 Belgian draft horses graze on a farm at Prophetstown State Park, Tippecanoe County, Indiana

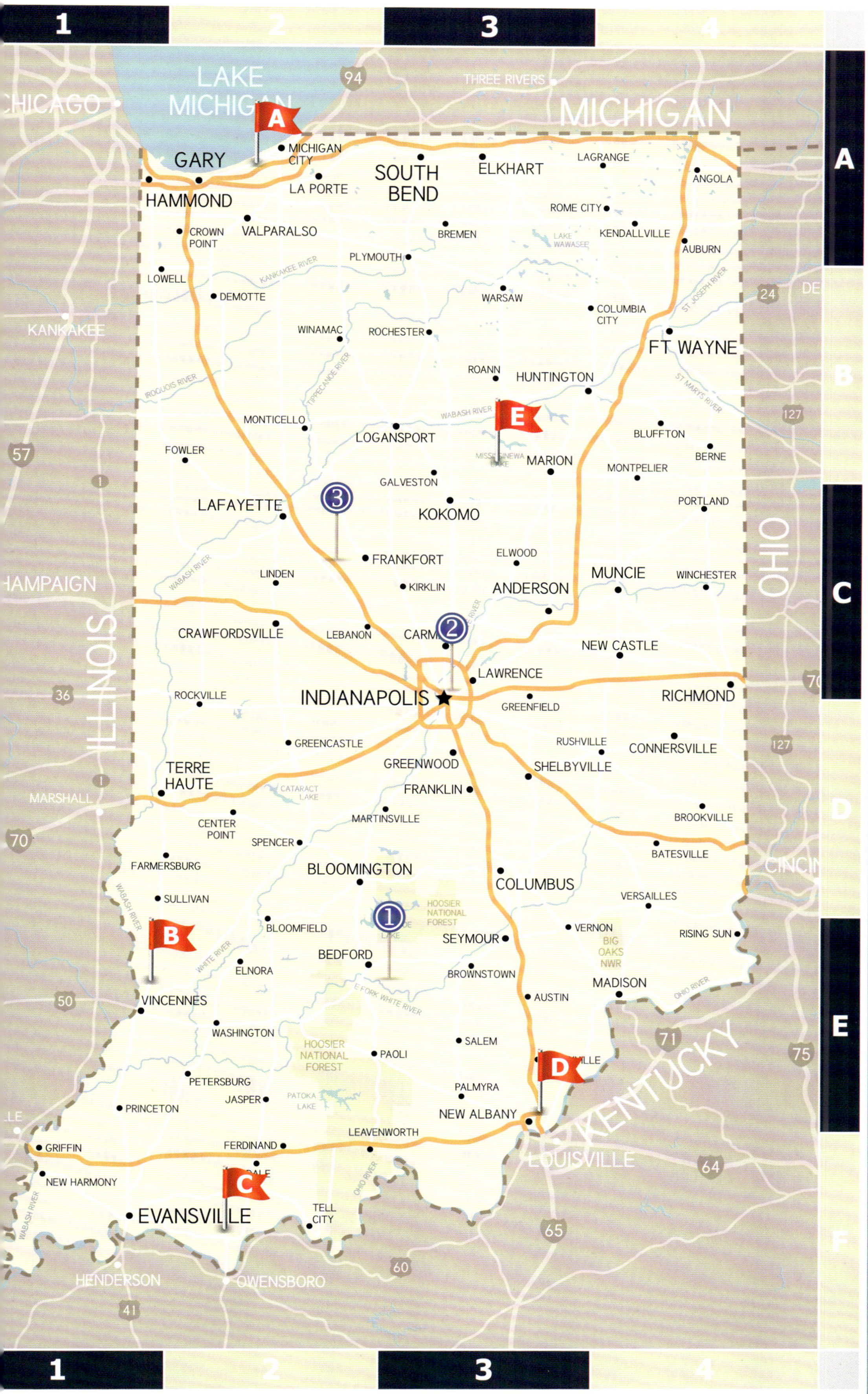

1 2 3 4

A B C D E F

LAKE MICHIGAN
CHICAGO
94
THREE RIVERS
MICHIGAN
GARY
MICHIGAN CITY
HAMMOND
LA PORTE
SOUTH BEND
ELKHART
LAGRANGE
ANGOLA
ROME CITY
CROWN POINT
VALPARALSO
BREMEN
LAKE WAWASEE
KENDALLVILLE
AUBURN
PLYMOUTH
LOWELL
DEMOTTE
KANKAKEE RIVER
WARSAW
COLUMBIA CITY
ST JOSEPH RIVER
24
KANKAKEE
WINAMAC
ROCHESTER
FT WAYNE
ROANN
HUNTINGTON
IROQUOIS RIVER
TIPPECANOE RIVER
ST MARYS RIVER
WABASH RIVER
MONTICELLO
127
LOGANSPORT
BLUFFTON
57
FOWLER
MISSISSINEWA LAKE
MARION
BERNE
MONTPELIER
GALVESTON
LAFAYETTE
KOKOMO
PORTLAND
OHIO
FRANKFORT
ELWOOD
LINDEN
MUNCIE
WINCHESTER
CHAMPAIGN
KIRKLIN
ANDERSON
ILLINOIS
CRAWFORDSVILLE
LEBANON
CARMEL
NEW CASTLE
LAWRENCE
36
ROCKVILLE
INDIANAPOLIS
GREENFIELD
RICHMOND
70
RUSHVILLE
GREENCASTLE
CONNERSVILLE
GREENWOOD
SHELBYVILLE
TERRE HAUTE
MARSHALL
CATARACT LAKE
FRANKLIN
BROOKVILLE
CENTER POINT
MARTINSVILLE
SPENCER
BATESVILLE
FARMERSBURG
BLOOMINGTON
COLUMBUS
CINCINNATI
SULLIVAN
HOOSIER NATIONAL FOREST
VERSAILLES
BLOOMFIELD
SEYMOUR
VERNON
RISING SUN
BEDFORD
BIG OAKS NWR
ELNORA
BROWNSTOWN
MADISON
WHITE RIVER
E FORK WHITE RIVER
OHIO RIVER
50
VINCENNES
AUSTIN
WASHINGTON
SALEM
71
HOOSIER NATIONAL FOREST
PAOLI
75
KENTUCKY
PETERSBURG
PALMYRA
JASPER
PATOKA LAKE
PRINCETON
NEW ALBANY
LEAVENWORTH
GRIFFIN
FERDINAND
LOUISVILLE
64
NEW HARMONY
EVANSVILLE
TELL CITY
65
HENDERSON
OWENSBORO
60
41

A

Indiana Dunes National Park

Come explore the 15 beautiful miles of the shore of Lake Michigan. There are over 50 miles of trails that cross the wondrous dunes, wetlands, prairies, and peaceful forests. God's glorious creation is everywhere on display!

B

George Rogers Clark National Historical Park

This park in Vincennes honors Lieutenant Colonel George Rogers Clark and the brave soldiers who marched with him in 1779 to capture Fort Sackville from the British. The memorial was completed in 1936.

E

Salamonie River State Forest

The name of the forest comes from a Native American word: O-sah-mo-nee. The word means "yellow paint." The native people once made yellow paint from the bloodroot plants here. Much of the forest was replanted back in the 1930s and is now protected.

C

Lincoln Boyhood National Memorial

Abraham Lincoln, the 16th president of the United States, grew up in southern Indiana. With just a short hike, you can explore the cabin and other buildings that are a part of this recreated 1820s farm.

D

Lewis & Clark National Historic Trail

Covering 16 states over 4,900 miles, the focus here is on what was once called the Indiana Territory. In 1803, Meriwether Lewis journeyed to Clarksville in the Indiana Territory to find his partner, William Clark.

IOWA

IOWA PREAMBLE

WE THE PEOPLE OF THE STATE OF IOWA, grateful to the ***Supreme Being*** for the blessings hitherto enjoyed, and feeling our dependence on Him for a continuation of those blessings, do ordain and establish a free and independent government, by the name of the State of Iowa, the boundaries whereof shall be as follows…

Statehood	1846 (29th state)
Population ranking	31st
Capital	Des Moines
State flower	Wild rose
State bird	Eastern goldfinch
Nickname	The Hawkeye State
Highest point	Hawkeye Point, 1,670 feet

Otto Frederick Rohwedder, who happened to be from Davenport, Iowa, invented the first single loaf bread-slicing machine in 1912. Though it was destroyed in a fire, he had a fully working machine ready to go by 1928. Now we say, "That's the greatest thing since sliced bread!"

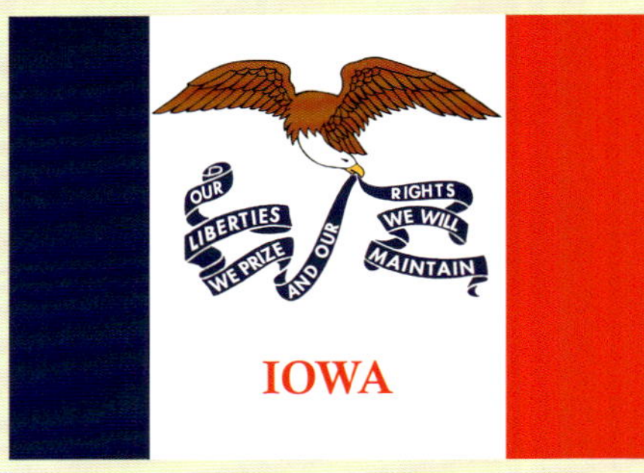

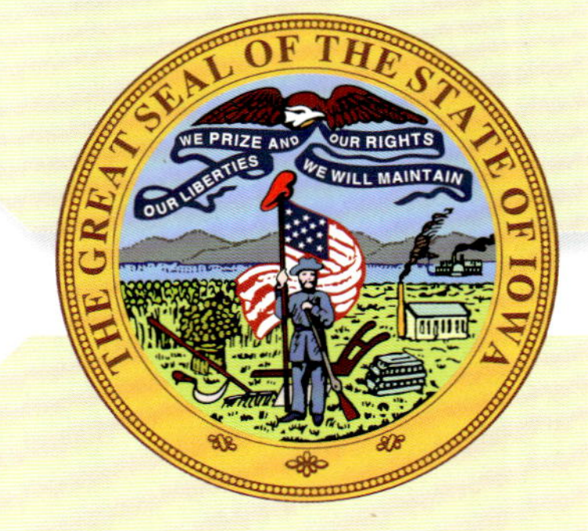

Iowa is in the Midwest. It became the 29th state in 1846. "The Song of Iowa" is their state song. And the state rock? That would be the geode!

① Come to Effigy Mounds National Monument, the only place in the country that has mounds in the shape of birds, mammals, and reptiles. And these mounds are thought to have been built over 2,000 years ago!

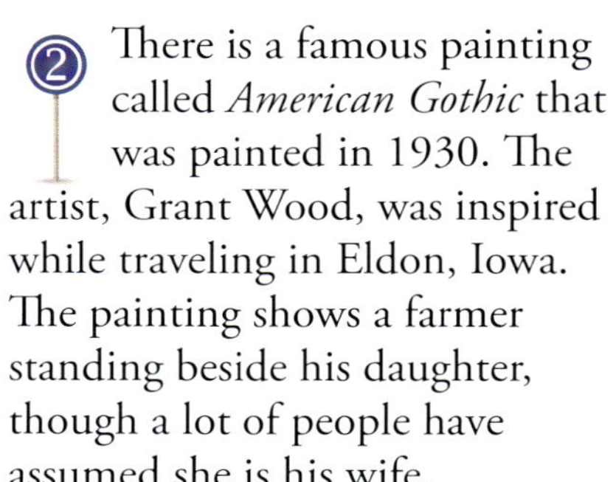

② There is a famous painting called *American Gothic* that was painted in 1930. The artist, Grant Wood, was inspired while traveling in Eldon, Iowa. The painting shows a farmer standing beside his daughter, though a lot of people have assumed she is his wife.

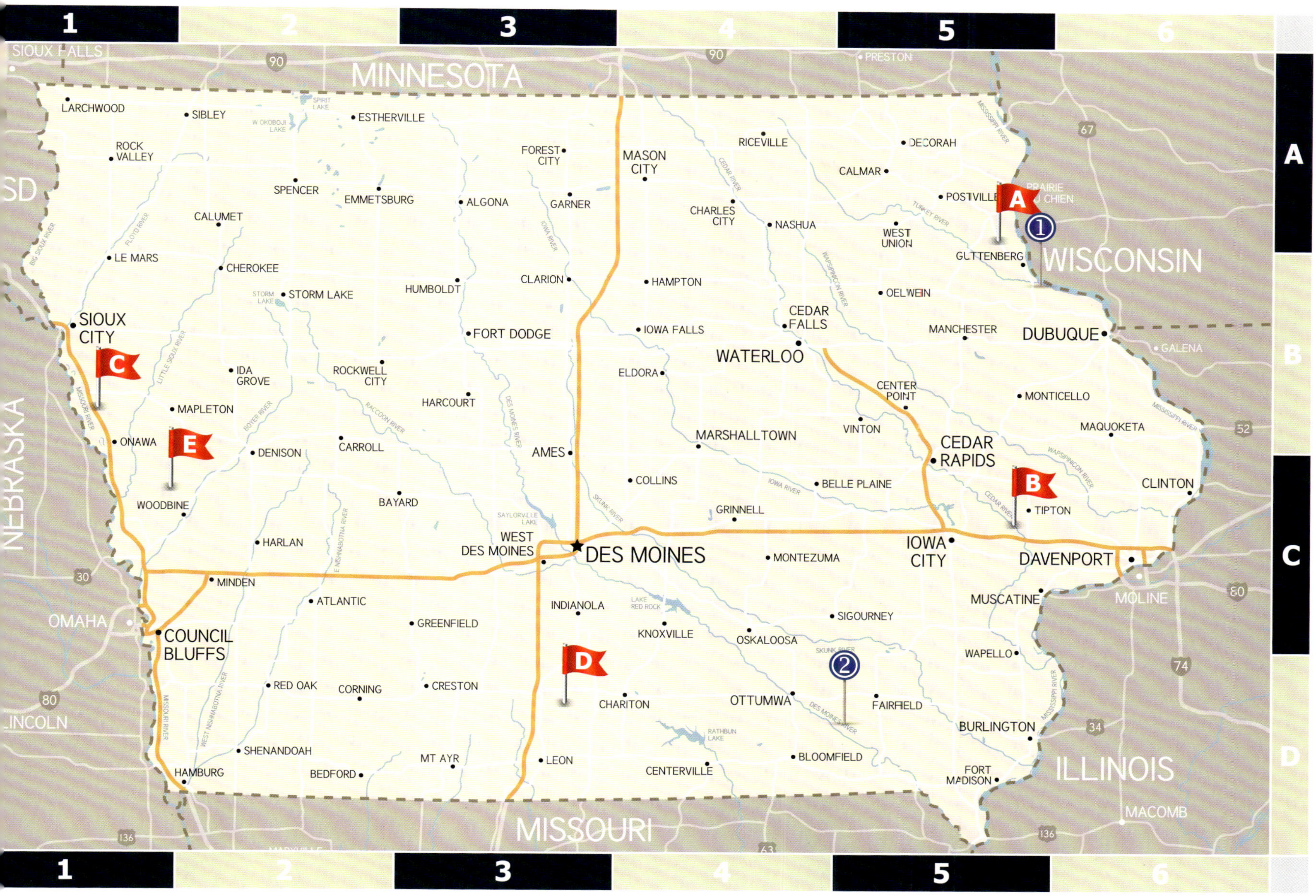

1 2 3 4 5 6

SIOUX FALLS
MINNESOTA
PRESTON
LARCHWOOD
SIBLEY
ESTHERVILLE
ROCK VALLEY
SD
SPENCER
EMMETSBURG
ALGONA
FOREST CITY
MASON CITY
GARNER
RICEVILLE
DECORAH
CALMAR
POSTVILLE
PRAIRIE DU CHIEN
CALUMET
CHARLES CITY
NASHUA
WEST UNION
GUTTENBERG
WISCONSIN
LE MARS
CHEROKEE
STORM LAKE
HUMBOLDT
CLARION
HAMPTON
OELWEIN
CEDAR FALLS
SIOUX CITY
FORT DODGE
IOWA FALLS
MANCHESTER
DUBUQUE
WATERLOO
GALENA
IDA GROVE
ROCKWELL CITY
ELDORA
CENTER POINT
MONTICELLO
HARCOURT
MAPLETON
MAQUOKETA
NEBRASKA
ONAWA
DENISON
CARROLL
AMES
MARSHALLTOWN
VINTON
CEDAR RAPIDS
COLLINS
BELLE PLAINE
CLINTON
WOODBINE
BAYARD
GRINNELL
TIPTON
HARLAN
WEST DES MOINES
DES MOINES
MONTEZUMA
IOWA CITY
DAVENPORT
MINDEN
MOLINE
OMAHA
ATLANTIC
INDIANOLA
MUSCATINE
COUNCIL BLUFFS
GREENFIELD
KNOXVILLE
SIGOURNEY
OSKALOOSA
WAPELLO
RED OAK
CORNING
CRESTON
CHARITON
OTTUMWA
FAIRFIELD
LINCOLN
BURLINGTON
SHENANDOAH
MT AYR
LEON
BLOOMFIELD
HAMBURG
BEDFORD
CENTERVILLE
FORT MADISON
ILLINOIS
MACOMB
MISSOURI
A B C D

WONDERS IN GOD'S WORLD

A Effigy Mounds National Monument

More than 200 ancient mounds that were built by native peoples are preserved here. These mounds are unique in their animal shapes and were featured in the America the Beautiful Quarters Program.

B Herbert Hoover National Historic Site

Herbert Hoover, the 31st president of the United States, grew up in West Branch, Iowa. At age nine, he was left an orphan and never lived in this area again. His young years did teach him the importance of hard work, honesty, and community.

C Lewis & Clark National Historic Trail

The journey of Lewis and Clark started over 200 years ago, at a time when the landscapes they encountered looked nothing like they do today. Iowa's portion of their trip follows the Missouri River from Council Bluffs to Sioux (pronounced "Sue") City.

D Stephens State Forest

This protected forest area covers 15,554 acres across five counties. Not only will you find a beautiful, diverse area of habitats, but you and your family can enjoy recreational opportunities as well.

E Loess Hills State Forest

The Loess (LOW-ess) protected area is 10,600 acres of forested land, as well as savannas and prairies. First set aside in 1986, the state plans to expand it to 20,000 acres.

KANSAS

KANSAS PREAMBLE

We, the people of Kansas, grateful to ***Almighty God*** for our civil and religious privileges, in order to insure the full enjoyment of our rights as American citizens, do ordain and establish this constitution of the state of Kansas, with the following boundaries, to wit: Beginning at a point on the western boundary of the state of Missouri, where the thirty-seventh parallel of north latitude crosses the same; thence running west on said parallel to the twenty-fifth meridian of longitude west from Washington; thence north on said meridian to the fortieth parallel of north latitude; thence east on said parallel to the western boundary of the state of Missouri; thence south with the western boundary of said state to the place of beginning.

Statehood	1861 (34th state)
Population ranking	35th
Capital	Topeka
State flower	Sunflower
State bird	Western meadowlark
Nickname	The Sunflower State
Highest point	Mount Sunflower, 4,041 feet

Kansas is a part of the Midwest Region. In 1861 it became the 34th state. Their state song is called "Home on the Range." And the state tree? The oak!

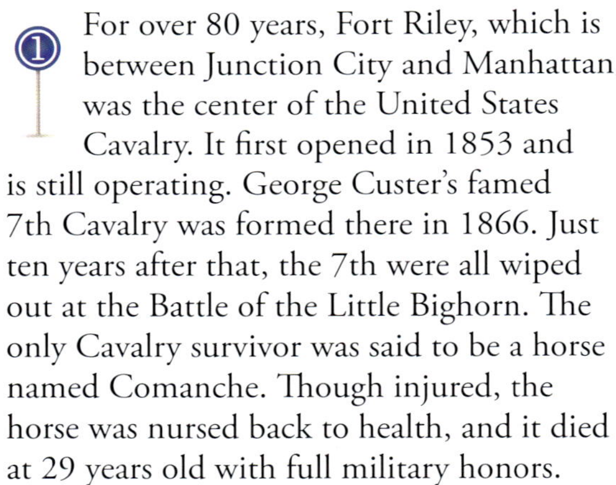

① For over 80 years, Fort Riley, which is between Junction City and Manhattan, was the center of the United States Cavalry. It first opened in 1853 and is still operating. George Custer's famed 7th Cavalry was formed there in 1866. Just ten years after that, the 7th were all wiped out at the Battle of the Little Bighorn. The only Cavalry survivor was said to be a horse named Comanche. Though injured, the horse was nursed back to health, and it died at 29 years old with full military honors.

② If you're driving along Highway 56 near Lyons, look for the monument to the first Christian martyr in what became the United States. Father Juan de Padilla came to this area with the explorer Coronado in 1541. This was some 80 years before the Pilgrims came to America.

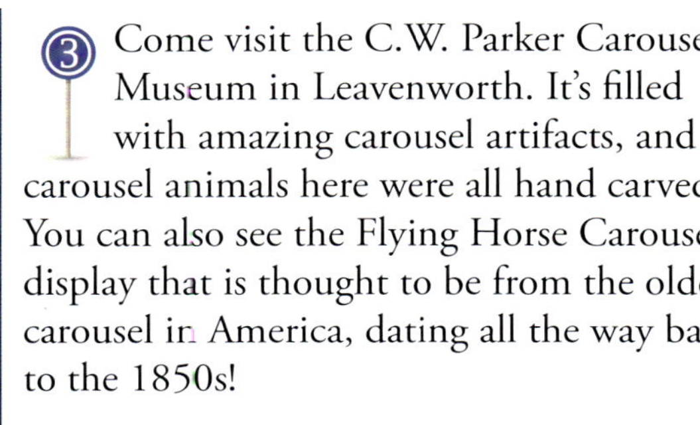

③ Come visit the C.W. Parker Carousel Museum in Leavenworth. It's filled with amazing carousel artifacts, and the carousel animals here were all hand carved. You can also see the Flying Horse Carousel display that is thought to be from the oldest carousel in America, dating all the way back to the 1850s!

1 2 3 4 5 6

NEBRASKA

MISSOURI

OKLAHOMA

A B C

ST FRANCIS • ATWOOD • NORTON • PHILLIPSBURG • SMITH CENTER • BELLEVILLE • MARYSVILLE • SUMMERFIELD • SENECA • HIAWATHA • TROY • ST JOSEPH

JENNINGS • EDMOND • KIRWIN RESERVOIR • LINN • FRANKFORT • KICKAPOO IND RES • HAVENSVILLE • ATCHISON

GOODLAND • COLBY • SELDEN • HOXIE • HILL CITY • WEBSTER LAKE • STOCKTON • OSBORNE • WACONDA LAKE • BELOIT • CONCORDIA • CLAY CENTER • TUTTLE CREEK LAKE • HOLTON • POTAWATOMI INDIAN RESERVATION • LEAVENWORTH

PLAINVILLE • HUNTER • MILTONVALE • MANHATTAN • MILFORD LAKE • KANSAS CITY • SILVER LAKE

OAKLEY • PARK • SALINE RIVER • LURAY • MINNEAPOLIS • TALMAGE • JUNCTION CITY • TOPEKA • LAWRENCE • KANSAS RIVER

RUSSELL SPRINGS • SHARON SPRINGS • GOVE • WAKEENEY • CEDAR BLUFF RESERVOIR • HAYS • RUSSELL • WILSON LAKE • LINCOLN • SALINA • ABILENE • ALTA VISTA • ESKRIDGE • CLINTON LAKE • OVERLAND PARK • BALDWIN CITY

SMOKY HILL RIVER • RANSOM • LIEBENTHAL • ELLSWORTH • KANOPOLIS LAKE • BRIDGEPORT • HERINGTON • COUNCIL GROVE LAKE • COUNCIL GROVE • POMONA LAKE • HILLSDALE LAKE • OTTAWA

TRIBUNE • LEOTI • SCOTT CITY • DIGHTON • NESS CITY • RUSH CENTER • HOISINGTON • BUSHTON • LINDSBORG • MARION RESERVOIR • MELVERN LAKE • OSAWATOMIE

GREAT BEND • LYONS • MCPHERSON • HILLSBORO • STRONG CITY • EMPORIA • WAVERLY

FRIEND • LARNED • FLORENCE • JOHN REDMOND RESERVOIR • COFFEY COUNTY LAKE • GARNETT • WELDA • MOUND

SYRACUSE • LAKIN • KALVESTA • JETMORE • GARDEN CITY • KINSLEY • ST JOHN • MACKSVILLE • HUTCHINSON • NEWTON • WALTON • WHITEWATER • MADISON • GRIDLEY • IOLA • BRONSON

ARKANSAS RIVER • CIMARRON • DODGE CITY • ARLINGTON • EL DORADO RESERVOIR • EUREKA • YATES CENTER • FORT SCOTT

ULYSSES • CHENEY RESERVOIR • BENTON • EL DORADO • FALL RIVER LAKE • TORONTO LAKE • CHANUTE

MANTER • COPELAND • BUCKLIN • GREENSBURG • PRATT • KINGMAN • WICHITA • AUGUSTA • SEVERY • BENEDICT • ENGLEVALE

SATANTA • MINNEOLA • SAWYER • ARNORAGOLD • VIOLA • DERBY • FREDONIA • PITTSBURG

CIMARRON NATIONAL GRASSLAND • MEADE • COLDWATER • MEDICINE LODGE • HARPER • WELLINGTON • WINFIELD • MOLINE • ELK CITY LAKE • PARSONS • NEOSHO RIVER

HUGOTON • ROLLA • LIBERAL • SITKA • ENGLEWOOD • ANTHONY • HARDTNER • ARKANSAS CITY • SEDAN • INDEPENDENCE • COFFEYVILLE • BAXTER SPRINGS

HOOKER • BUFFALO • MIAMI

WONDERS IN GOD'S WORLD

A Brown v. Board of Education National Historic Site

Public schools in America used to be segregated, which meant that white students and black students met at different places. The people that were part of the case that is celebrated here helped end legal segregation.

B Fort Scott National Historic Site

This fort is named after General Winfield Scott. The fort served as a military base in 1850 and then as a supply base and place of security during difficult times.

C Nicodemus National Historic Site

After the Civil War ended, those who had been slaves were freed but had little or nothing that was their own to begin a new life. Many of them came to the "promised land" of Kansas to start a new life. This site tells of their histories.

D Pony Express National Historic Trail

Between 1860 and 1861, young men rode horses from Missouri to California, carrying mail. They could do this on a relay system that took only 10 days!

E Santa Fe National Historic Trail

Before the railroad came in 1880, this trail that started up in 1821 helped people travel from Franklin, Missouri, to Santa Fe, New Mexico. Explore the adventure!

KENTUCKY

KENTUCKY PREAMBLE

We, the people of the Commonwealth of Kentucky, grateful to ***Almighty God*** for the civil, political and religious liberties we enjoy, and invoking the continuance of these blessings, do ordain and establish this Constitution.

Statehood	1792 (15th state)
Population ranking	26th
Capital	Frankfort
State flower	Goldenrod
State bird	Kentucky cardinal
Nickname	The Bluegrass State
Highest point	Black Mountain, 4,145 feet

The Kentucky Horse Park is not only a working horse farm but also an educational theme park. If you love horses, you'll love their International Museum of the Horse, their Southern Lights holiday festival, and their special competitions here in Lexington.

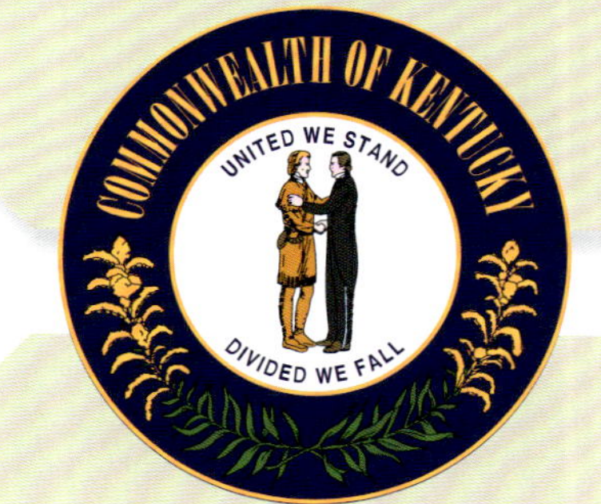

Kentucky is a state in the American South. As the 15th state, they received their statehood in 1792. "My Old Kentucky Home" is their state song. And the state dance? That would be clogging!

① It's interesting that both Abraham Lincoln, who became President of the Union, and Jefferson Davis, who became President of the Confederacy, both were born in Kentucky. Lincoln was born on Sinking Spring Farm, and Davis was born in Fairview.

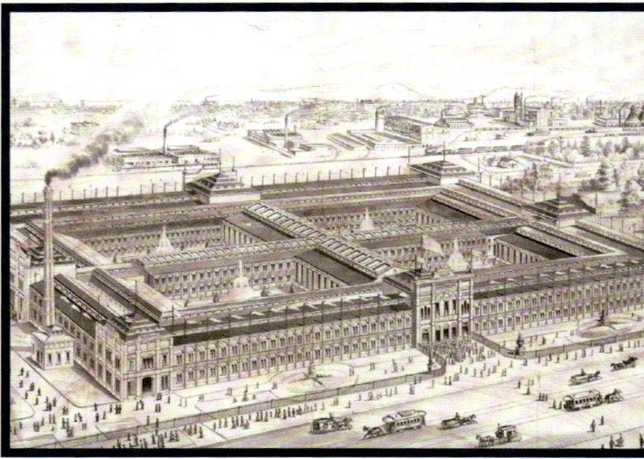

② Thomas Edison was an amazing inventor who was homeschooled, taught his math, reading, and writing by his mother. He introduced his incandescent light bulb to the people at the Southern Exposition in Louisville in 1883.

③ The Ark Encounter features a full-size reproduction of Noah's Ark, built according to the dimensions given in the Bible and filled with unique features that teach about the Genesis Flood. It's 510 feet long, 85 feet wide, and 51 feet high, and you can visit it in Grant County in Williamstown, Kentucky.

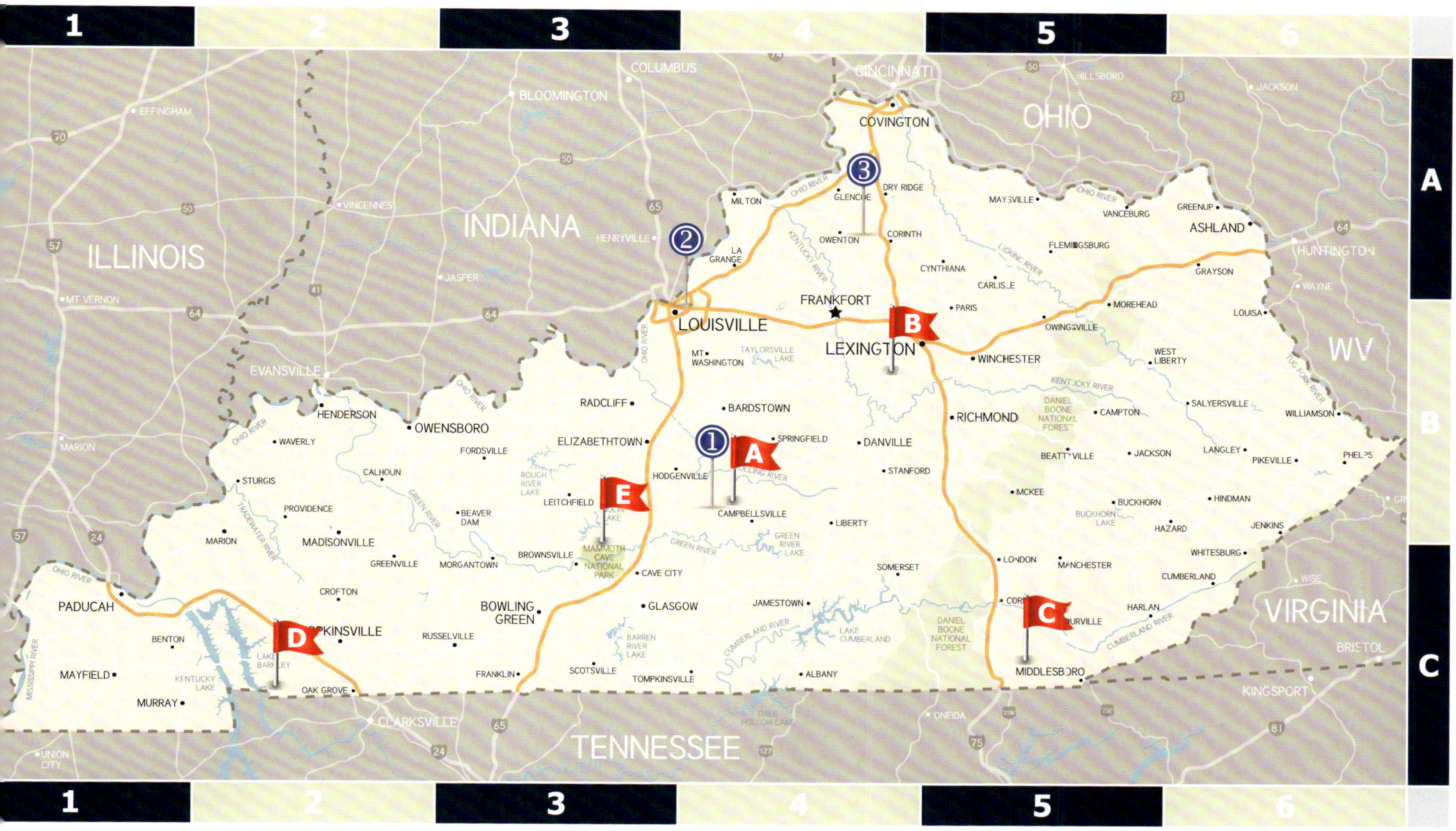

1 2 3 4 5 6

A B C

ILLINOIS
INDIANA
OHIO
WV
VIRGINIA
TENNESSEE

CINCINNATI
COVINGTON
COLUMBUS
BLOOMINGTON
EFFINGHAM
VINCENNES
JASPER
MT VERNON
EVANSVILLE
MARION
HENRYVILLE
MILTON
GLENCOE
DRY RIDGE
LA GRANGE
OWENTON
CORINTH
MAYSVILLE
VANCEBURG
GREENUP
ASHLAND
HUNTINGTON
FLEMINGSBURG
GRAYSON
CYNTHIANA
CARLISLE
FRANKFORT
LOUISVILLE
PARIS
MOREHEAD
OWINGSVILLE
LOUISA
WAYNE
LEXINGTON
MT WASHINGTON
TAYLORSVILLE LAKE
WINCHESTER
WEST LIBERTY
RADCLIFF
BARDSTOWN
RICHMOND
HENDERSON
OWENSBORO
ELIZABETHTOWN
SPRINGFIELD
DANVILLE
CAMPTON
SALYERSVILLE
WILLIAMSON
WAVERLY
FORDSVILLE
HODGENVILLE
STANFORD
BEATTYVILLE
JACKSON
LANGLEY
PIKEVILLE
STURGIS
CALHOUN
LEITCHFIELD
CAMPBELLSVILLE
MCKEE
BUCKHORN
HINDMAN
PROVIDENCE
BEAVER DAM
LIBERTY
HAZARD
JENKINS
MARION
MADISONVILLE
BROWNSVILLE
MAMMOTH CAVE NATIONAL PARK
LONDON
MANCHESTER
WHITESBURG
GREENVILLE
MORGANTOWN
CAVE CITY
SOMERSET
CUMBERLAND
CROFTON
PADUCAH
BOWLING GREEN
GLASGOW
JAMESTOWN
HARLAN
HOPKINSVILLE
BENTON
RUSSELVILLE
LAKE CUMBERLAND
DANIEL BOONE NATIONAL FOREST
BRISTOL
MAYFIELD
FRANKLIN
SCOTSVILLE
TOMPKINSVILLE
ALBANY
MIDDLESBORO
KINGSPORT
MURRAY
OAK GROVE
CLARKSVILLE
ONEIDA
UNION CITY
OHIO RIVER
GREEN RIVER
CUMBERLAND RIVER
KENTUCKY RIVER
KENTUCKY LAKE

1 2 3 4 5 6

WONDERS IN GOD'S WORLD

A

Abraham Lincoln Birthplace National Historical Park

Referred to as the first Lincoln Memorial, this structure was built on the traditional birthplace of Abraham Lincoln, our 16th president. His early life here growing up in a small log cabin helped shape his godly character.

B

Camp Nelson National Monument

The camp was initially set up as a supply depot and hospital for the Union army during the Civil War. It soon became a recruiting center for African American soldiers, and if they were escaped slaves, it would often include their wives and children.

C

Cumberland Gap National Historical Park

Come hike or camp at a place that once was considered the gateway to the west. Native Americans traveled these woods, as well as pioneers and settlers. The beauty of God's creation is still stunning.

D

Fort Donelson National Battlefield

This area includes both Fort Donelson and Fort Heiman, which became significant battle sites for General Ulysses S. Grant and his troops who captured three Confederate forts in 1862. The area is spread out between Kentucky and Tennessee.

E

Mammoth Cave National Park

The park preserves both the massive cave system, as well as part of the Green River valley and hill country of south-central Kentucky. The world's longest known cave system, Mammoth Cave has had 400 miles of the cave system explored.

LOUISIANA

LOUISIANA PREAMBLE

We, the people of Louisiana, grateful to ***Almighty God*** for the civil, political, economic, and religious liberties we enjoy, and desiring to protect individual rights to life, liberty, and property; afford opportunity for the fullest development of the individual; assure equality of rights; promote the health, safety, education, and welfare of the people; maintain a representative and orderly government; ensure domestic tranquility; provide for the common defense; and secure the blessings of freedom and justice to ourselves and our posterity, do ordain and establish this constitution.

Statehood	1812 (18th state)
Population ranking	25th
Capital	Baton Rouge
State flower	Magnolia
State bird	Eastern brown pelican
Nickname	The Pelican State / The Bayou State
Highest point	Driskill Mountain, 535 feet

Louisiana is considered part of the South. It became the 18th state in 1812. Their state song is "Give Me Louisiana." And the state doughnut? The beignet!

Louisiana is known for its bayous. But just what is a bayou? Well, it's a French name that comes from a Choctaw word: *bayuk*. *Bayuk* means slow-moving river or small stream.

① The area around the town of Jean Lafitte was once a hiding place for pirates. This included the pirate Jean Lafitte himself. He helped the United States win the battle of New Orleans.

The fishing industry of Louisiana is a major part of the state's economy. In fact, one out of every seventy jobs in the state is connected to the seafood industry.

② Have you ever seen the Superdome in New Orleans? It's the world's largest fixed dome structure. During Hurricane Katrina, it was transformed into a storm shelter for thousands of people who fled their homes.

Eastern brown pelican

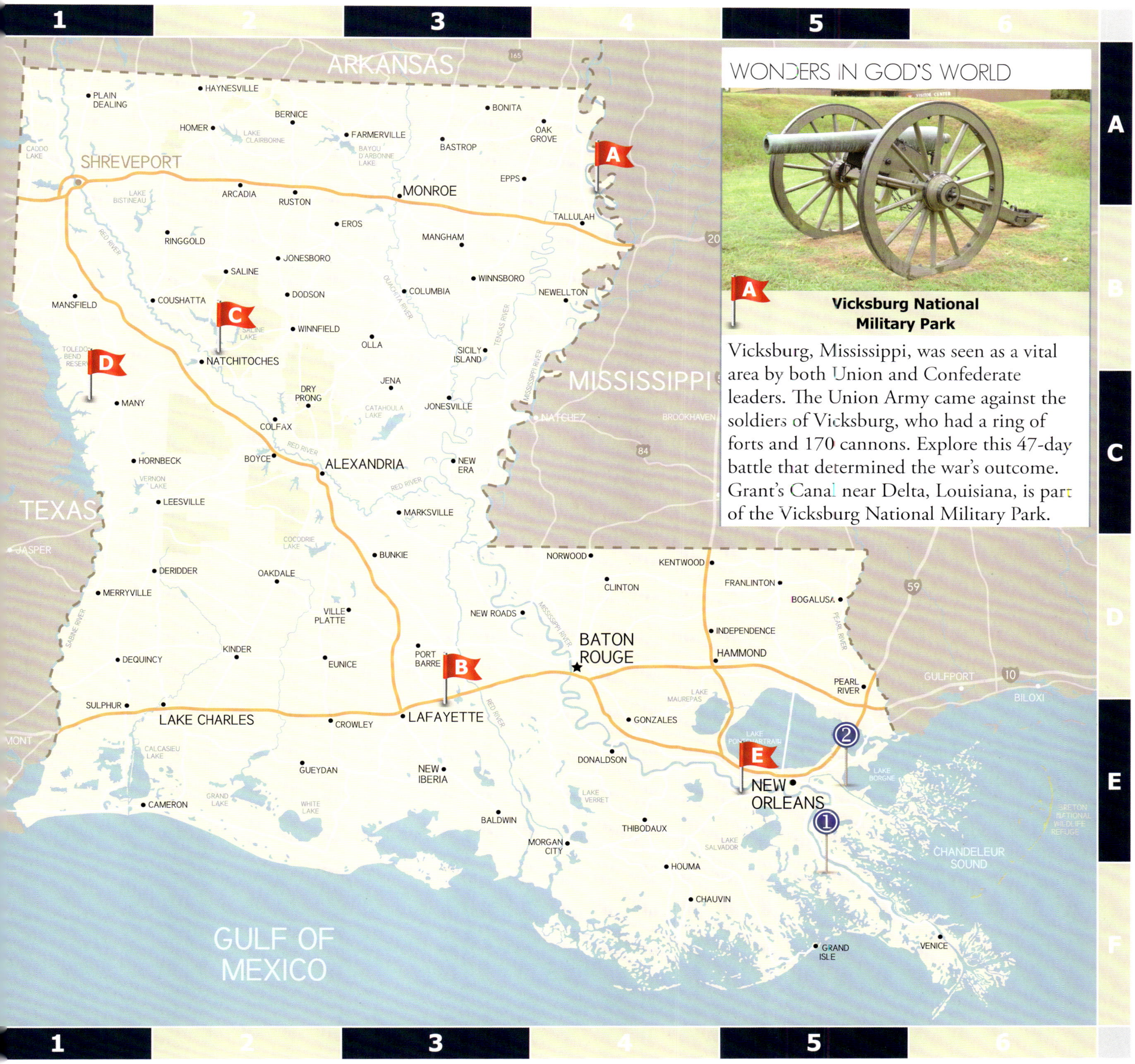

1 3 5

ARKANSAS

PLAIN DEALING
HAYNESVILLE
CADDO LAKE
HOMER
LAKE CLAIBORNE
BERNICE
FARMERVILLE
BAYOU D'ARBONNE LAKE
BONITA
BASTROP
OAK GROVE
SHREVEPORT
LAKE BISTINEAU
ARCADIA
RUSTON
MONROE
EPPS
TALLULAH
EROS
MANGHAM
RINGGOLD
JONESBORO
SALINE
WINNSBORO
MANSFIELD
COUSHATTA
DODSON
COLUMBIA
NEWELLTON
SALINE LAKE
WINNFIELD
OLLA
SICILY ISLAND
TOLEDO BEND RESERVOIR
NATCHITOCHES
JENA
MISSISSIPPI
MANY
DRY PRONG
CATAHOULA LAKE
JONESVILLE
NATCHEZ
BROOKHAVEN
COLFAX
RED RIVER
BOYCE
ALEXANDRIA
NEW ERA
HORNBECK
VERNON LAKE
LEESVILLE
MARKSVILLE
TEXAS
JASPER
COCODRIE LAKE
BUNKIE
NORWOOD
KENTWOOD
DERIDDER
OAKDALE
CLINTON
FRANLINTON
MERRYVILLE
BOGALUSA
VILLE PLATTE
NEW ROADS
INDEPENDENCE
BATON ROUGE
HAMMOND
KINDER
PORT BARRE
DEQUINCY
EUNICE
GULFPORT
PEARL RIVER
BILOXI
SULPHUR
LAKE CHARLES
LAFAYETTE
LAKE MAUREPAS
GONZALES
CROWLEY
CALCASIEU LAKE
LAKE PONTCHARTRAIN
DONALDSON
GUEYDAN
NEW IBERIA
NEW ORLEANS
LAKE BORGNE
CAMERON
GRAND LAKE
WHITE LAKE
LAKE VERRET
BALDWIN
THIBODAUX
MORGAN CITY
LAKE SALVADOR
BRETON NATIONAL WILDLIFE REFUGE
CHANDELEUR SOUND
HOUMA
CHAUVIN
GULF OF MEXICO
GRAND ISLE
VENICE

1 3 5

A B C D E F

WONDERS IN GOD'S WORLD

A Vicksburg National Military Park

Vicksburg, Mississippi, was seen as a vital area by both Union and Confederate leaders. The Union Army came against the soldiers of Vicksburg, who had a ring of forts and 170 cannons. Explore this 47-day battle that determined the war's outcome. Grant's Canal near Delta, Louisiana, is part of the Vicksburg National Military Park.

B Atchafalaya National Heritage Area

The Atchafalaya (ah-CHAFF-ah-lie-ah) area of Louisiana is filled with bayous, rivers, and the largest river swamp in America. You will see some of the most unique landscapes, including the ancient live oaks and massive cypress, and wildlife like alligators and bears.

C Cane River Creole National Historical Park

This area was established in 1994 and is home to the unique culture of the Creoles, who are descended from both the French and Spanish peoples. Explore the history of two French Creole cotton plantations, including 65 historic structures and artifacts.

D El Camino Real de los Tejas National Historic Trail

Study this trail that has a 300-year history. It originally ran from Mexico City, Mexico, all the way to the Louisiana border near the Sabine River and was known as the ancient Spanish colonial royal road.

E New Orleans Jazz National Historical Park

The park was created to celebrate jazz — its origins and legacy as a musical art form of America. They host live jazz concerts that provide both entertainment and educational opportunities.

MAINE

MAINE PREAMBLE

We the people of Maine, in order to establish justice, insure tranquility, provide for our mutual defense, promote our common welfare, and secure to ourselves and our posterity the blessings of liberty, acknowledging with grateful hearts the goodness of the ***Sovereign Ruler of the Universe*** in affording us an opportunity, so favorable to the design; and, imploring ***God's*** aid and direction in its accomplishment, do agree to form ourselves into a free and independent State, by the style and title of the State of Maine and do ordain and establish the following Constitution for the government of the same.

Statehood	1820 (23rd state)
Population ranking	42nd
Capital	Augusta
State flower	White pinecone and tassel
State bird	Chickadee
Nickname	The Pine Tree State
Highest point	Mount Katahdin, 5,268 feet

Maine is in the Northeast Region. In 1820, Maine became the 23rd state. "State of Maine" is their official song. And the state crustacean? That would be the lobster! Out of all fifty states, Maine is the only state with just one syllable.

It is actually known when the first ship was built in the Americas. It was constructed by Popham colonists, it was called *Virginia*, and it was launched on the Kennebec River in 1607.

1. The first sawmill in what would become the United States was opened in 1623. It was on the Piscataqua (piz-cah-TALK-wah) River near York, Maine.

2. The very first incorporated city in America was called Gorgeana, and this was in 1642. Portions of this first city became what is today called York, Maine.

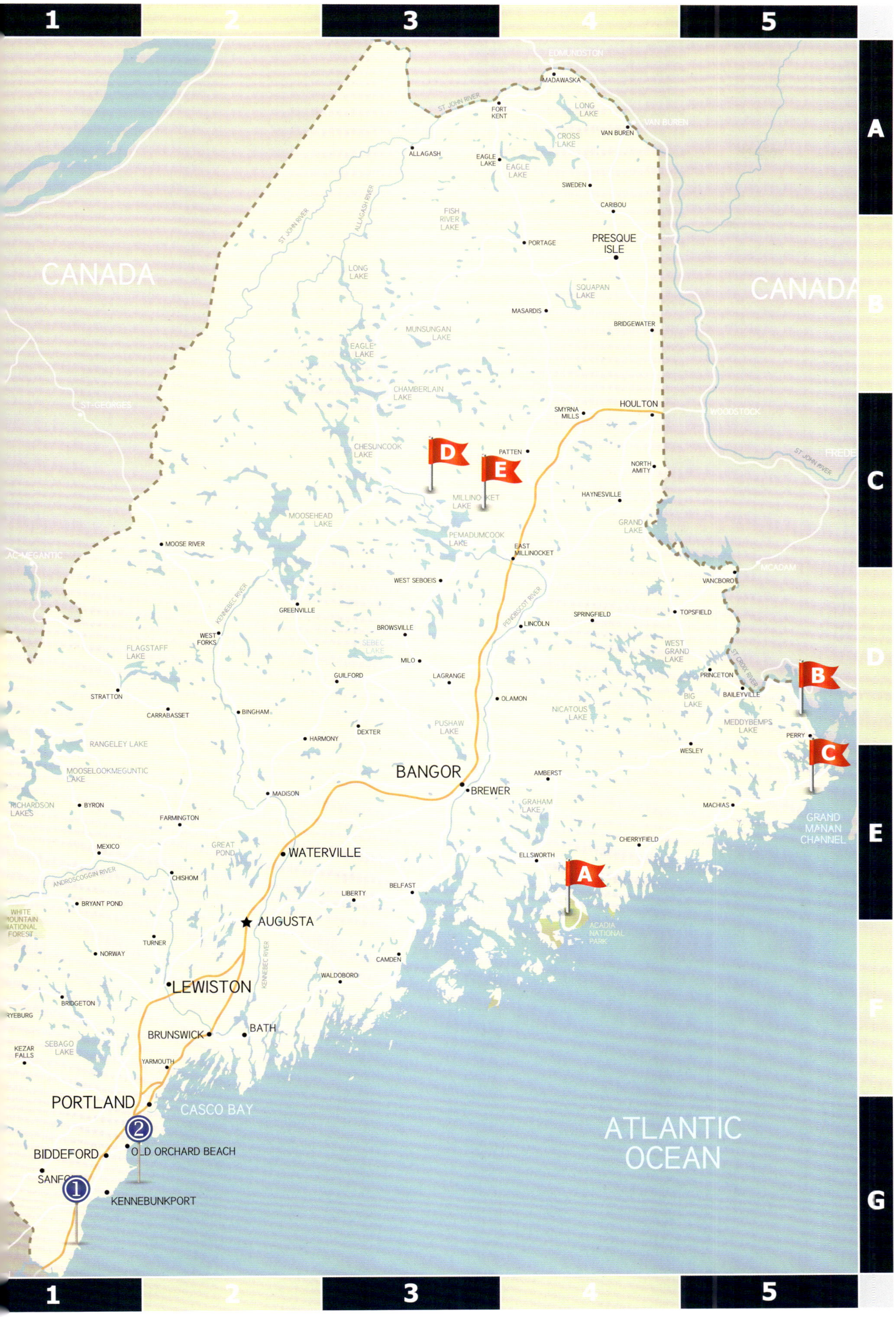

Acadia National Park

This park has around 3.5 million visitors each year, which makes it one of the top ten most-visited national parks in America. Come see the wondrous beauty God created with scenic coastlines, 158 miles of hiking trails, and 45 miles of roads created for carriages!

Saint Croix Island International Historic Site

Discover the history of this area that was defined during the winter of 1604–1605. Pierre Dugua's French expedition was trapped on Saint Croix Island, with 35 of the 75 men dying. Native people came in the spring and brought game to trade and brought hope as well.

Roosevelt Campobello International Park

When he was growing up, Franklin D. Roosevelt used to summer on Campobello Island. He later became the 32nd president of the United States, but this place connecting Lubec, Maine, and New Brunswick, Canada, was always special to him.

Appalachian National Scenic Trail

This amazing trail is a 2,180-mile-long footpath that crosses through amazing scenic areas over 14 states. The trail was planned and completed by private citizens between 1921 and 1937, but the National Park Service oversees it now.

Katahdin Woods & Waters National Monument

There are 87,563 acres of forests, mountains, and rivers. This fairly new monument has a somewhat old name that comes from the language of the Penobscot Native peoples and means "the greatest mountain."

MARYLAND

MARYLAND PREAMBLE

We, the People of the State of Maryland, grateful to ***Almighty God*** for our civil and religious liberty, and taking into our serious consideration the best means of establishing a good Constitution in this State for the sure foundation and more permanent security thereof, declare…

Statehood	1788 (7th state)
Population ranking	19th
Capital	Annapolis
State flower	Black-eyed Susan
State bird	Baltimore oriole
Nickname	The Old Line State / The Free State
Highest point	Hoye-Crest, the summit on Backbone Mountain, 3,360 feet

The Book Thing of Baltimore is a bookstore that allows you to simply take their books for free. It was started as a way to provide books for impoverished students, but anyone can come by.

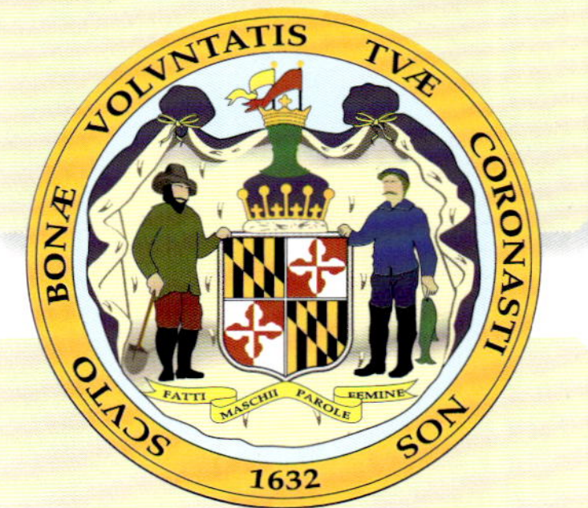

Maryland is in the South Region of the U.S. It became the 7th state in 1788. The state song is "Maryland, My Maryland." And the state folk dance? That's the square dance!

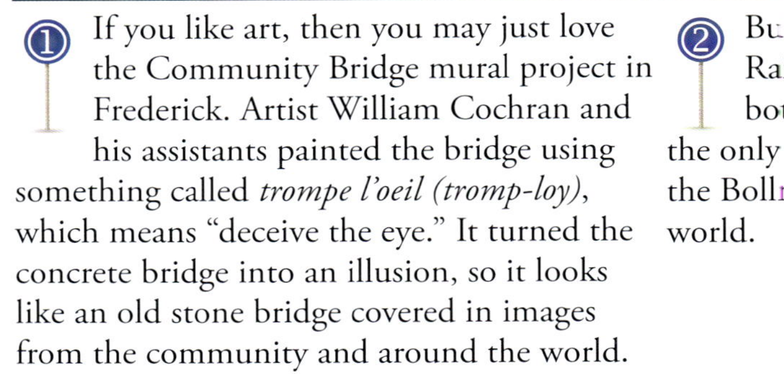

① If you like art, then you may just love the Community Bridge mural project in Frederick. Artist William Cochran and his assistants painted the bridge using something called *trompe l'oeil (tromp-loy)*, which means "deceive the eye." It turned the concrete bridge into an illusion, so it looks like an old stone bridge covered in images from the community and around the world.

② Built in 1869, the Bollman Truss Railroad Bridge in Savage is made of both cast iron and wrought iron. It's the only open railroad bridge, formerly called the Bollman truss, that's left anywhere in the world.

③ At the founding of the United States, the leaders wanted to create a capital city that wasn't part of a state, so as not to be unfair to other states. Maryland gave up some of its land to help form Washington, D.C., our country's capital. Virginia gave up some land as well, but it was given back to the state in 1846.

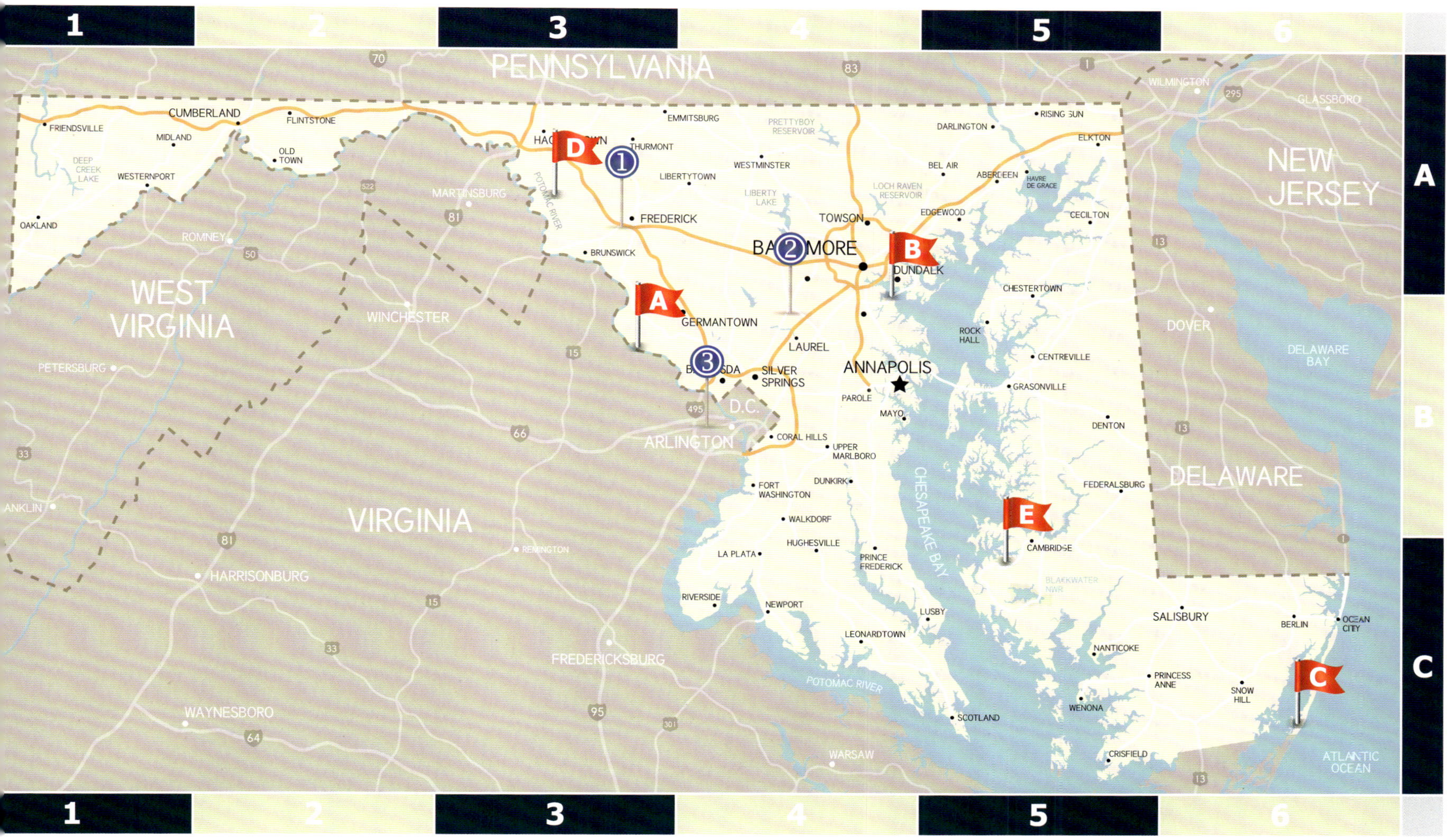

WONDERS IN GOD'S WORLD

A Clara Barton National Historic Site

Clara Barton was the founder of the American Red Cross. This historic site honors her amazing life. The house that is in Glen Echo was her home, the headquarters for the American Red Cross, and a warehouse for their disaster relief supplies.

B Star-Spangled Banner National Historic Trail

The trail crosses 560 miles of land and water between Maryland; Virginia; and Washington, D.C. Much of the history of the War of 1812 is addressed, with a focus on the story of our National Anthem. You can see the almost 200-year-old, 30-by-34-foot flag that inspired the lyrics at the National Museum of American History.

C Assateague Island National Seashore

Come explore the beautiful beach areas, the salt marshes, and the forests that thrive in this wild area. From here you're only a few hours' drive from Baltimore, Philadelphia, or Washington. The Chincoteague Pony or Assateague horse is a wild breed that lives here.

D Antietam National Battlefield

The area commemorates the Civil War Battle of Antietam. There were 23,000 soldiers killed, wounded, or missing after 12 hours of fighting on September 17, 1862. See the battlefield, visitor center, field hospital museum, and a national military cemetery.

E Harriet Tubman Underground Railroad National Historical Park

Established in 2013, this park honors the legacy of Harriet Tubman, who helped guide nearly 70 enslaved people to freedom in the north. The "Railroad" was a network of people helping slaves start new lives as free people.

MASSACHUSETTS

MASSACHUSETTS PREAMBLE

We, therefore, the people of Massachusetts, acknowledging, with grateful hearts, the goodness of the great ***Legislator*** of the universe, in affording us, in the course of ***His*** providence, an opportunity, deliberately and peaceably, without fraud, violence or surprise, of entering into an original, explicit, and solemn compact with each other; and of forming a new constitution of civil government, for ourselves and posterity; and devoutly imploring ***His*** direction in so interesting a design, do agree upon, ordain and establish the following Declaration of Rights, and Frame of Government, as the Constitution of the Commonwealth of Massachusetts.

Statehood	1788 (6th state)
Population ranking	15th
Capital	Boston
State flower	Mayflower
State bird	Chickadee
Nickname	The Bay State / The Old Colony State
Highest point	Mount Greylock, 3,490 feet

Massachusetts is a part of the Northeast Region. In 1788 it became the 6th state. The state anthem is "All Hail to Massachusetts." There is also a state polka, called "Say Hello to Someone from Massachusetts." And the state artist? Norman Rockwell!

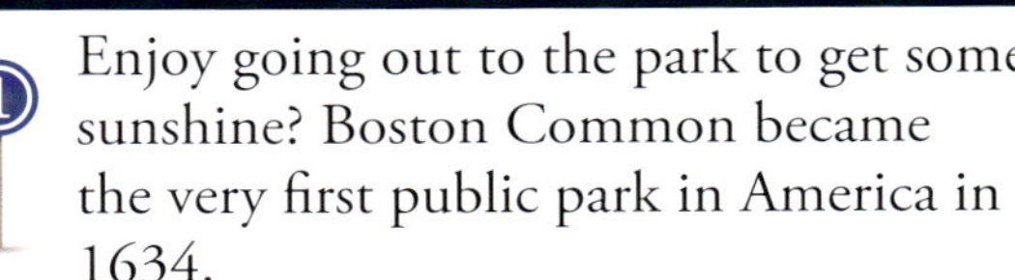

1. Enjoy going out to the park to get some sunshine? Boston Common became the very first public park in America in 1634.

2. The first college established in North America was Harvard University. It was founded in 1636.

3. The USS *Constitution*, sometimes known as "Old Ironsides," is the world's oldest commissioned vessel still floating. It was first launched in 1797. Now you can find the ship at Charlestown Navy Yard.

4. The first game of basketball was on December 21, 1891. It was played in Springfield, and that's where you can find the Naismith Memorial Basketball Hall of Fame, built in 1959.

Public transportation in big cities, like buses and taxis, has become a very important way to get around. Boston completed the first subway system in the United States in 1897. It was just 1 ½ miles long!

WONDERS IN GOD'S WORLD

A Blackstone River Valley National Historical Park

This park is in parts of both Rhode Island and Massachusetts. It was created to help preserve and protect the industrial heritage of this region because the Blackstone River area was a significant part of the American Industrial Revolution.

B Boston African American National Historic Site

This site honors the history of the African American community that was a part of Boston's fight against slavery and injustice in the 1800s. You will see the 1806 African Meeting House, the oldest standing black church in America, and more.

C New Bedford Whaling National Historical Park

New Bedford was the world's major whaling port during the 19th century. You can discover so much about this town and the whaling history here through the visitor center, a whaling museum, a special schooner, and so much more.

D Longfellow House Washington's Headquarters National Historic Site

Before it was the home of the famous poet Henry Wadsworth Longfellow, this house served as the headquarters for General George Washington. Come explore the history and literature of the region.

E Cape Cod National Seashore

Here the great Outer Beach is protected, which includes 40 miles of beach, marshes, and ponds, and all the diverse creatures that live here. The area was set aside on August 7, 1961 by president John F. Kennedy.

MICHIGAN

MICHIGAN PREAMBLE

We, the people of the State of Michigan, grateful to ***Almighty God*** for the blessings of freedom, and earnestly desiring to secure these blessings undiminished to ourselves and our posterity, do ordain and establish this constitution.

Statehood	1837 (26th state)
Population ranking	10th
Capital	Lansing
State flower	Apple blossom
State bird	Robin
Nickname	The Wolverine State
Highest point	Mount Arvon, 1,979 feet

The largest freshwater spring in Michigan is called Kitch-iti-kipi, which means "big cold water." This 40-foot-deep pool fills with a fresh 10,000 gallons of water every minute.

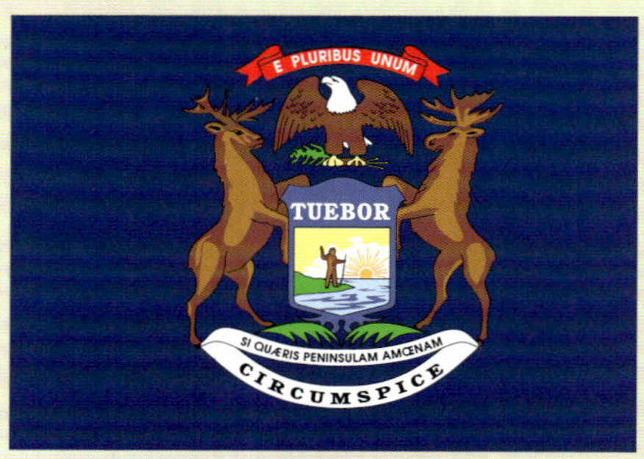

Michigan is considered part of the Midwest and is divided into two sections called peninsulas. In 1837 it became the 26th state. The official state song is called "My Michigan." And the state fossil? That would be the mastodon!

① The *J. W. Westcott II* is a mail delivery boat that brings letters and packages to ships while they are out on the water. They have been operating the service since 1874 and are headquartered in Detroit. It has the only floating ZIP code in the United States!

② There are a lot of zoos in America, but one of the first to feature "cageless," open exhibits that allow animals to roam with more freedom was the Detroit Zoo. It opened in 1928.

Detroit is known as Motor City because of its history of automaking. This 1913 photograph shows workers at the Ford Motor Company in Detroit, working on an early assembly line.

1 2 3 4 5 6

LAKE SUPERIOR

CANADA

MICHIGAN

WISCONSIN

LAKE MICHIGAN

LAKE HURON

LAKE ERIE

INDIANA

OHIO

LANSING

DETROIT

GRAND RAPIDS

WONDERS IN GOD'S WORLD

A Pictured Rocks National Lakeshore

Considered America's first National Lakeshore, you can explore the beaches, hike over nearly 100 miles of trails, look at towering sandstone cliffs, and see the beauty of the northern woodlands.

B Keweenaw National Historical Park

The Keweenaw (KEY-when-ah) was mined for copper for over a thousand years. The native peoples used it for their tools, and later the immigrants of the 1800s mined and developed the industry that thrived here. There is no more mining, but you can see the marks.

C Isle Royale National Park

Surrounded by Lake Superior, this isolated island is a wonder for hikers, backpackers, kayakers, and scuba divers. Everywhere you step, God's wonders are on display.

D River Raisin National Battlefield Park

Discover the history of the January battles of 1813 that took place here. It is the only National Battlefield Park in America that focuses on the War of 1812.

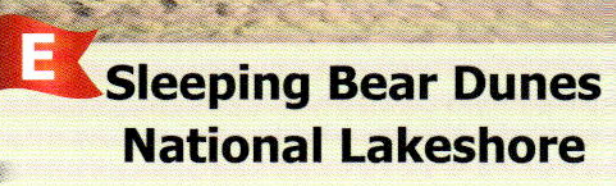

E Sleeping Bear Dunes National Lakeshore

Come see the beauty of these sandy beaches, bluffs that rise 450 feet above Lake Michigan, thick forests, inland lakes, and more. The high dunes take you to where you can look out over the wonders of the lake.

MINNESOTA

MINNESOTA PREAMBLE

We, the people of the state of Minnesota, grateful to ***God*** for our civil and religious liberty, and desiring to perpetuate its blessings and secure the same to ourselves and our posterity, do ordain and establish this Constitution.

Statehood	1858 (32nd state)
Population ranking	22nd
Capital	St. Paul
State flower	Pink and white lady's slipper
State bird	Common loon
Nickname	The Land of 10,000 Lakes / The North Star State
Highest point	Eagle Mountain, 2,302 feet

If you like Viking history, you might want to visit the Hjemkomst Center in Moorhead. Hjemkomst means "homecoming" in Norwegian, and the center has a replica of a Viking ship and a stave church that both honor the Scandinavian heritage of this area.

Minnesota can be found in the Midwest Region. It became the 32nd state in 1858. The state song here is "Hail! Minnesota." And the state muffin? The blueberry muffin!

① Open pit mining is used when the rocks or minerals you're needing are near the surface of the earth. One of the world's first open-pit mines was the Hull-Rust-Mahoning Mine in Hibbing. It was opened in 1895 and is still the largest such mine in Minnesota.

② The city of Excelsior is where you'll find the Old Log Theatre. It's the oldest professional theater in the state of Minnesota.

③ Do you like staying indoors? If you do, you would love the Minneapolis Skyway System. It's a whole 80 city blocks (over 11 miles) of the downtown area. You can eat, live, shop, and work without ever going outside. That's the longest continuous indoor system in the world.

④ The Little House on the Prairie children's book series was written by Laura Ingalls Wilder between 1932 and 1943. They were based on her life growing up in a pioneer family. Parts of her story unfolded near Walnut Grove, Minnesota, as discussed in *On the Banks of Plum Creek*.

WONDERS IN GOD'S WORLD

A **Grand Portage National Monument**

Located on the north shore of Lake Superior, the center helps preserve the heritage of the native peoples of this region and tells the history of the British fur trading activity that took place here.

B **North Country National Scenic Trail**

The trail will soon cover eight states from North Dakota, through Minnesota, and all the way to Vermont. It extends some 4,600 miles, making it the longest of the 11 National Scenic Trails in the U.S.

C **Pipestone National Monument**

The area is just north of the city of Pipestone in southwestern Minnesota. Learn how American Indians have quarried pipestone at this site for generations in order to make their sacred pipes.

D **Saint Croix National Scenic Riverway**

The St. Croix and Namekagon (NAM-uh-KAH-gun) rivers flow through 255 miles of God's beautiful creation teeming with life. Find adventure in hiking, boating, fishing, and more!

E **Voyageurs National Park**

Over 40 percent of the Voyageurs Park is water, creating a maze of connected water highways. You might want to bring your own boat or reserve a boat in order to get around.

MISSISSIPPI

MISSISSIPPI PREAMBLE

We, the people of Mississippi in convention assembled, grateful to ***Almighty God***, and invoking his blessing on our work, do ordain and establish this constitution.

Statehood	1817 (20th state)
Population ranking	34th
Capital	Jackson
State flower	Magnolia
State bird	Mockingbird
Nickname	The Magnolia State
Highest point	Woodall Mountain, 807 feet

The word "evangel" means "good news," and back in the early 19th century, a movement called the Great Revival began in the backwoods of Kentucky, quickly spreading across Mississippi and sharing the good news of Christ. The evangelical churches grew in large numbers during this time and were known for including people from all backgrounds to worship together.

Image above is of the old flag, as the new state flag has not yet been adopted.

THE GREAT SEAL OF THE STATE OF MISSISSIPPI ★ IN GOD WE TRUST ★

Mississippi is a state in the American South. In 1817 it became the 20th state. "Go, Mississippi" is the state song. And the state fossil? The prehistoric whale!

① One of the oldest games in America is stickball. It was a game that could last for several days. The Choctaw Indians of Mississippi played the game, and you can still see demonstrations of it every July in Choctaw.

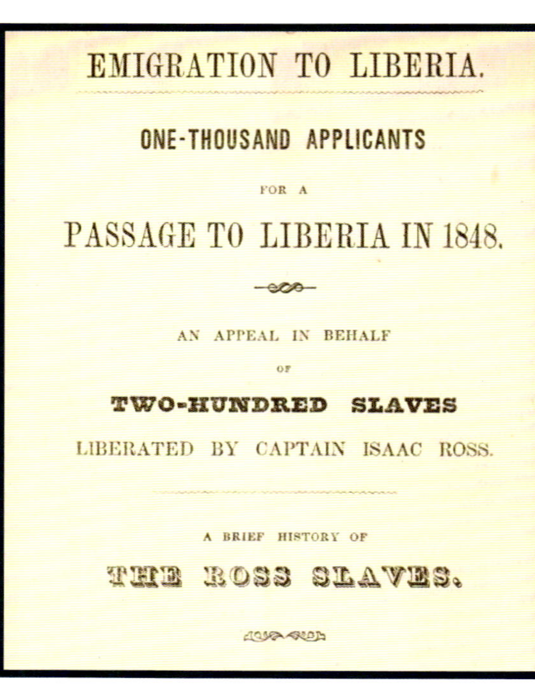

EMIGRATION TO LIBERIA.

ONE-THOUSAND APPLICANTS

FOR A

PASSAGE TO LIBERIA IN 1848.

AN APPEAL IN BEHALF

OF

TWO-HUNDRED SLAVES

LIBERATED BY CAPTAIN ISAAC ROSS.

A BRIEF HISTORY OF

THE ROSS SLAVES.

② When he died in 1836, Captain Isaac Ross, who had lived in Jefferson County, Mississippi, left it in his will for his slaves to be set free. He had them sent back to Africa, and there they helped found the country of Liberia.

③ The Mississippi River is the second-longest river in North America. It flows for 2,350 miles, is as wide as 11 miles at one point, and is considered the nation's chief waterway.

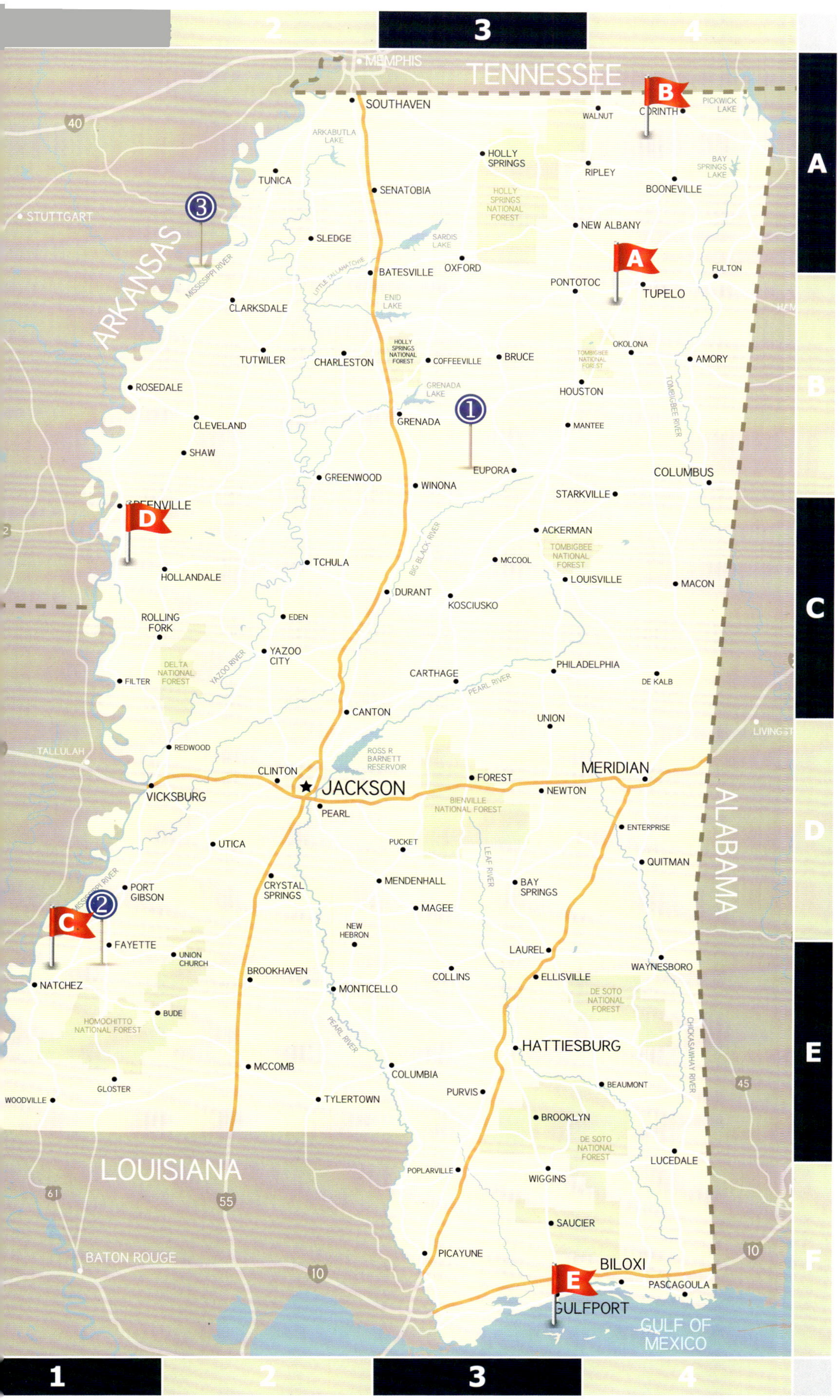

2 3 4

TENNESSEE
MEMPHIS
SOUTHAVEN
WALNUT
CORINTH
PICKWICK LAKE
ARKABUTLA LAKE
HOLLY SPRINGS
RIPLEY
BOONEVILLE
BAY SPRINGS LAKE
TUNICA
SENATOBIA
HOLLY SPRINGS NATIONAL FOREST
STUTTGART
ARKANSAS
SLEDGE
SARDIS LAKE
NEW ALBANY
BATESVILLE
OXFORD
PONTOTOC
TUPELO
FULTON
CLARKSDALE
ENID LAKE
MISSISSIPPI RIVER
TUTWILER
CHARLESTON
HOLLY SPRINGS NATIONAL FOREST
COFFEEVILLE
BRUCE
TOMBIGBEE NATIONAL FOREST
OKOLONA
AMORY
ROSEDALE
GRENADA LAKE
HOUSTON
CLEVELAND
GRENADA
MANTEE
TOMBIGBEE RIVER
SHAW
EUPORA
GREENWOOD
WINONA
COLUMBUS
STARKVILLE
GREENVILLE
ACKERMAN
TOMBIGBEE NATIONAL FOREST
MCCOOL
LOUISVILLE
MACON
TCHULA
BIG BLACK RIVER
HOLLANDALE
DURANT
KOSCIUSKO
ROLLING FORK
EDEN
YAZOO CITY
DELTA NATIONAL FOREST
YAZOO RIVER
CARTHAGE
PHILADELPHIA
DE KALB
FILTER
PEARL RIVER
CANTON
UNION
TALLULAH
ROSS R. BARNETT RESERVOIR
LIVINGSTON
REDWOOD
CLINTON
FOREST
MERIDIAN
VICKSBURG
JACKSON
NEWTON
PEARL
BIENVILLE NATIONAL FOREST
ENTERPRISE
ALABAMA
UTICA
PUCKETT
QUITMAN
CRYSTAL SPRINGS
MENDENHALL
LEAF RIVER
BAY SPRINGS
PORT GIBSON
MAGEE
NEW HEBRON
FAYETTE
LAUREL
UNION CHURCH
WAYNESBORO
BROOKHAVEN
MONTICELLO
COLLINS
ELLISVILLE
NATCHEZ
DE SOTO NATIONAL FOREST
BUDE
HOMOCHITTO NATIONAL FOREST
HATTIESBURG
CHICKASAWHAY RIVER
MCCOMB
COLUMBIA
BEAUMONT
GLOSTER
PURVIS
WOODVILLE
TYLERTOWN
BROOKLYN
LOUISIANA
DE SOTO NATIONAL FOREST
LUCEDALE
POPLARVILLE
WIGGINS
SAUCIER
BATON ROUGE
PICAYUNE
BILOXI
PASCAGOULA
GULFPORT
GULF OF MEXICO

A B C D E F

1 2 3 4

A

Tupelo National Battlefield

Established in 1929, this battlefield is dedicated to the remembrance of the July 1864 Civil War battle that was fought here. There was no true victory for either side, but the Union forces did keep the Confederate army from capturing railroads.

B

Shiloh National Military Park

Covers the history of suffering brought about when over 100,000 soldiers fought here, on both the Shiloh (TN) and Corinth (MS) battlefields during the Civil War. Some 23,746 soldiers died here, more than the number who died in all the U.S. wars prior to this combined. This statue from the park shows Chaplain Alexander handing a book to a child.

C

Natchez National Historical Park

The Natchez were the native peoples who lived in this area when the first Europeans came. The park speaks of their history, as well as the region's development over the years, including the pre– and post–Civil War times.

D

Mississippi Delta National Heritage Area

This special area preserves and promotes the culture, history, and landscape of the Mississippi Delta. This area in the northwestern section of the state is famous for its blues music and the distinctive culture that thrives here.

E

Gulf Islands National Seashore

Established in 1971, this protected coastline has so much to see and do. The Mississippi portion of the park has a historic fort and beautiful barrier islands. Want something to do? Well, there is biking, boating, camping, fishing, hiking, swimming, and more.

MISSOURI

MISSOURI PREAMBLE

We, the people of Missouri, with profound reverence for the ***Supreme Ruler of the Universe***, and grateful for ***His*** goodness, do establish this Constitution for the better government of the state.

Statehood	1821 (24th state)
Population ranking	18th
Capital	Jefferson City
State flower	Hawthorn
State bird	Bluebird
Nickname	The Show-Me State
Highest point	Taum Sauk Mountain, 1,772 feet

Missouri is in the Midwest Region. It became the 24th state in 1821. The song "Missouri Waltz" is the state song. And the state animal? The Missouri mule!

1. The most powerful earthquake to strike the lower 48 states happened in 1811. It was centered in New Madrid, Missouri, registered 7.5 to 8.1, shook more than one million square miles of the country, and could be felt as far as 1,000 miles away!

2. Kansas City has come to be known as the City of Fountains. In fact, it is said to have more fountains than any city in the world except for Rome. If you go to Kansas City in April, you can be a part of the Fountain Day festivities as fountains are turned back on after winter.

3. Some say the first real Wild West gunfight happened in the downtown square of Springfield, Missouri, in 1865. "Wild Bill" Hickok shot and killed Davis Tutt in a quick-draw shootout after a gambling dispute.

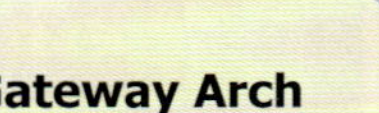

Gateway Arch

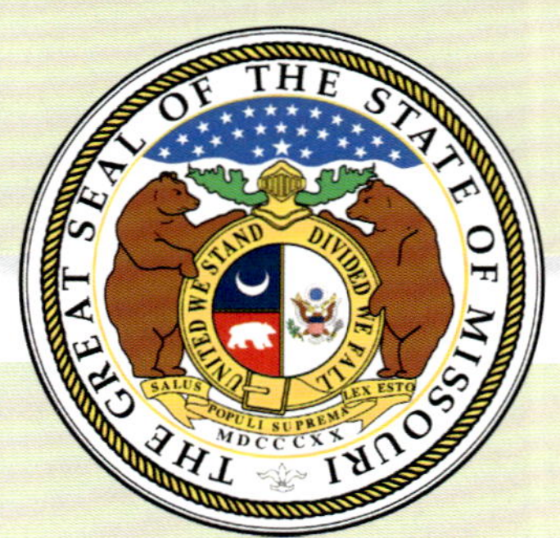

4. Sheldon "Red" Chaney cut a window into the side of his Springfield restaurant in 1947, creating the first drive-thru restaurant. The restaurant served hamburgers along the famous Route 66 and fed hungry drivers until it closed in 1984.

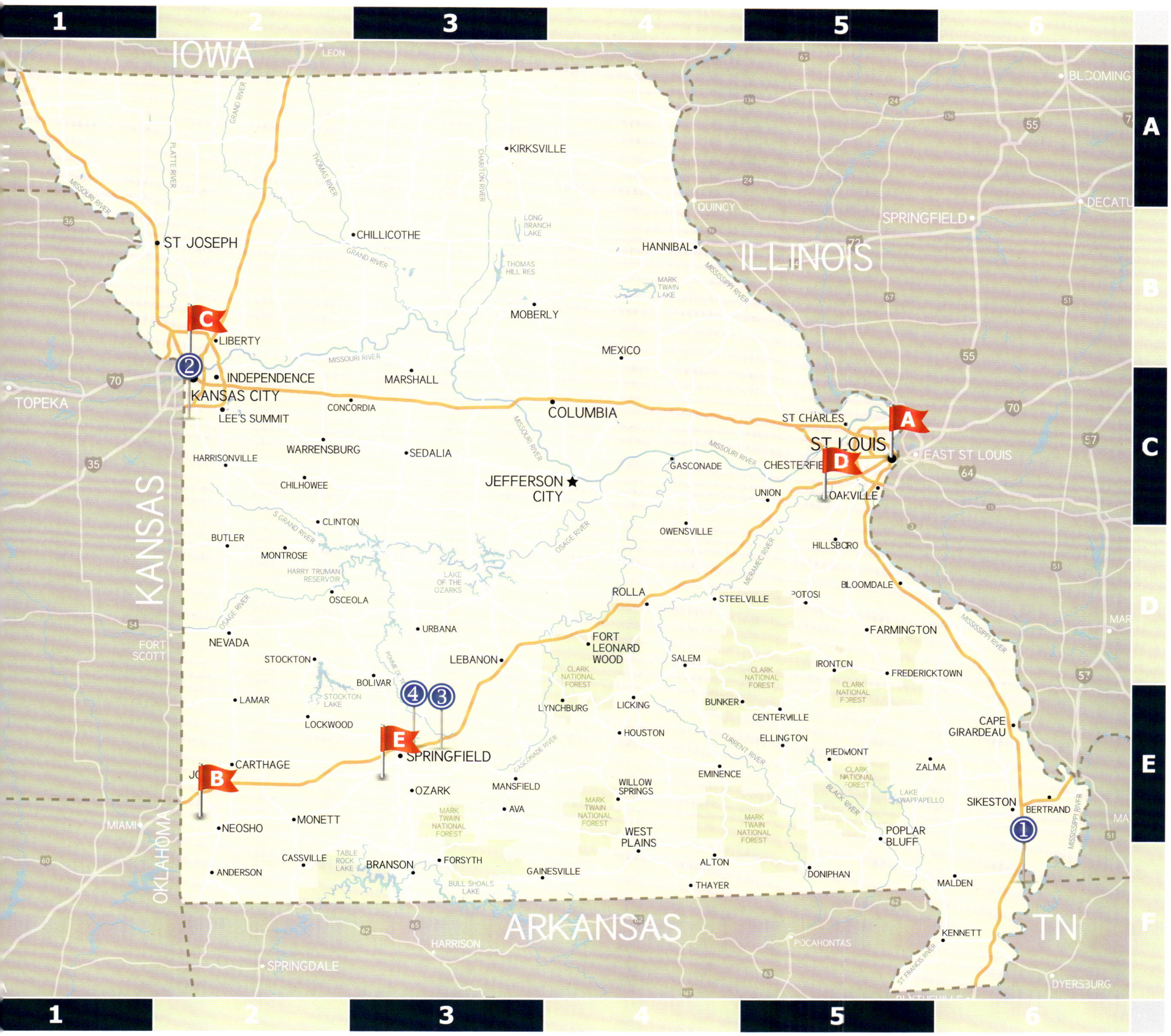

IOWA
ILLINOIS
KANSAS
OKLAHOMA
ARKANSAS
TN

ST JOSEPH
KIRKSVILLE
CHILLICOTHE
HANNIBAL
MOBERLY
MEXICO
LIBERTY
INDEPENDENCE
KANSAS CITY
MARSHALL
LEE'S SUMMIT
CONCORDIA
COLUMBIA
ST CHARLES
ST LOUIS
CHESTERFIELD
OAKVILLE
WARRENSBURG
SEDALIA
JEFFERSON CITY
GASCONADE
UNION
ROLLA
SPRINGFIELD
CARTHAGE
JOPLIN
BRANSON
CAPE GIRARDEAU
SIKESTON
POPLAR BLUFF

WONDERS IN GOD'S WORLD

A Gateway Arch National Park

Construction of the Arch was begun in 1963. It was completed in 1965 and is the tallest structure in Missouri. The park area consists of the Gateway Arch, the Museum of Westward Expansion, and St. Louis' Old Courthouse.

B George Washington Carver National Monument

This childhood home of the famous educator, humanitarian, and scientist is the first unit of the National Park Service dedicated to an African American. Carver was a Christian who believed he could integrate faith with science.

C Harry S Truman National Historic Site

The site includes the Truman Home in Independence, Missouri, and the Truman Farm Home in Grandview, Missouri. Truman was the 33rd president of the United States and lived in the home from 1919 until his death in 1972.

D Ulysses S. Grant National Historic Site

Grant is remembered most as the victorious Civil War general of the Union army and the 18th president of the United States. The site is located just 10 miles southwest of St. Louis and includes five historic structures.

E Wilson's Creek National Battlefield

The battlefield is not far from Springfield, Missouri. The area preserves the site of the first major Civil War battle fought west of the Mississippi River in 1861. General Nathaniel Lyon was killed here, the first Union general killed in action.

MONTANA

MONTANA PREAMBLE

We the people of Montana grateful to ***God*** for the quiet beauty of our state, the grandeur of our mountains, the vastness of our rolling plains, and desiring to improve the quality of life, equality of opportunity and to secure the blessings of liberty for this and future generations do ordain and establish this constitution.

Statehood	1889 (41st state)
Population ranking	43rd
Capital	Helena
State flower	Bitterroot
State bird	Western meadowlark
Nickname	The Treasure State / Big Sky Country
Highest point	Granite Peak, 12,807 feet

There is only one road that goes through the heart of Glacier National Park and it's called Going-to-the-Sun Road. Finished in 1932, this two-lane roadway is said to pass through some of the most beautiful landscapes in North America.

Montana is in the West Region. In 1889 it became the 41st state. It has a state ballad called "Montana Melody." And the state fossil? The Duck-billed Dinosaur!

Before Montana became a state, a lot of people came here in search of silver and gold!

Montana is filled with wide open spaces and is known as big sky country. It shouldn't be too surprising that cattle ranching is a big deal. It's very important for the economy.

① Every spring, up to 8,000 white pelicans migrate up from Texas, Louisiana, and Mexico on their way to Medicine Lake in northeastern Montana. Some of them have a wingspan of up to nine feet!

Something called the Continental Divide cuts through Montana. This means that rivers to the west of the divide flow into the Pacific Ocean and rivers to the east of it flow into the Atlantic Ocean.

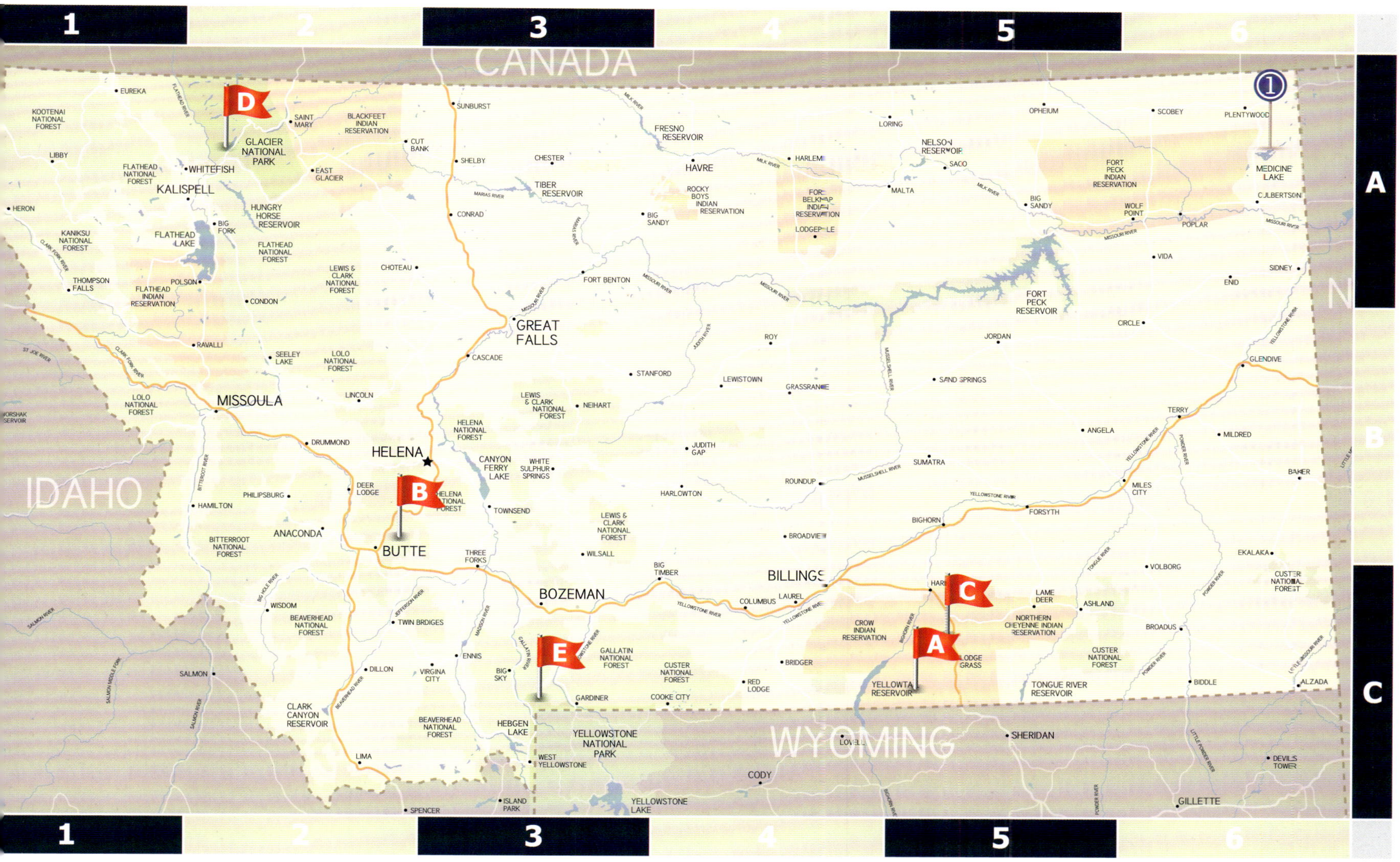

WONDERS IN GOD'S WORLD

A Bighorn Canyon National Recreation Area

The wonder of God's creation is everywhere to be seen in this 120,000-acre park. Established in 1966 after the completion of the Yellowtail Dam, part of the area connects visitors to Bighorn Lake that was created by the dam.

B Grant-Kohrs Ranch National Historic Site

Created in 1972 as a historic site, it celebrates hardworking cattleman from the 1850s through more recent history. What makes it even more interesting to visit is that it's an actual working ranch where you can get hands-on experience.

C Little Bighorn Battlefield National Monument

The area memorializes the U.S. Army's 7th Cavalry and the Lakotas and Cheyennes in one of the last efforts of the native peoples to preserve their freedom. The battle happened over June 25th and 26th in 1876.

D Glacier National Park

Come to the park to see forests, alpine meadows, massive mountain regions, and wondrous lakes. And if you like to walk, there are over 700 miles of trails to explore. Experience over one million acres of land with hundreds of different animals to see.

E Yellowstone National Park

Diverse with wildlife and plant life, as well as with hydrothermal wonders, Yellowstone became the first U.S. national park on March 1, 1872. It is so large that it covers parts of Wyoming, Montana, and Idaho.

NEBRASKA

NEBRASKA PREAMBLE

We, the people, grateful to ***Almighty God*** for our freedom, do ordain and establish the following declaration of rights and frame of government, as the Constitution of the State of Nebraska.

Statehood	1867 (37th state)
Population ranking	37th
Capital	Lincoln
State flower	Goldenrod
State bird	Western meadowlark
Nickname	The Cornhusker State
Highest point	Panorama Point, 5,427 feet

The first coast-to-coast road in America was opened in 1913. Called the Lincoln Highway, it ran from New York's Times Square to San Francisco's Lincoln Park across 13 states. In Nebraska, a portion of it remains, and this 3-mile section is paved with brick.

Nebraska is a part of the Midwest. It became the 37th state in 1867. The official song is called "Beautiful Nebraska." And the state fish? The channel catfish!

1 In the 1800s, Nebraska's Chimney Rock was one of the most mentioned landmarks of travelers on the Oregon Trail. Some of the original settlers here were called sodbusters because they would use sod to build their homes.

Nebraska is the only state in the Union with something called a unicameral legislature. That's a state government with only one house or chamber of leaders. All the other states have a bicameral system of government with two governing bodies.

The U.S. Congress passed something called the Homestead Act in 1862. This stated that any 21-year-old citizen or immigrant wanting to be a citizen could lay claim to 160 acres of land out west known as the Great American Prairie, including parts of Nebraska. If they could pay a filing fee, farm the land, and live on it for five years, it would become their land.

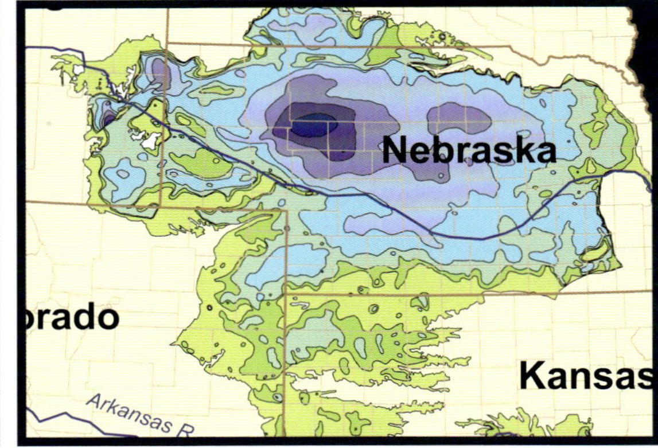

Do you know what an aquifer is? Well, it's an underground lake or water supply. Nebraska has a part of the nation's largest, called the Ogallala Aquifer. It's so big that it's also under parts of Colorado, Kansas, New Mexico, Oklahoma, South Dakota, Texas, and Wyoming.

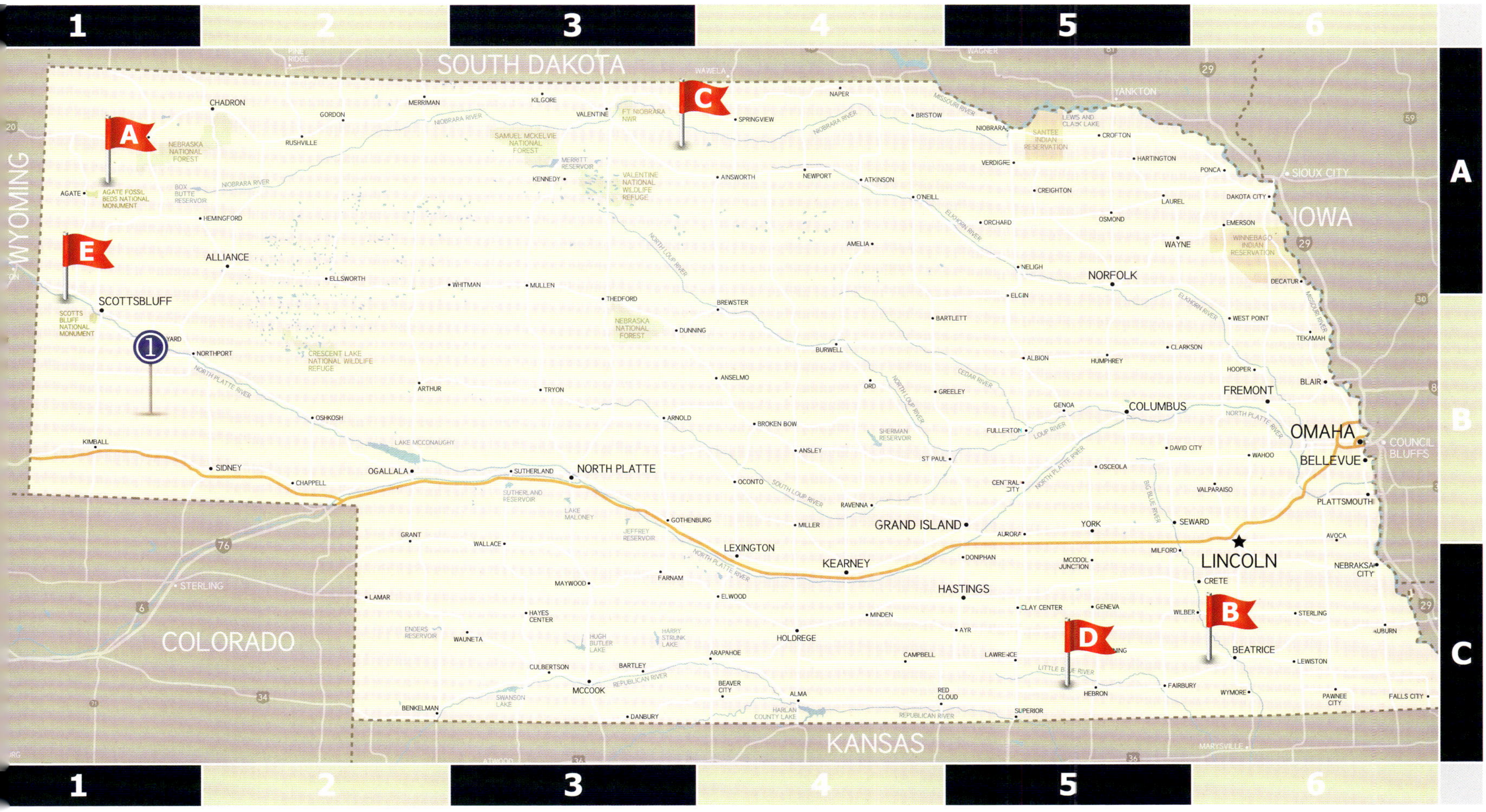

1 2 3 4 5 6

A B C

SOUTH DAKOTA

WYOMING

IOWA

COLORADO

KANSAS

SCOTTSBLUFF

ALLIANCE

NORTH PLATTE

OGALLALA

NORFOLK

COLUMBUS

FREMONT

OMAHA

BELLEVUE

GRAND ISLAND

KEARNEY

LEXINGTON

HASTINGS

LINCOLN

BEATRICE

1 2 3 4 5 6

WONDERS IN GOD'S WORLD

Agate Fossil Beds National Monument

During the 1890s, scientists began digging up bones in this area, something the Lakota Sioux had already found. Some of the mammals discovered here are the miohippus (my-oh-hip-pus), ancestor of the modern horse, and menoceras (men-oh-SEER-us), a small rhino.

Homestead National Monument of America

The Homestead Act of 1862 helped draw millions of people to the frontier territory. Families, freed slaves, immigrants, and others came to receive their free land. Almost any man or woman had a chance to make a new life.

Niobrara National Scenic River

The 76 miles of the Niobrara (nigh-UH-brair-uh) river area contains diverse wildlife, beautiful waterfalls, fossil resources, and areas for rafting and recreation. If you like to go canoeing, it's known as one of the best places to canoe in America.

Pony Express National Historic Trail

From April 1860 to October 1861, the Pony Express delivery took mail back and forth from St. Joseph, Missouri, to Sacramento, California, some 1,800 miles. Rock Creek Station in Fairbury, Nebraska, has reconstructed buildings from that era.

Scotts Bluff National Monument

The bluff rises some 800 feet over the North Platte River. It has stood as a landmark for Native Americans and immigrants traveling to Oregon and California.

NEVADA

NEVADA PREAMBLE

We the people of the State of Nevada Grateful to ***Almighty God*** for our freedom in order to secure its blessings, insure domestic tranquility, and form a more perfect Government, do establish this Constitution.

Statehood	1864 (36th state)
Population ranking	32nd
Capital	Carson City
State flower	Sagebrush
State bird	Mountain bluebird
Nickname	The Silver State
Highest point	Boundary Peak, 13,147 feet

The area that is now the state of Nevada was once called Washoe by the mountain men who traveled here. It was based on the native people called the Washoe or Wa She Shu who lived here and whose name meant "people from here."

Nevada is in the West Region of the U.S. In 1864 it became the 36th state. "Home Means Nevada" is the state song. And the state artifact? The Tule duck decoy!

In the 1870s, camels were used here as pack animals because much of the area is desert. In fact, Nevada gets the least amount of rain of any state in the country. Camels were first used by the military in 1855 but eventually were sold to private collectors.

Gold is very valuable, often a part of wedding rings and other special jewelry. Nevada is the largest gold-producing state in America. You can tour the gold ore mill at Eldorado Canyon Mining District south of Las Vegas, Nevada.

2 The ichthyosaur happens to be Nevada's official state fossil. Berlin-Ichthyosaur State Park was constructed around the fossilized remains of these mysterious reptiles. They were found in a mining camp from the 1890s.

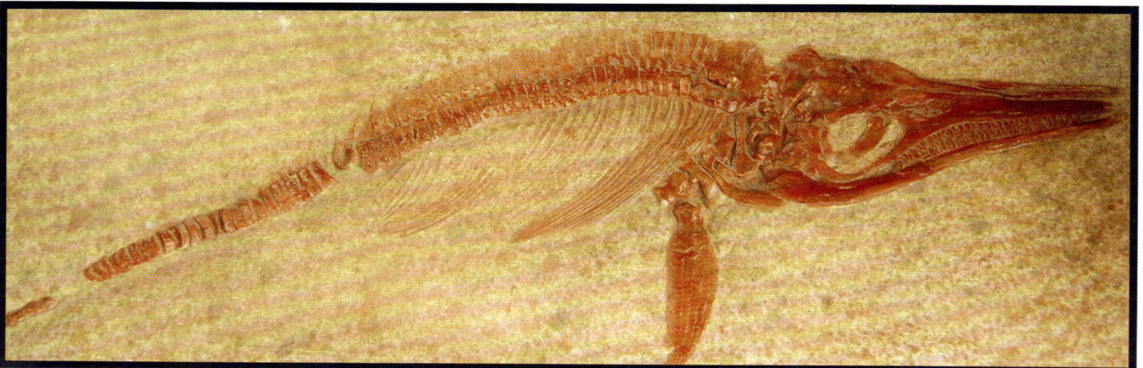

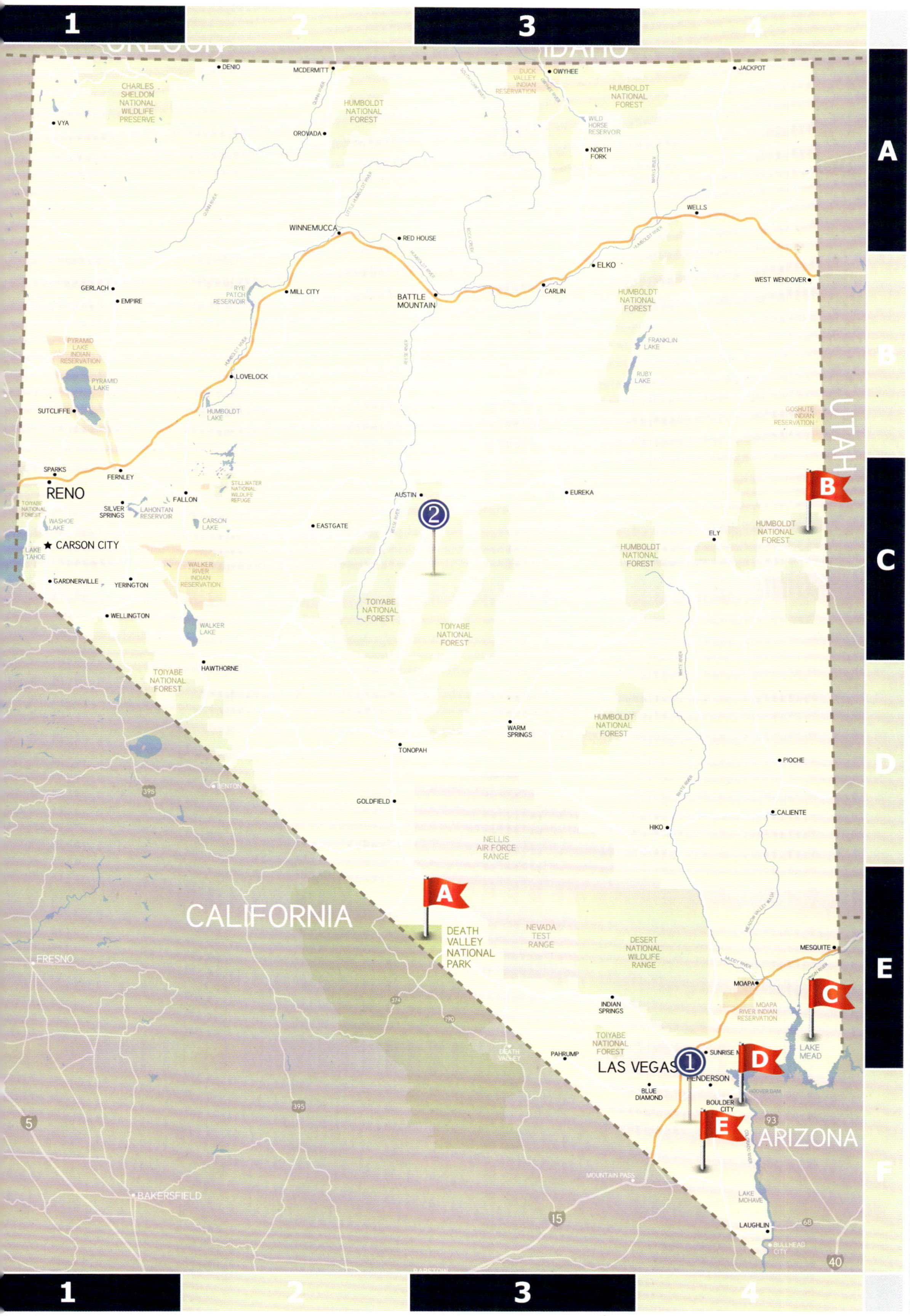

1 2 3 4

A B C D E F

RENO

CARSON CITY

CALIFORNIA

UTAH

ARIZONA

LAS VEGAS

HENDERSON

DEATH VALLEY NATIONAL PARK

LAKE MEAD

WINNEMUCCA

ELKO

WELLS

BATTLE MOUNTAIN

TONOPAH

ELY

A Death Valley National Park

Want to visit the hottest national park? What about the driest? How about the lowest in elevation? Well, just come to Death Valley and experience all three. The park is below sea level, has a steady drought, the summer heat is intense, and it's amazing.

B Great Basin National Park

Established in 1986, there is so much to explore here. Discover the dry desert, subterranean passages, ancient bristlecone pines, sage-covered foothills, vivid starry skies, and the 13,063-foot summit of Wheeler Peak.

C Lake Mead National Recreation Area

This was America's first national recreation area. The park has nine wilderness areas and plenty to do, including swimming, boating, hiking, cycling, camping, and fishing, all within the 1.5 million acres.

D Tule Springs Fossil Beds National Monument

Established in 2014, the site is just north of Las Vegas and has Ice Age discoveries, including mammoths and lions that once roamed the area.

E Old Spanish National Historic Trail

The old trail crossed between Santa Fe, New Mexico, all the way to Los Angeles, California. The trail is approximately 700 miles long and passes through high mountain regions, deserts, and deep canyons.

NEW HAMPSHIRE

NEW HAMPSHIRE PREAMBLE

Part I. Art. I. Sec. V: Every individual has a natural and unalienable right to worship ***God*** according to the dictates of his own conscience, and reason; and no subject shall be hurt, molested, or restrained, in his person, liberty, or estate, for worshipping ***God*** in the manner and season most agreeable to the dictates of his own conscience...

Statehood	1788 (9th state)
Population ranking	41st
Capital	Concord
State flower	Purple lilac
State bird	Purple finch
Nickname	The Granite State
Highest point	Mount Washington, 6,228 feet

New Hampshire can be found in the Northeast Region. It became the 9th state in 1788, though it was the first to declare its independence from England. It has two official state songs: "Old New Hampshire" and "Live Free or Die." They also have 8 other honorary state songs. And the state beverage? Apple cider!

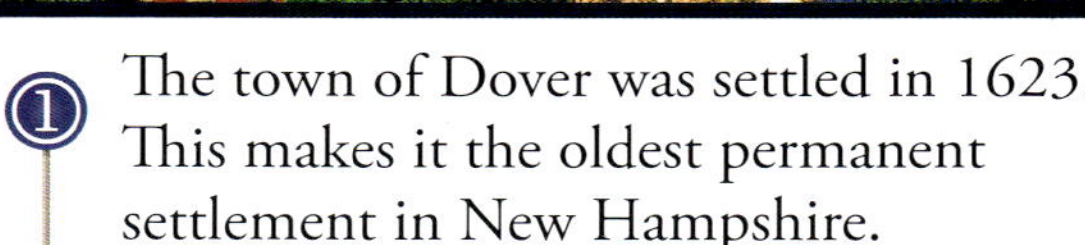

① The town of Dover was settled in 1623. This makes it the oldest permanent settlement in New Hampshire.

② In 1833, Peterborough established the first free public library in the United States. It was paid for by local taxes.

Autumn foliage and snow on the slopes of Mount Washington

It wasn't until 1909 that New Hampshire officially adopted a state flag. Before that the state had numerous regimental flags to represent the state.

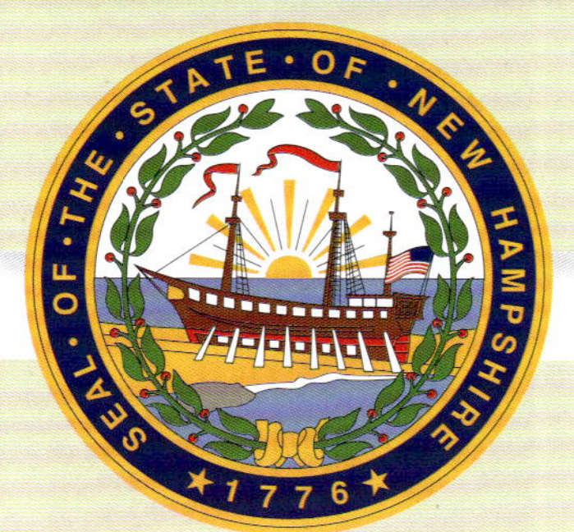

Appalachian National Scenic Trail

This scenic trail crosses over 2,000 miles of wooded areas, mountainous regions, and beautiful meadowlands. Though it was first conceived in 1921, it was built by private citizens, who completed it in 1937.

Floating Island National Landmark

Floating Island is a floating heath bog. The bog is surrounded by mixed bog swamp forest, as well as rivers and ponds. This wondrous display of God's creation is filled with amazing creatures, including bald eagles and osprey.

Pondicherry Wildlife Refuge National Landmark

The wildlife refuge is home to creatures that thrive in the marshes and bogs here. You will find two warm water ponds here, with forests around them, and a diverse variety of birds.

Rhododendron Natural Area National Landmark

Rhododendrons are beautiful, flowering bushes, and they flourish here. The landmark has the largest, thriving stand of rhododendrons in central and southern New England.

Winter in Portsmouth

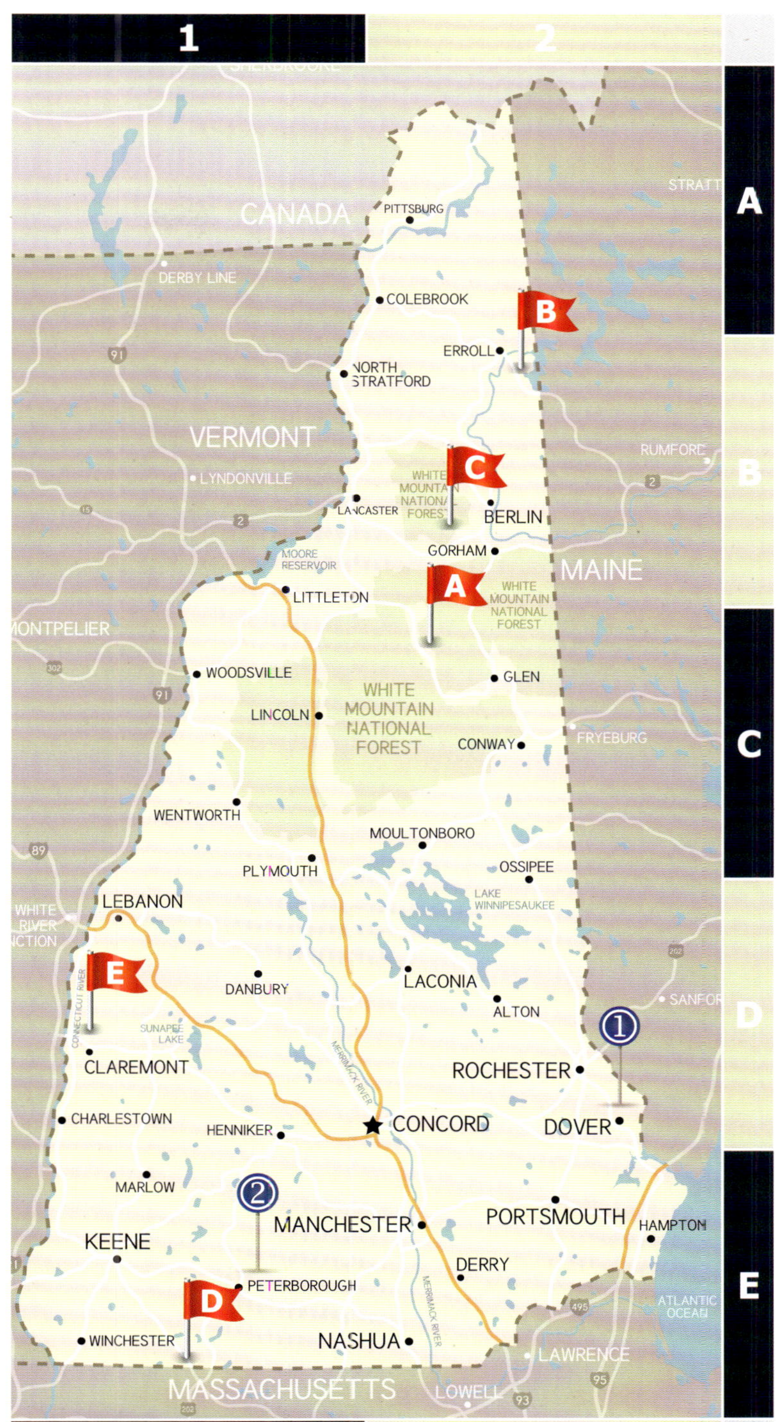

Saint-Gaudens National Historical Park

Augustus Saint-Gaudens was one of America's greatest sculptors. Here you can explore his home, studios, and gardens and see over 100 of his artworks. There are also summer concerts, special art classes, and nature trails to enjoy.

NEW JERSEY

NEW JERSEY PREAMBLE

We, the people of the State of New Jersey, grateful to ***Almighty God*** for the civil and religious liberty which ***He*** hath so long permitted us to enjoy, and looking to ***Him*** for a blessing upon our endeavors to secure and transmit the same unimpaired to succeeding generations, do ordain and establish this Constitution.

Statehood	1787 (3rd state)
Population ranking	11th
Capital	Trenton
State flower	Blue violet
State bird	Eastern goldfinch
Nickname	The Garden State
Highest point	High Point, 1,803 feet

Sometime in the 1630s, mining began in the Sterling Mine of Ogdenburg. It ended up being the last working mine in New Jersey when it closed in 1986. Now you can visit it to see the glowing fluorescent rocks of this historic zinc mine.

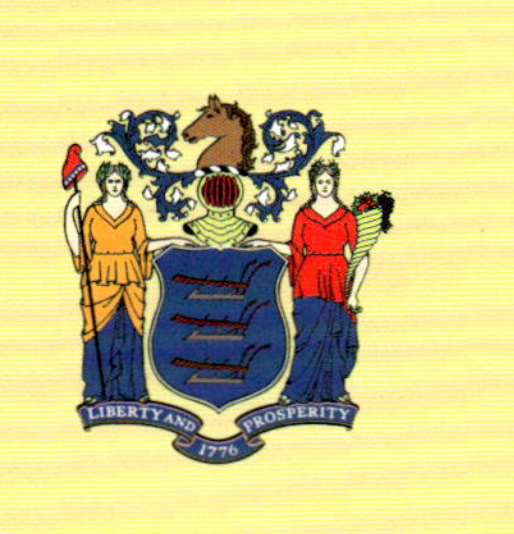

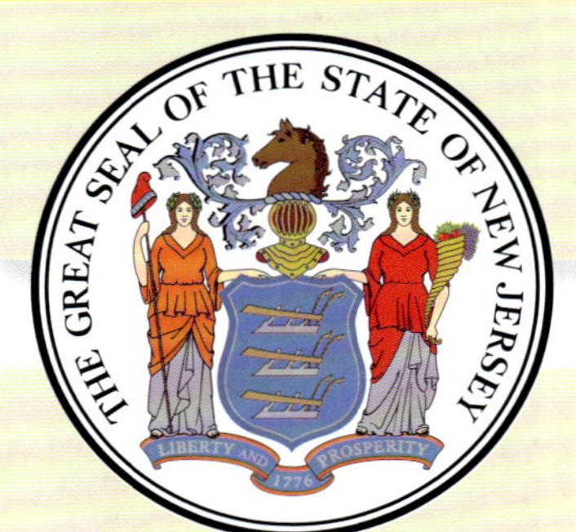

New Jersey is considered part of the Northeast. In 1787 it became the 3rd state. It is the only state without a state song or anthem. They do have a state reptile: the bog turtle!

① In 1879 while in his Menlo Park laboratory, Thomas Edison invented the electric light bulb, as well as the phonograph (record player), the motion picture projector, and many other things. The Menlo Park lab was one of the first labs that existed to design practical inventions. Edison later lived and worked in West Orange from 1886 until he died in 1931.

② Paleontology is the scientific study of dinosaur fossils. It began in the U.S. in 1858 when a nearly complete skeleton of a dinosaur was discovered in Haddonfield, New Jersey. The *Hadrosaurus foulkii* (had-row-SOAR-us folk-eye) eventually became the official New Jersey state dinosaur.

Brooklyn Bridge

③ John Roebling opened a factory in Trenton, New Jersey, in 1848 to meet the demands for his wire rope. He and his two sons then used it to build a suspension bridge across the gorge of the Niagara River. They went on to build the Brooklyn Bridge and other U.S. suspension bridges.

Crossroads of the American Revolution National Heritage Area

The special area is focused on the American Revolution and New Jersey's historic places that are connected to it. This includes the meeting place of the Continental Congress when they declared peace in 1783. Nassau Hall at Princeton is pictured.

Paterson Great Falls National Historical Park

Paterson was America's first planned industrial city when it was established in 1792. The 77-foot Great Falls on the Passaic River helped power the mills here that made cotton fabrics, locomotives, airplane engines, and more.

New Jersey Pinelands National Reserve

In 1978, this area was established as the country's first National Reserve. It includes over a million acres with over 700,000 residents and has everything from wetlands to historic villages and berry farms.

Thomas Edison National Historical Park

Come see the laboratory and home of Thomas Edison, who helped create so much of what we enjoy today. From the light bulb to the phonograph, movie camera, and electric power distribution, Edison worked to make our lives better.

Ellis Island National Monument

Twelve million immigrants passed through this area from 1892 to 1954. Here you can find a museum that unfolds the stories and dreams of so many of these people coming to America to find a better life.

NEW MEXICO

NEW MEXICO PREAMBLE

We, the people of New Mexico, grateful to ***Almighty God*** for the blessings of liberty, in order to secure the advantages of a state government, do ordain and establish this constitution.

Statehood	1912 (47th state)
Population ranking	36th
Capital	Santa Fe
State flower	Yucca
State bird	Roadrunner
Nickname	The Land of Enchantment
Highest point	Wheeler Peak, 13,167 feet

It is said that there may be more than 400 ghost towns in New Mexico. Most were mining towns that drew people seeking gold, silver, or copper, while others were small farming towns. At some point in their history, everyone left, leaving only the abandoned buildings. Some of the abandoned mines were known by names like Calamity Jane, Mystic Lode, and Confidence.

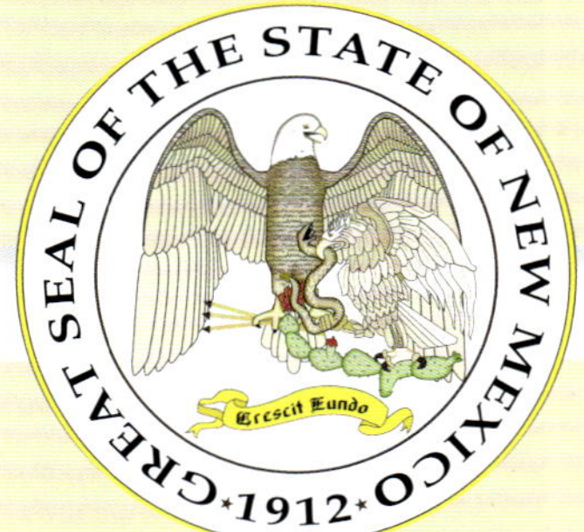

New Mexico is a part of the West Region. It became the 47th state in 1912. The state song is called "O Fair New Mexico." It also has a Spanish state song, which is "Así es Nuevo México" ("That's How New Mexico Is"). And the state clean-up mascot? The dusty roadrunner!

1 Santa Fe is the oldest capital city in America. In fact, the Palace of Governors here was built way back in 1610, making it the oldest continuously occupied public building in the country.

2 The desert of the White Sands National Monument is not made up of typical sand. It is actually 275 square miles of the world's largest gypsum dunefield.

There have been thousands of Anasazi sites found by archeologists, which include stone towers and stone cliff dwellings. The Anasazi people created an amazing civilization here from about A.D. 500 until nearly 1500. They are the ancestors of the Pueblo people who live here today. Their name in Navajo actually means "ancient enemy" and is considered a hurtful title now.

3 Go to Carlsbad Caverns near nightfall and you may just see a few of the tens of thousands of bats that call the caves home. The largest chamber in the caverns has a massive floor space of over 357,400 square feet!

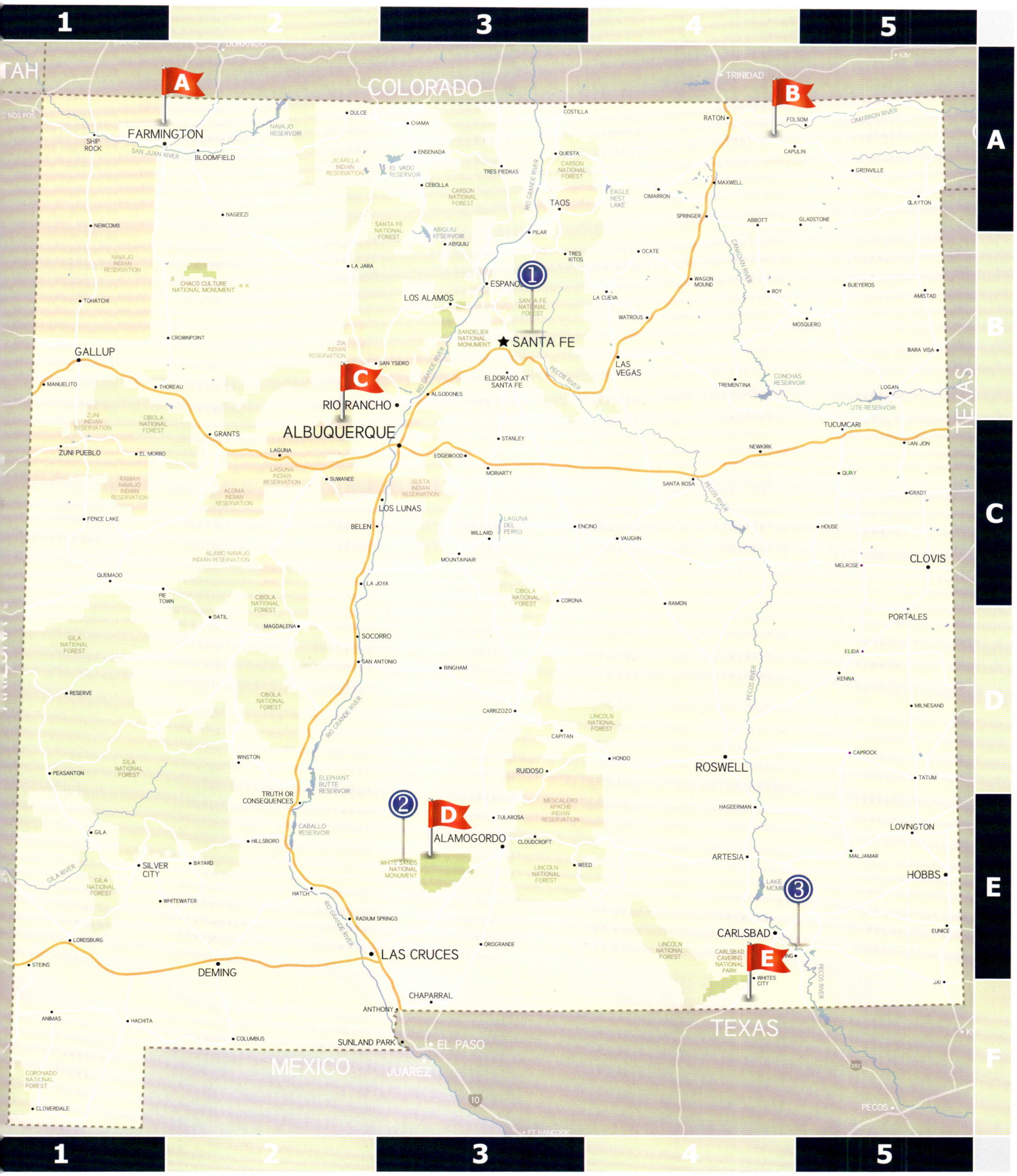

A Aztec Ruins National Monument

These ruins are over 900 years old. You will find what is left of this ancestral Pueblo society, including the Great House with over 400 stone rooms. Certain buildings have been reconstructed as well, like the Great Kiva, a Hopi word that means "ceremonial chamber."

E Carlsbad Caverns National Park

Underneath the beautiful desert lie 119 caves, which can be experienced with self-guided or ranger-guided tours. You can come in the evening to watch thousands of bats emerge to devour their insect dinners or come at dawn to watch them fly back home.

B Capulin Volcano National Monument

Many come here to drive up the volcano road, but you will also have an opportunity to see mule deer, elk, black bears, and even some mountain lions. Charles Goodnight and Oliver Loving drove cattle to Fort Sumner and Capulin Volcano, becoming a part of the 1860s Goodnight-Loving Trail.

C Petroglyph National Monument

Petroglyphs are carvings on stone made by people long ago. The petroglyphs here were carved in this volcanic rock by Native Americans, as well as Spanish people who passed through here 400 to 700 years ago.

D White Sands National Monument

The white sands of gypsum here simply shine and sparkle in the sun. Along with all the natural wonders protected in the area, there are sometimes missile tests that will shut down the only road into the dunefield. Stay safe!

NEW YORK

NEW YORK PREAMBLE

We The People of the State of New York, grateful to ***Almighty God*** for our Freedom, in order to secure its blessings, DO ESTABLISH THIS CONSTITUTION.

Statehood	1788 (11th state)
Population ranking	4th
Capital	Albany
State flower	Rose
State bird	Bluebird
Nickname	The Empire State
Highest point	Mount Marcy, 5,343 feet

The *New York Post*, a newspaper printed in New York City, was begun in 1801. It was originally called the *New York Evening Post* by its creator Alexander Hamilton, who was the nation's first secretary of the treasury and the author of the Federalist Papers, special documents about the United States.

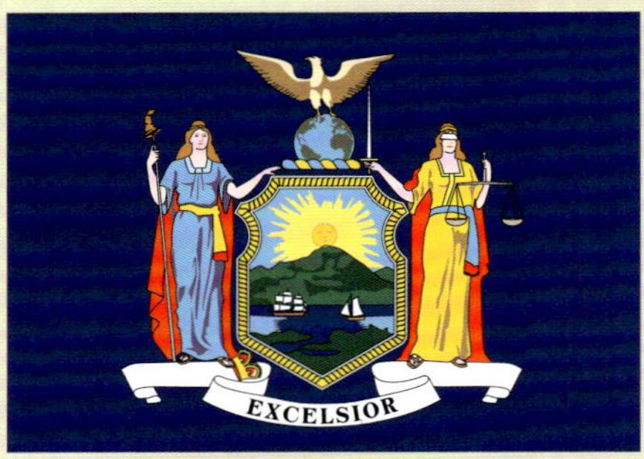

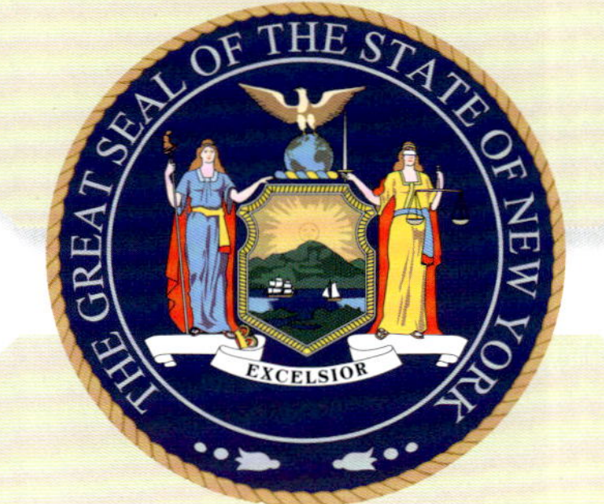

New York is in the Northeast, and New York City is the largest city in that region and in the whole United States. It became the 11th state in 1788. It has a state hymn of remembrance called "Here Rests in Honored Glory." And the state dog? Working canines!

1. In 1789, George Washington took his oath as president in New York City on the balcony at Federal Hall on Wall Street.

2. The Genesee River is one of the few rivers in the world that flows south to north. The most famous river that does this is the Nile in Egypt.

3. The *North River Steamboat*, better known as the *Clermont*, made its first voyage in 1807. Traveling from New York City to Albany, it became the first successful steamboat to be used for commercial water transportation. All this while traveling at the wild speed of 5 miles per hour!

4. New York City has a total of 850 miles of subway track, and this is one of the world's oldest public transportation systems. Opening in 1904, the subway operates 24 hours a day every single day of the year.

5. The world's smallest church can be found in Oneida (oh-NYE-duh). Cross Island Chapel has floor dimensions of 51 inches by 81 inches. The church floats on a pond and has just enough room for the bride, the groom, and the minister.

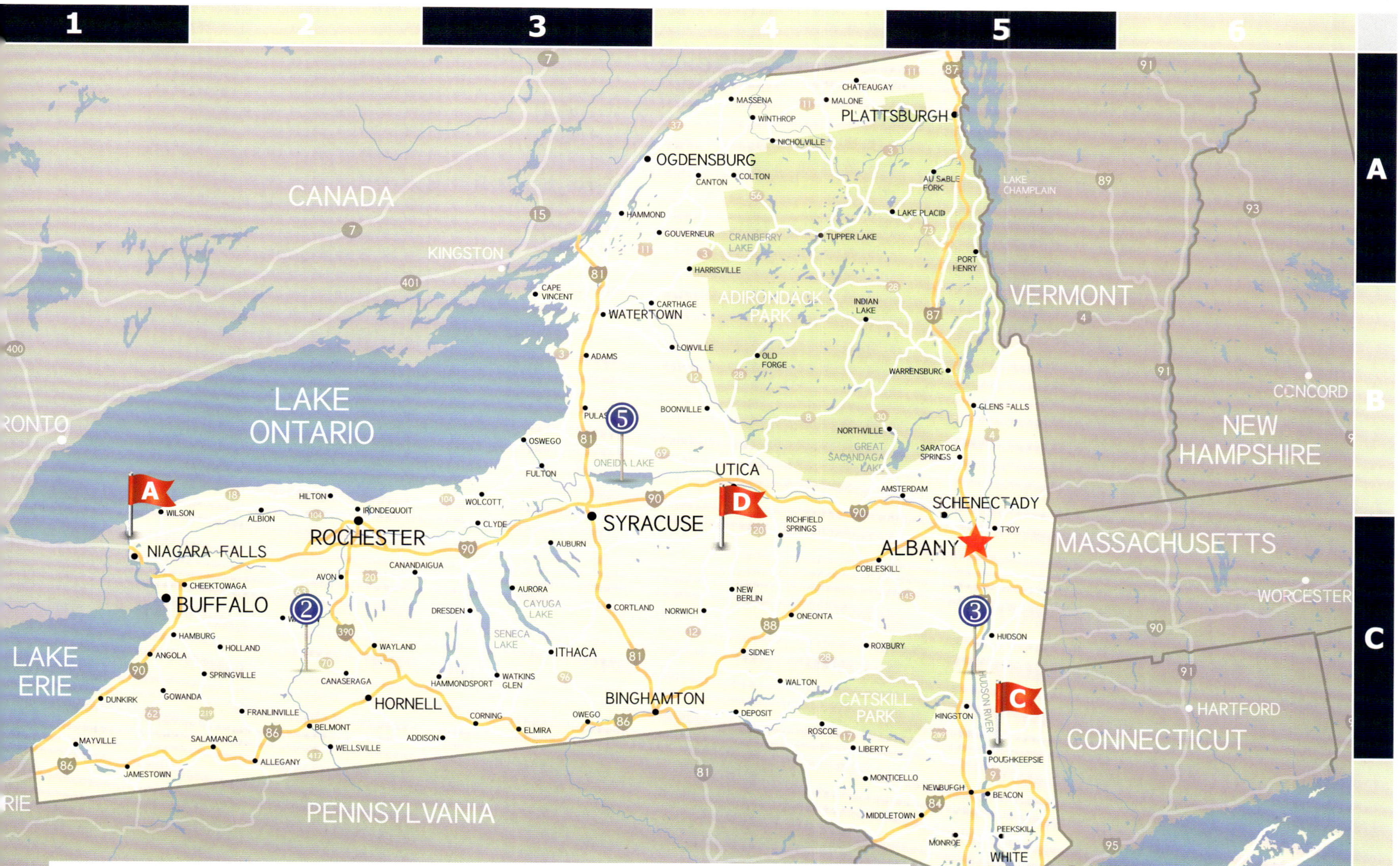

WONDERS IN GOD'S WORLD

A Niagara Falls National Heritage Area

The mission of this heritage area is to preserve, protect, and promote the historic, natural, and cultural resources that exist from Niagara Falls to Old Fort Niagara. Such a beautiful display of God's creation!

B Fire Island National Seashore

This United States National Seashore helps protect some 26 miles of the Fire Island area and a 30-mile section of the long barrier island. This beautiful area also supports artists through an artist-in-residence program.

C Eleanor Roosevelt National Historic Site

Established in 1977, this is the only National Historic Site dedicated to a first lady. It is connected to the Roosevelt family estate located in Hyde Park, New York. You can visit historic buildings across the 181 acres of land.

D Erie Canalway National Heritage Corridor

With more than 500 miles of waterways, you can explore the characteristic locks and low-lying bridges of the Erie Canal. There are some 34 national historic landmarks across the area.

E Statue of Liberty National Monument

It was on October 28, 1886 that the Statue of Liberty was first dedicated. Then in 1924, it was designated as a national monument. The monument includes Liberty Island and Ellis Island.

NORTH CAROLINA

NORTH CAROLINA PREAMBLE

We, the people of the State of North Carolina, grateful to ***Almighty God***, the ***Sovereign Ruler of Nations***, for the preservation of the American Union and the existence of our civil, political and religious liberties, and acknowledging our dependence upon ***Him*** for the continuance of those blessings to us and our posterity, do, for the more certain security thereof and for the better government of this State, ordain and establish this Constitution.

Statehood	1789 (12th state)
Population ranking	9th
Capital	Raleigh
State flower	Dogwood
State bird	Cardinal
Nickname	The Tar Heel State / Old North State
Highest point	Mount Mitchell, 6,684 feet

North Carolina can be found in the South. In 1789 it became the 12th state. The state song is "The Old North State." And the state carnivorous plant? The Venus Flytrap!

① The town of New Bern was founded in 1710. This Swiss and German settlement was named in honor of the founder's home, Bern, Switzerland.

② At 480 feet high, Fontana Dam is the tallest dam in the Eastern United States.

③ Built in 1895, the Biltmore House in Asheville is the largest home in America. It has 250 rooms and extensive gardens to explore, if you have the time.

④ Labeled as the nation's safest beach, White Lake near Elizabethtown is known for its white sandy bottom and very clear waters. It's also known for having no currents and no tides.

⑤ Hiram Rhoades Revels was born in Fayetteville in 1827. He was the first African American member of the United States Congress.

WONDERS IN GOD'S WORLD

A Fort Raleigh National Historic Site

The site preserves the history of this region, all the way back to the first New World settlements in 1584. There is also a record here of the Native Americans and African Americans who make Roanoke Island their home.

B Cape Hatteras National Seashore

There are more than 70 miles of shoreline here that stretch from Bodie Island all the way to Ocracoke Island. There are beautiful areas of peace and places for all kinds of recreational activities. Make time for the wildlife, including sea turtles and deer.

C Moores Creek National Battlefield

Come and hear the story of what took place in the early morning of February 27, 1776 when the patriots here fought back the loyalist forces trying to take back this area of North Carolina for England.

D Wright Brothers National Memorial

After working for four years to research and develop their idea, Wilbur and Orville Wright came to Kitty Hawk for the steady winds. Here they achieved the first successful airplane flight on December 17, 1903. The rest is history.

E Great Smoky Mountains National Park

This is the most visited national park in the United States. Here you will find a wondrous diversity of wildlife and plants and the pure joy of the forests and mountains often covered in the bluish haze that gives the area its name.

NORTH DAKOTA

NORTH DAKOTA PREAMBLE

We, the people of North Dakota, grateful to ***Almighty God*** for the blessings of civil and religious liberty, do ordain and establish this constitution.

Statehood	1889 (39th or 40th state)
Population ranking	47th
Capital	Bismarck
State flower	Wild prairie rose
State bird	Western meadowlark
Nickname	The Flickertail State / The Roughrider State / Peace Garden State
Highest point	White Butte, 3,508 feet

In 1987, North Dakota passed a bill that made English the official state language. The United States does not have an official national language.

North Dakota is a state in the Midwest. It became the 39th state in 1889. "North Dakota Hymn" is the state song. And the state beverage? That would be milk!

① The International Peace Garden is in both the United States and Canada. Created in 1932, it celebrates the friendship of the two nations.

② There is a town named Rugby in North Dakota that is said to be the geographical center of North America. If you go there, look for the rock obelisk that is about 15 feet tall and that has a flag of the U.S. and a Canadian flag next to it to mark the location.

In 1889, North and South Dakota were both admitted as states at the exact same time, so no one really knows which was the 39th state and which was the 40th state. It was a tie!

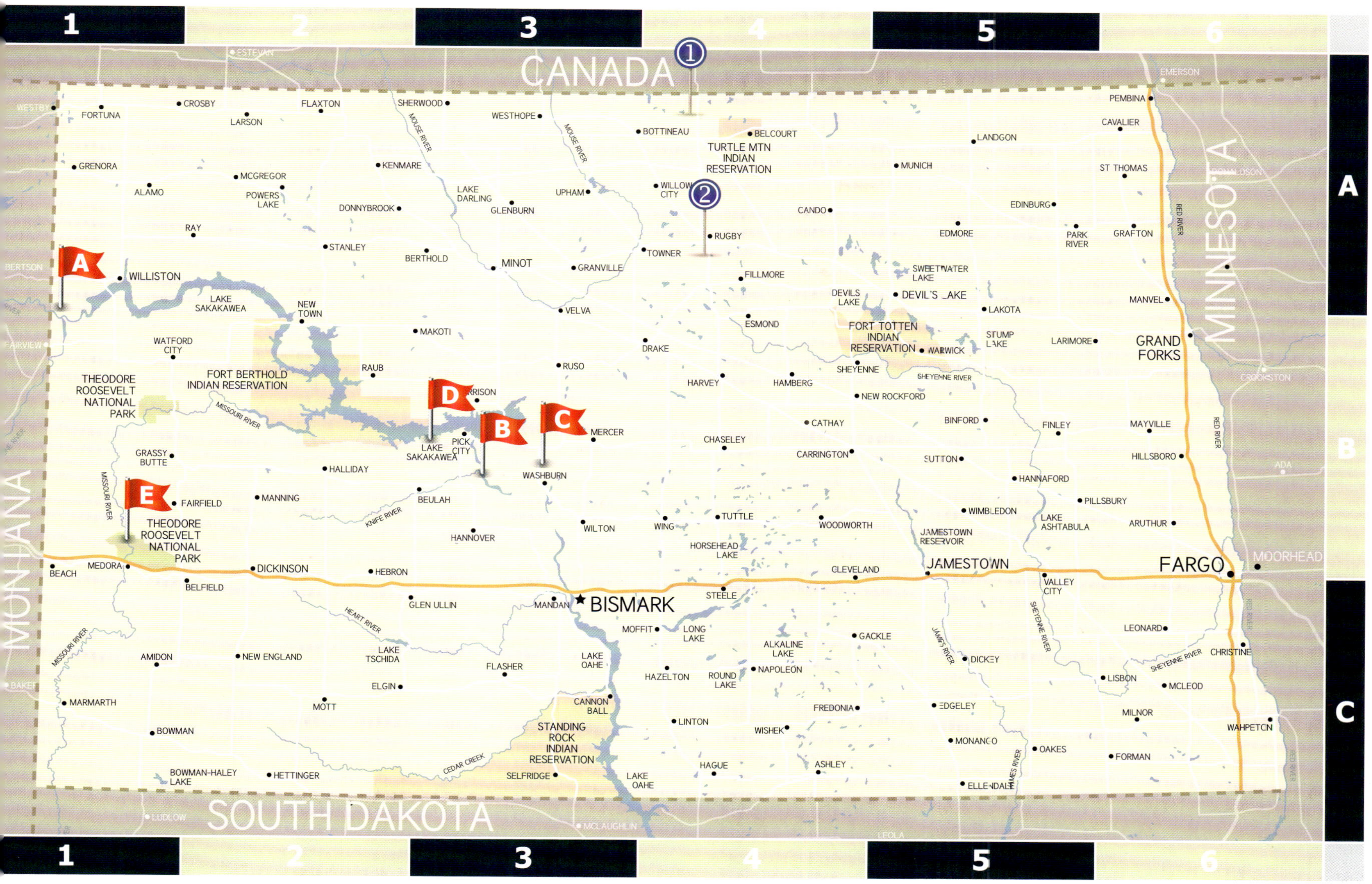

1 2 3 4 5 6

A B C

CANADA

MONTANA

MINNESOTA

SOUTH DAKOTA

FORTUNA CROSBY FLAXTON SHERWOOD WESTHOPE BOTTINEAU BELCOURT PEMBINA CAVALIER LANDGON

TURTLE MTN INDIAN RESERVATION

GRENORA MCGREGOR KENMARE MUNICH ST THOMAS ALAMO POWERS LAKE LAKE DARLING GLENBURN UPHAM WILLOW CITY CANDO EDINBURG DONNYBROOK RAY STANLEY BERTHOLD MINOT GRANVILLE TOWNER RUGBY EDMORE PARK RIVER GRAFTON

WILLISTON LAKE SAKAKAWEA NEW TOWN VELVA FILLMORE SWEETWATER LAKE DEVILS LAKE DEVIL'S LAKE LAKOTA MANVEL

WATFORD CITY MAKOTI ESMOND FORT TOTTEN INDIAN RESERVATION WARWICK STUMP LAKE LARIMORE GRAND FORKS DRAKE

THEODORE ROOSEVELT NATIONAL PARK FORT BERTHOLD INDIAN RESERVATION RAUB RUSO HARVEY HAMBERG SHEYENNE NEW ROCKFORD

GARRISON PICK CITY LAKE SAKAKAWEA MERCER CHASELEY CATHAY BINFORD FINLEY MAYVILLE CARRINGTON SUTTON HILLSBORO

GRASSY BUTTE HALLIDAY WASHBURN HANNAFORD PILLSBURY FAIRFIELD MANNING BEULAH TUTTLE WIMBLEDON LAKE ASHTABULA ARUTHUR THEODORE ROOSEVELT NATIONAL PARK HANNOVER WILTON WING HORSEHEAD LAKE WOODWORTH JAMESTOWN RESERVOIR

BEACH MEDORA DICKINSON HEBRON CLEVELAND JAMESTOWN FARGO MOORHEAD BELFIELD STEELE VALLEY CITY GLEN ULLIN MANDAN BISMARK

MOFFIT LONG LAKE GACKLE LEONARD AMIDON NEW ENGLAND LAKE TSCHIDA FLASHER LAKE OAHE ALKALINE LAKE DICKEY CHRISTINE NAPOLEON HAZELTON ROUND LAKE LISBON MCLEOD ELGIN MARMARTH MOTT CANNON BALL FREDONIA EDGELEY MILNOR

BOWMAN STANDING ROCK INDIAN RESERVATION LINTON WISHEK MONANGO WAHPETON OAKES FORMAN BOWMAN-HALEY LAKE HETTINGER SELFRIDGE LAKE OAHE HAGUE ASHLEY ELLENDALE

WONDERS IN GOD'S WORLD

A Fort Union Trading Post National Historic Site

The fort was the most important fur trading post on the Upper Missouri River between 1828 and 1867. Come see a partial reconstruction of the post where Northern Plains Indian Tribes came to trade furs for goods from around the world.

B Knife River Indian Villages National Historic Site

Established in 1974, this site helps preserve the history of the Hidatsa Northern Plains Indians who hunted bison and farmed in villages in this area. The Big Hidatsa (hee-DAT-suh) village is thought to have been started around 1600.

C Lewis & Clark National Historic Trail

Discover the history of this part of the trail that extends some 4,900 miles, seeing the dynamic sights of God's beautiful creation as they saw it and understanding better the story of the native peoples they met along the route.

D North Country National Scenic Trail

If you like, just call it the N.C.T. like the locals do. This footpath is a whopping 4,600 miles of wonder, going from Crown Point in eastern New York to Lake Sakakawea State Park in North Dakota. It's the longest of the 11 scenic trails in America.

E Theodore Roosevelt National Park

Named after president Theodore (Teddy) Roosevelt, who also had the Teddy Bear named after him, the park is made up of three separate areas of the Badlands covering 70,446 acres. This is the only national park named for a single person.

OHIO

OHIO PREAMBLE

We, the people of the State of Ohio, grateful to ***Almighty God*** for our freedom, to secure its blessings and promote our common welfare, do establish this Constitution.

Statehood	1803 (17th state)
Population ranking	7th
Capital	Columbus
State flower	Scarlet carnation
State bird	Cardinal
Nickname	The Buckeye State
Highest point	Campbell Hill, 1,550 feet

James Mastronardo, a 12-year old, won an Ohio contest to suggest a state motto. He thought it should be "With God All Things Are Possible," and it became the official motto of Ohio in 1959. The American Civil Liberties Union filed a lawsuit in 1997 to stop the motto from being used because it mentions God, but various federal courts sided with the state, and it is still used today.

Ohio is in the Midwest Region. In 1803 it became the 17th state. The state song is called "Beautiful Ohio." And the state fossil? The Isotelus Trilobite!

① Thomas A. Edison was born in Milan, Ohio. He developed the incandescent light bulb and many other inventions. Cleveland, Ohio, became the world's first city to use electric lights, specifically the arc lamp, for lighting their streets in 1879.

② Oberlin College was founded in 1833. This was the first interracial college in America, which opened its doors to black students in 1835. It was also the first college to grant bachelor's degrees to women in a coeducational program in 1841.

③ There is a large mound that looks like a serpent out near Locust Grove. Created by the native people hundreds of years ago, the mound is over 1,000 feet long.

A First Ladies National Historic Site

This historic site in Canton honors the legacies of the first ladies of the United States. There are two properties connected to the site, which are the home of former First Lady Ida Saxton-McKinley and a small visitor center.

E James A. Garfield National Historic Site

Located in Mentor, Ohio, and established in 1966, the site preserves the estate of late James Abram Garfield, who was the 20th president of the United States. Come see the first presidential library created in his honor.

B Cuyahoga Valley National Park

Not far from Cleveland, the park is a beautiful getaway where you can see wildlife and native plants along the Cuyahoga (kai-uh-HO-guh) River. This 32,572-acre park was initially protected in 1974.

C National Aviation Heritage Area

This amazing national site is made up of more than 15 aviation locations around the Dayton area. The main focus is on the Wright Brothers and their workshop, honoring their legacy of flight.

D William Howard Taft National Historic Site

William Howard Taft was the 27th president of the United States. He was also the 10th chief justice of the United States. Come see the 1835 home where he was born and spent much of his childhood.

OKLAHOMA

OKLAHOMA PREAMBLE

Invoking the guidance of ***Almighty God***, in order to secure and perpetuate the blessing of liberty; to secure just and rightful government; to promote our mutual welfare and happiness, we, the people of the State of Oklahoma, do ordain and establish this Constitution.

Statehood	1907 (46th state)
Population ranking	28th
Capital	Oklahoma City
State flower	Oklahoma rose
State bird	Scissor-tailed flycatcher
Nickname	The Sooner State
Highest point	Black Mesa, 4,975 feet

In the 1930s a terrible drought hit the Midwestern United States, something that came to be called the Dust Bowl. Because it impacted large farming areas, over a million residents of Oklahoma ended up moving to California, many of them poor farm workers. At the time, people began calling them “Okies,” which was not considered a nice term. Later, the children and grandchildren of these families began using the term with pride.

Oklahoma is a part of the South. It became the 46th state in 1907. The official state song is “Oklahoma,” and the official state children’s song is “Oklahoma, My Native Land.” And the state flying mammal? The Mexican Free-tailed Bat!

① Sequoyah’s Cabin near Akins may seem like a typical frontier log house, but it has an amazing history. The Native American Sequoyah, known also as George Gist, lived here between 1829 and 1844. He was the teacher who created a written language for the Cherokee Nation in 1821.

② Gordon Matthews was an American inventor who was born in Tulsa, Oklahoma. He is credited with inventing voice mail, which can record a voice message if someone calls and you can’t answer your phone.

Oklahoma has the largest Native American population of any state in the U.S. There are around 276,000 people here who represent various tribes, including the Caddo, Comanche, Osage, Ute, and Wichita. Oklahoma is actually home to 39 distinct tribes.

Two Native American Chickasaw warriors hunting. (Sculptures at the Chickasaw Cultural Center in Sulphur, Oklahoma.)

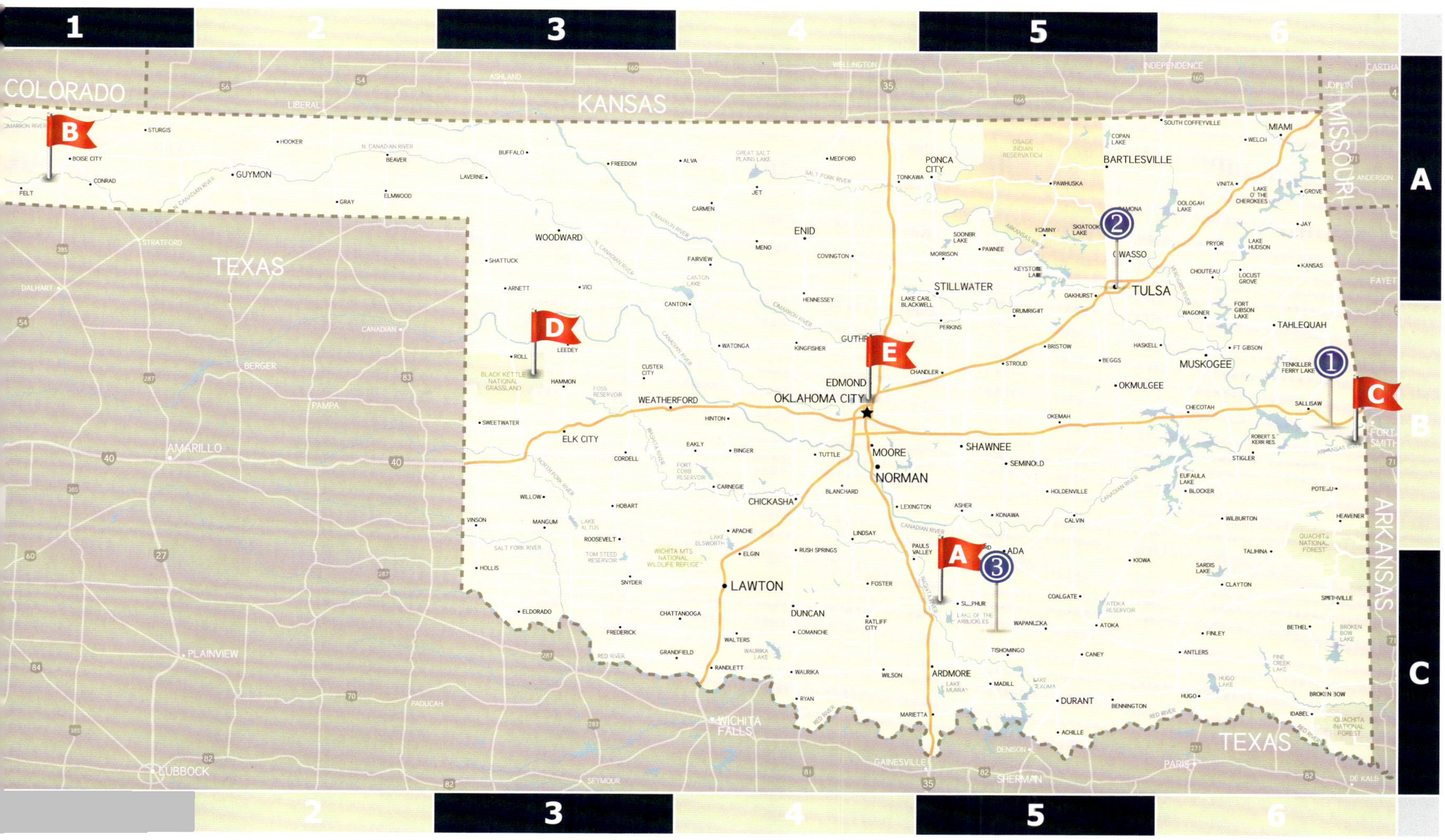

WONDERS IN GOD'S WORLD

A Chickasaw National Recreation Area

The Chickasaw Nation encountered Hernando de Soto in 1540, but they were here long before that. This recreational area has been a peaceful place of refuge all that time, with mineral springs, forests, wildlife, and more.

B Santa Fe National Historic Trail

This historic trail of the 19th century winds through 5 states. It started in Franklin, Missouri, and connected with Santa Fe, New Mexico. It was started around 1821 and thrived until the coming of the railroad in 1880.

C Fort Smith National Historic Site

Partly in Arkansas and partly in Oklahoma, this site connects you to almost 80 years of history. Fort Smith began in 1817, so this area saw the expansion of the west. You can still see traces of the old road that connected it to Fort Towson.

D Washita Battlefield National Historic Site

The Washita (wosh-EE-taw) site preserves the history and honors the lives of those lost during the battle that occurred here. On November 27, 1868, Lt. Colonel George Armstrong Custer led his 7th Cavalry into a morning attack against a Cheyenne village.

E Oklahoma City National Memorial

This beautiful place of reflection honors the victims, survivors, and rescuers impacted during the bombing of the Alfred P. Murrah Federal Building on April 19, 1995. It is a sobering reminder of how quickly our lives can be taken.

OREGON

OREGON BILL OF RIGHTS, ARTICLE I. SECTION 2

All men shall be secure in the Natural right, to worship ***Almighty God*** according to the dictates of their own consciences.

Statehood	1859 (33rd state)
Population ranking	27th
Capital	Salem
State flower	Oregon grape
State bird	Western meadowlark
Nickname	The Beaver State
Highest point	Mount Hood, 11,249 feet

The first church was built in Oregon City back in 1844. This is remembered as the first Protestant church on the West Coast of what is now the United States. Oregon City was built up along the Willamette River at the ending point of the Oregon Trail. It was the first U.S. city west of the Rockies to become incorporated.

Oregon is in the West Region of the U.S. In 1859 it became the 33rd state. "Oregon, My Oregon" is the state song. And the state chainsaw carving capital? That would be Reedsport!

① Tillamook is home to Oregon's largest cheese factory. Starting in 1909 in the Tillamook Valley, they now make ice cream, sour cream, yogurt, and more and are still owned by the farmers.

② Founded in 2004, the Historic Carousel and Museum has created a world class carousel complex in Albany, Oregon. They are constructing a fully functional carousel that will hold 52 hand-carved and painted animals. It's wonderful that people get to volunteer to help create and restore the beautiful pieces.

③ Starting in Independence, Missouri, and going all the way to Oregon City, Oregon, the Oregon trail crossed some 2,400 miles of territory. It was the longest of the overland routes used to go out West. There weren't cars, trains, or planes back then, so the slow-moving wagons could take up to 6 months to travel all that distance.

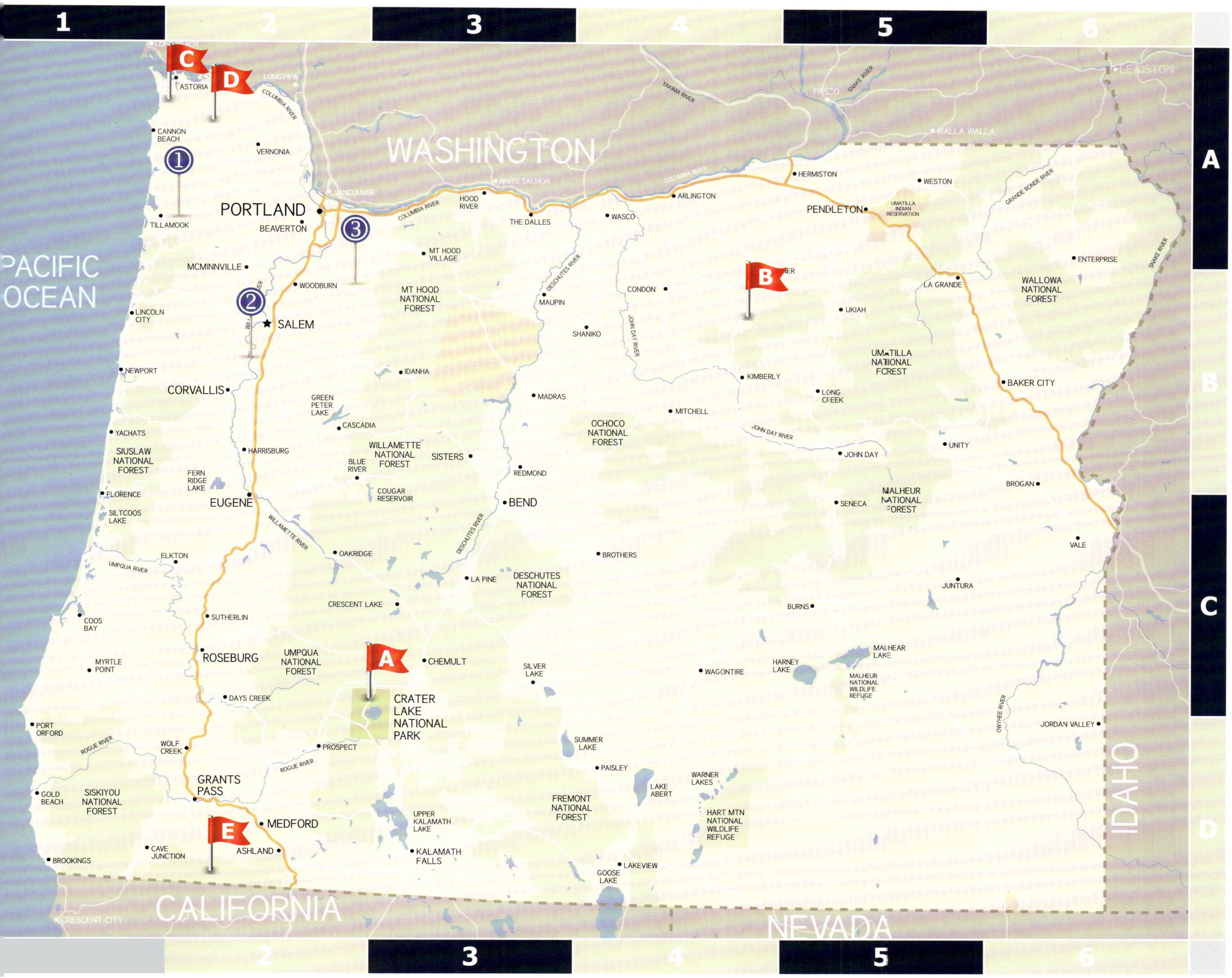

1 2 3 4 5 6

A B C D

PACIFIC OCEAN
WASHINGTON
IDAHO
CALIFORNIA
NEVADA

ASTORIA
LONGVIEW
COLUMBIA RIVER
CANNON BEACH
VERNONIA
TILLAMOOK
PORTLAND
BEAVERTON
VANCOUVER
HOOD RIVER
WHITE SALMON
THE DALLES
WASCO
ARLINGTON
HERMISTON
PASCO
SNAKE RIVER
YAKIMA RIVER
WALLA WALLA
WESTON
PENDLETON
UMATILLA INDIAN RESERVATION
GRANDE RONDE RIVER
LEWISTON
ENTERPRISE
WALLOWA NATIONAL FOREST
LA GRANDE
UKIAH
UMATILLA NATIONAL FOREST
BAKER CITY
MCMINNVILLE
WOODBURN
MT HOOD VILLAGE
MT HOOD NATIONAL FOREST
DESCHUTES RIVER
MAUPIN
CONDON
SHANIKO
JOHN DAY RIVER
LINCOLN CITY
SALEM
NEWPORT
IDANHA
CORVALLIS
GREEN PETER LAKE
CASCADIA
MADRAS
KIMBERLY
LONG CREEK
MITCHELL
OCHOCO NATIONAL FOREST
YACHATS
SIUSLAW NATIONAL FOREST
HARRISBURG
WILLAMETTE NATIONAL FOREST
BLUE RIVER
SISTERS
REDMOND
JOHN DAY
UNITY
FERN RIDGE LAKE
FLORENCE
SILTCOOS LAKE
EUGENE
COUGAR RESERVOIR
BEND
SENECA
MALHEUR NATIONAL FOREST
BROGAN
WILLAMETTE RIVER
OAKRIDGE
BROTHERS
VALE
ELKTON
UMPQUA RIVER
LA PINE
DESCHUTES NATIONAL FOREST
JUNTURA
CRESCENT LAKE
COOS BAY
SUTHERLIN
BURNS
MYRTLE POINT
ROSEBURG
UMPQUA NATIONAL FOREST
CHEMULT
SILVER LAKE
WAGONTIRE
HARNEY LAKE
MALHEAR LAKE
MALHEUR NATIONAL WILDLIFE REFUGE
DAYS CREEK
CRATER LAKE NATIONAL PARK
PORT ORFORD
ROGUE RIVER
WOLF CREEK
PROSPECT
SUMMER LAKE
OWYHEE RIVER
JORDAN VALLEY
GRANTS PASS
PAISLEY
WARNER LAKES
GOLD BEACH
SISKIYOU NATIONAL FOREST
LAKE ABERT
FREMONT NATIONAL FOREST
HART MTN NATIONAL WILDLIFE REFUGE
MEDFORD
UPPER KALAMATH LAKE
CAVE JUNCTION
ASHLAND
KALAMATH FALLS
BROOKINGS
LAKEVIEW
GOOSE LAKE
CRESCENT CITY

WONDERS IN GOD'S WORLD

A Crater Lake National Park

Come see the deepest lake in the United States, with water so clear and blue filling the hollow cavity of an ancient volcano. Established in 1902, the park includes the caldera of Crater Lake and the shadow of what remains of Mount Mazama after it erupted.

B John Day Fossil Beds National Monument

Visitors here can see the remains of life preserved during the Great Flood, including fossils of plants and animals. There are not only exhibits to view, but a working lab and scenic drives to explore the area in which the fossils have been uncovered.

C Lewis & Clark National Historical Park

This final leg of the Lewis and Clark journey includes 12 sites along the beautiful Pacific coastal road. Stand where they stood when they first glimpsed the ocean and when they began building their shelter for winter.

D Oregon National Historic Trail

Here is another ending to a very long trail. The 2,170-mile Oregon trail that thousands came across wound its way to the beautiful valleys where so many established their homes and settled down. There is so much to see and do here at Fort Clatsop.

E Oregon Caves National Monument & Preserve

If you travel to the northern Siskiyou Mountains of Oregon, you may well run across this 4,554-acre park. You can explore the caves if you wish, which will lead you to marble passageways and a huge room 220 feet beneath the surface.

PENNSYLVANIA

PENNSYLVANIA PREAMBLE

WE, the people of the Commonwealth of Pennsylvania, grateful to ***Almighty God*** for the blessings of civil and religious liberty, and humbly invoking ***His*** guidance, do ordain and establish this Constitution.

Statehood	1787 (2nd state)
Population ranking	5th
Capital	Harrisburg
State flower	Mountain laurel
State bird	Ruffed grouse
Nickname	The Keystone State
Highest point	Mount Davis, 3,213 feet

In 1943, two NFL teams merged because so many players had left for military service in World War II. The teams who merged were the Pittsburgh Steelers and the Philadelphia Eagles. For one season they played as the Steagles.

Pennsylvania is considered part of the Northeast. It became the 2nd state in 1787. The state song is simply called "Pennsylvania." And the state insect? That's the firefly!

① The first U.S. Mint, which makes money, was established in Philadelphia in 1792 with the Coinage Act. Coins have been made there ever since.

② The Philadelphia Zoo is considered the first true zoo in the United States. It was chartered in 1859 and opened its doors in 1874. At that time, it had 1,000 animals and cost 25 cents to get in.

③ The citizens of Punxsutawney (punks-ah-TAW-nee) are excited to share their town, billed as the weather capital of the world, with its weather-forecasting groundhog, Punxsutawney Phil. Every February 2nd, they gather together on Groundhog Day to celebrate the coming of spring.

④ The Declaration of Independence was approved by Congress in Philadelphia on July 4, 1776 and signed primarily on August 2, 1776. This is celebrated across America every July 4th as America's Independence Day.

WONDERS IN GOD'S WORLD

A Allegheny Portage Railroad National Historic Site

First opened in 1834, this was the rail line that first connected Philadelphia with Pittsburgh through the Allegheny (al-ah-GAIN-ee) Mountains. It was 36 miles long, helped connect the canal system, and operated from 1834 to 1854.

B Delaware & Lehigh National Heritage Corridor

The corridor is a 165-mile national heritage area that goes across eastern Pennsylvania. It will connect you to many histories here, including the Lehigh and Susquehanna (suss-kwah-HANN-uh) Railroad, the Lehigh Canal, and the Delaware Canal.

C Edgar Allan Poe National Historic Site

Edgar Allan Poe was an American writer who lived and wrote in this Spring Garden neighborhood of Philadelphia for six years. Though he struggled with anxiety and depression, as well as his wife's illness, he was very happy here.

D Gettysburg National Military Park

Learn about the Battle of Gettysburg that took place during the Civil War in 1863. Explore the battlefield area, several non-battle areas, and the Gettysburg National Cemetery. There are some 43,000 artifacts of the war on display.

E Valley Forge National Historical Park

Take a trip back — way back to the winter of 1777 to 1778. Valley Forge was the encampment of the Continental Army under the command of General George Washington. See the historical buildings, recreated camps, museums, and more.

RHODE ISLAND

RHODE ISLAND PREAMBLE

We, the people of the State of Rhode Island and Providence Plantations, grateful to ***Almighty God*** for the civil and religious liberty which ***He*** hath so long permitted us to enjoy, and looking to ***Him*** for a blessing upon our endeavors to secure and to transmit the same, unimpaired, to succeeding generations, do ordain and establish this Constitution of government.

Statehood	1790 (13th state)
Population ranking	44th
Capital	Providence
State flower	Violet
State bird	Rhode Island Red hen
Nickname	The Ocean State
Highest point	Jerimoth Hill, 811 feet

The Rhode Island Charter of 1663 stated that a civil state is strongest when it allows people to have religious freedom. The people here have supported that ever since. The first Baptist congregation in what has become the United States was started in Providence in 1638. The oldest Jewish house of worship, the Touro Synagogue in Newport, was built in 1763. And one of the oldest Quaker meeting places was built here in 1699.

Rhode Island is in the Northeast Region. In 1790 it became the 13th state. The state song is called "Rhode Island, It's for Me." And the state appetizer? That's calamari!

① It has been said that the first circus in the United States was in Newport, Rhode Island, which included trick riding on horses. This seaside town was a place many went to for relaxation in the 1770s. The circus ended in 1774 with the war approaching.

Roger Williams, who was the founder of Rhode Island, created the first working model of democracy in America after being banished from Plymouth, Massachusetts. He strongly believed that people should have freedom of religion, that the American Indians should be treated fairly, and that slavery should be ended.

② Block Island was spotted by the Italian navigator Giovanni da Verrazzano in 1524. It was later named for a Dutch explorer, Adriaen Block, who had come this way in 1614. Block Island was finally admitted as part of Rhode Island in 1664.

Blackstone River Valley National Historical Park

This is connected to the historical park in Massachusetts, and both focus on America's industrial heritage that helped this area thrive. Everything started changing back then, and you can see just how much when you're here.

John H. Chafee Blackstone River Valley

Stretching across 24 mill towns, this heritage corridor helps you understand part of the reason why America began to change from living on farms to working in factories. This is an image of the power systems at Wilkinson Mill.

Roger Williams National Memorial

Roger Williams helped found Rhode Island. He wanted to create a place where people could have religious freedom. In 1636, he helped the state become a refuge for people to come and worship without needing government approval.

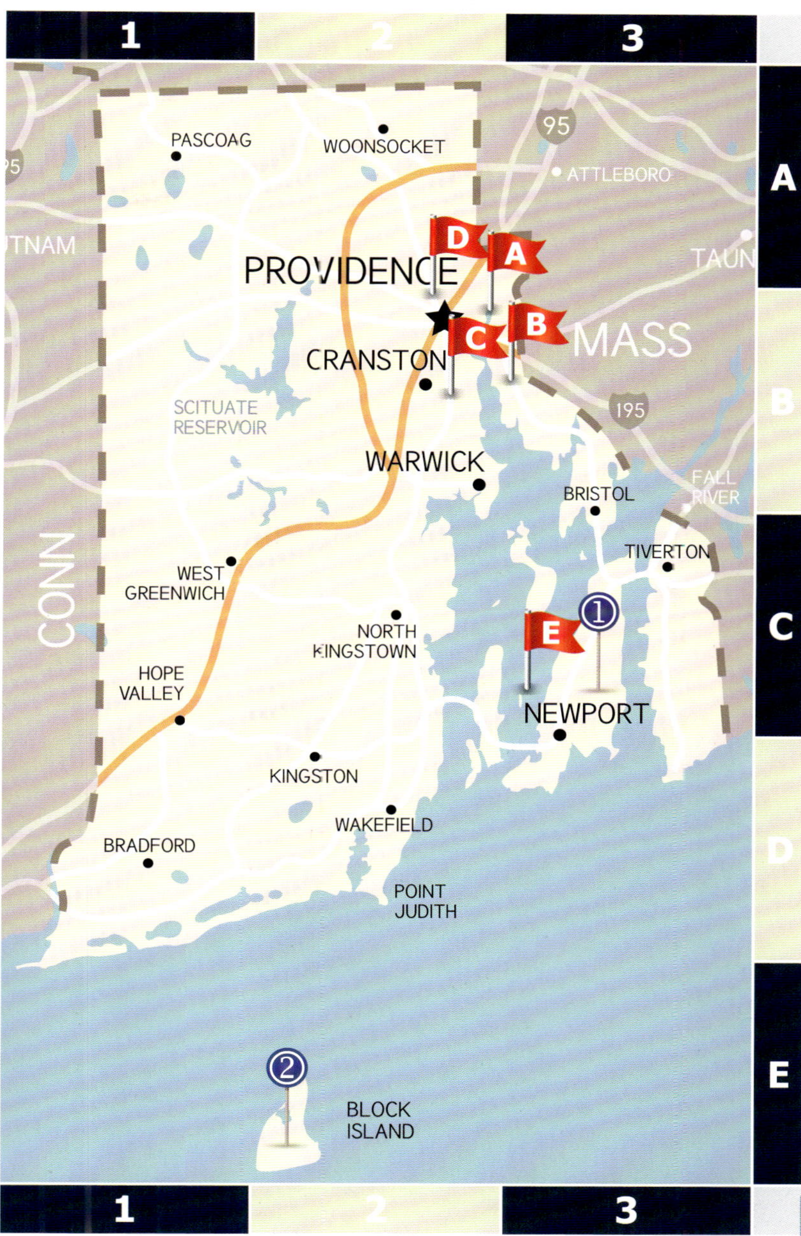

Washington-Rochambeau National Historic Trail

The Washington-Rochambeau (raw-shawn-BOW) trail is 680 miles of roadways that were used by the Continental Army under George Washington during the Revolutionary War. There are signs and exhibits that share the story of the U.S. and French working together here.

Touro Synagogue National Historic Site

This is the oldest synagogue in the United States. Built in 1763 in Newport, it has been a significant place of community and connection for the Jewish people here since before the United States became a nation.

SOUTH CAROLINA

SOUTH CAROLINA PREAMBLE

We, the people of the State of South Carolina, in Convention assembled, grateful to ***God*** for our liberties, do ordain and establish this Constitution for the preservation and perpetuation of the same.

Statehood	1788 (8th state)
Population ranking	23rd
Capital	Columbia
State flower	Carolina jessamine
State bird	Carolina wren
Nickname	The Palmetto State
Highest point	Sassafras Mountain, 3,560 feet

Golf has been big here since the first ship brought golf balls and clubs across the sea from Scotland in 1743. The South Carolina Golf Club was formed in 1786, which established America's first golf course, called Harleston Green.

South Carolina is a state in the American South. It became the 8th state in 1788. It has two state songs, one called "Carolina" and one called "South Carolina on My Mind." And the state hospitality beverage? That's South Carolina–grown tea!

① Each spring and summer, Bomb Island on Lake Murray becomes a home for thousands of Purple Martins. These birds return to the island to stay for the summer. The island has been declared a bird sanctuary, with as many as 750,000 of the birds coming here each year.

② Come to the Riverbanks Zoological Park in Columbia. Why? Well, you can see where more than 2,000 animals thrive, many of them in special natural habitats that don't have bars or cages. Take a look at the botanical gardens as well to see some 4,300 native and exotic plants on display. So much to see of God's creation!

③ South Carolina is called the Palmetto State, and there's good reason for that. The Palmetto tree symbolizes the defeat of the British army on Sullivan's Island on June 28, 1776. The British were firing cannon balls at the fort being defended by American troops, a fort made of Palmetto logs. The trees are spongy, so the logs simply deflected the cannon balls. They still celebrate the day as Carolina Day because the British army was stopped from taking over Charleston Harbor.

Palmetto trees in Charleston, South Carolina

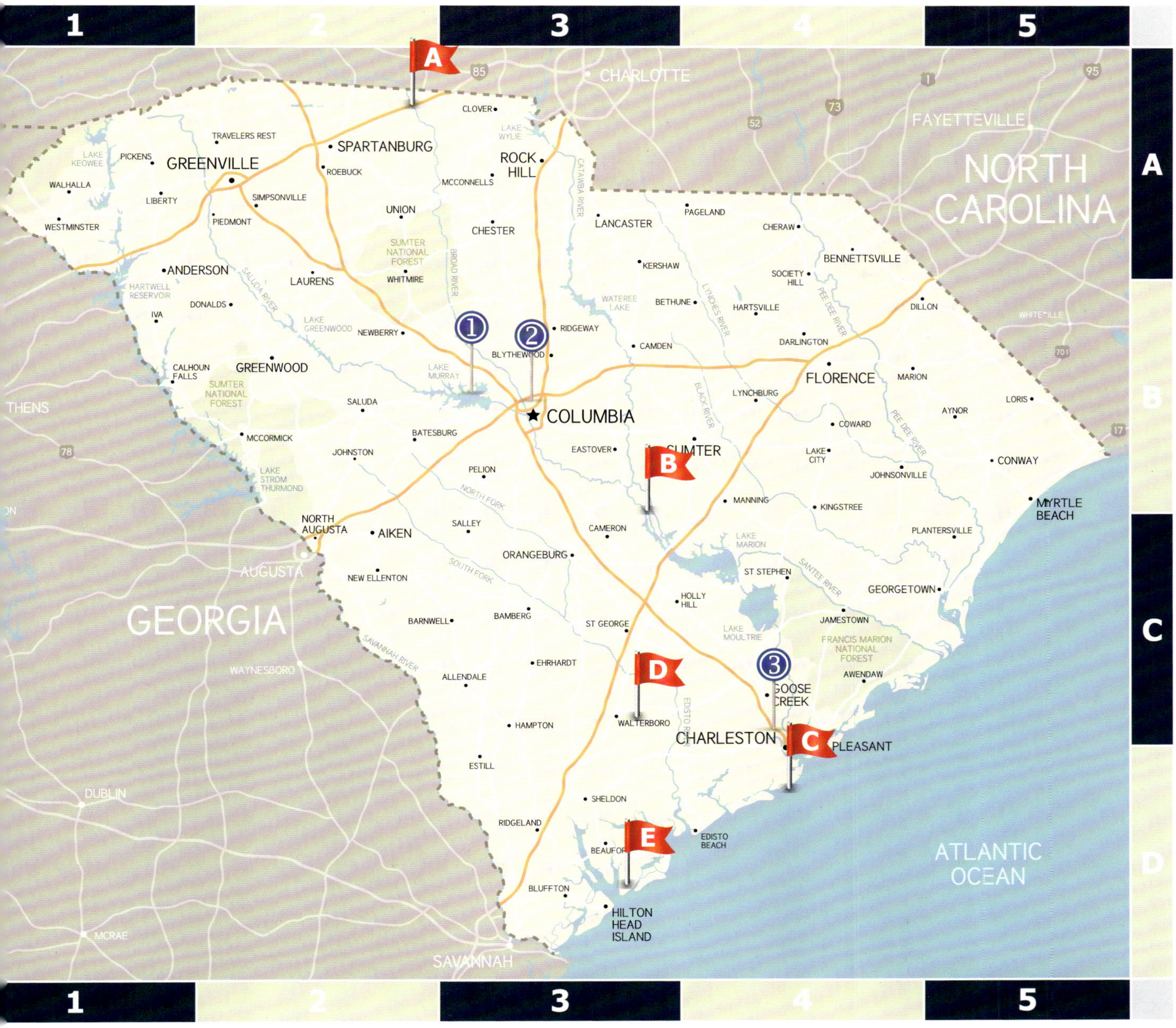

1 2 3 4 5

A B C D

CHARLOTTE
FAYETTEVILLE
NORTH CAROLINA
CLOVER
LAKE WYLIE
TRAVELERS REST
SPARTANBURG
LAKE KEOWEE
PICKENS
GREENVILLE
ROCK HILL
ROEBUCK
MCCONNELLS
WALHALLA
LIBERTY
SIMPSONVILLE
UNION
CATAWBA RIVER
PAGELAND
WESTMINSTER
PIEDMONT
LANCASTER
CHESTER
CHERAW
SUMTER NATIONAL FOREST
BROAD RIVER
KERSHAW
BENNETTSVILLE
ANDERSON
LAURENS
WHITMIRE
SOCIETY HILL
HARTWELL RESERVOIR
SALUDA RIVER
WATEREE LAKE
BETHUNE
HARTSVILLE
DILLON
DONALDS
IVA
LAKE GREENWOOD
NEWBERRY
RIDGEWAY
LYNCHES RIVER
PEE DEE RIVER
CAMDEN
DARLINGTON
BLYTHEWOOD
CALHOUN FALLS
GREENWOOD
LAKE MURRAY
FLORENCE
MARION
SUMTER NATIONAL FOREST
SALUDA
COLUMBIA
LYNCHBURG
AYNOR
LORIS
THENS
BATESBURG
COWARD
MCCORMICK
JOHNSTON
EASTOVER
SUMTER
BLACK RIVER
LAKE CITY
CONWAY
JOHNSONVILLE
LAKE STROM THURMOND
PELION
NORTH FORK
MANNING
KINGSTREE
MYRTLE BEACH
NORTH AUGUSTA
AIKEN
SALLEY
CAMERON
PLANTERSVILLE
ORANGEBURG
LAKE MARION
AUGUSTA
SOUTH FORK
ST STEPHEN
SANTEE RIVER
NEW ELLENTON
GEORGETOWN
GEORGIA
HOLLY HILL
BARNWELL
BAMBERG
ST GEORGE
JAMESTOWN
LAKE MOULTRIE
FRANCIS MARION NATIONAL FOREST
SAVANNAH RIVER
WAYNESBORO
EHRHARDT
ALLENDALE
AWENDAW
GOOSE CREEK
EDISTO RIVER
WALTERBORO
HAMPTON
CHARLESTON
PLEASANT
ESTILL
DUBLIN
SHELDON
RIDGELAND
EDISTO BEACH
BEAUFORT
ATLANTIC OCEAN
BLUFFTON
HILTON HEAD ISLAND
MCRAE
SAVANNAH

1 2 3 4 5

Kings Mountain National Military Park

The battle that took place here on Kings Mountain on October 7, 1780 was a vital American victory during the Revolutionary War. Explore the area where this significant battle took place that helped secure American independence.

Congaree National Park

Ready for this? This park happens to be the largest tract of old growth bottomland hardwood forest that remains in the United States. The trees you'll see here are also some of the tallest in the eastern U.S., making this such a beautiful display of God's creation.

Fort Sumter and Fort Moultrie National Historical Park

Fort Sumter and Fort Moultrie (mole-tree) were central sites at the beginning of the Civil War. When South Carolina seceded from the Union in 1860, the battles for this area began. Come see the history of the area come to life for you.

South Carolina National Heritage Corridor

This beautiful expanse of wondrous creation crosses 17 counties that go from the Appalachian Mountains all the way to the Atlantic Ocean. Come learn about the state's history, agricultural innovation, African American history, and more.

Reconstruction Era National Historical Park

The Reconstruction era was the historic period between 1861 and 1898. This is when the nation was trying to integrate the millions of African Americans into society after they were given back their freedom during and after the Civil War.

SOUTH DAKOTA

SOUTH DAKOTA PREAMBLE

We, the people of South Dakota, grateful to ***Almighty God*** for our civil and religious liberties, in order to form a more perfect and independent government, establish justice, insure tranquillity, provide for the common defense, promote the general welfare and preserve to ourselves and to our posterity the blessings of liberty, do ordain and establish this Constitution for the state of South Dakota.

Statehood	1889 (39th or 40th state)
Population ranking	46th
Capital	Pierre
State flower	Pasqueflower
State bird	Ring-necked pheasant
Nickname	The Coyote State / Mount Rushmore State
Highest point	Black Elk Peak, 7,244 feet

A tunnel along the George S. Mickelson Trail in the Black Hills

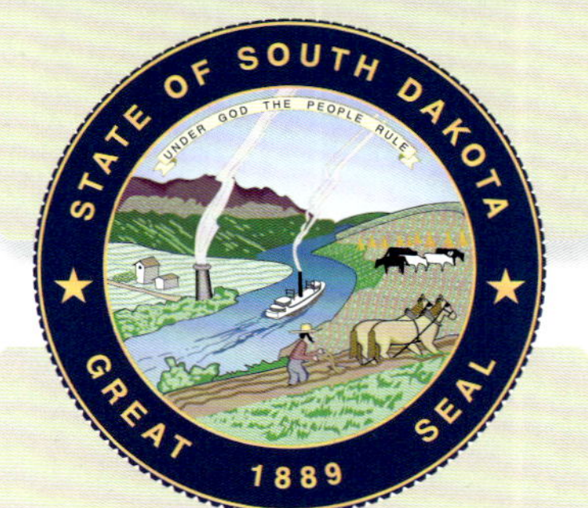

South Dakota is a part of the Midwest. In 1889 it became the 39th state. The state song is "Hail, South Dakota!" And the state bread? That would be fry bread!

The only venomous snake native to South Dakota is the Prairie Rattlesnake. Its colors vary from a light brown to a green with a yellow belly. During the very cold winters up here, they find holes or dens to shelter in until spring brings warmer weather again.

1 Want to know where the deepest underground laboratory is in the United States? Well, that would be the Sanford Underground Research Facility in Lead, South Dakota. They do experiments and studies on things such as dark matter, biology, geology, and physics. Just how big is it? Well, there are 7,700 acres of it underground, with 370 miles of underground shafts and more carved out, all to a depth of almost 5,000 feet.

Mount Rushmore has the faces of George Washington, Thomas Jefferson, Theodore Roosevelt, and Abraham Lincoln carved into it. Each face is around 60 feet high, with each nose measuring a whopping 20 feet long. The sculptor, Gutzon Borglum, and his son began the work on Mount Rushmore in 1927, finishing in 1941. This now priceless Shrine to Democracy cost only $1 million dollars to make!

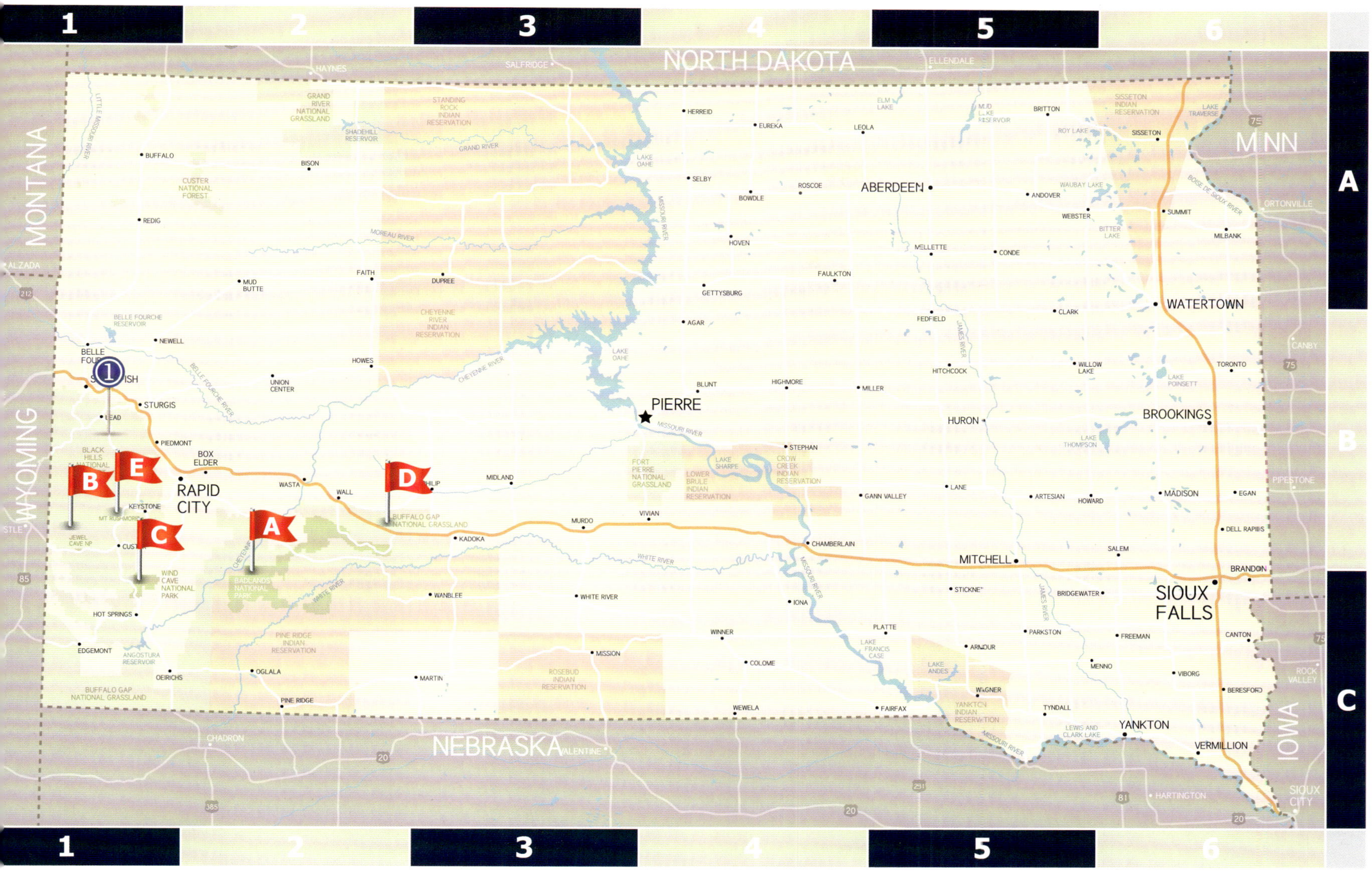

1
2
3
4
5
6
A
B
C
NORTH DAKOTA
MONTANA
WYOMING
NEBRASKA
IOWA
MINN
ABERDEEN
WATERTOWN
PIERRE
BROOKINGS
HURON
RAPID CITY
MITCHELL
SIOUX FALLS
YANKTON
VERMILLION
STURGIS
BOX ELDER
KEYSTONE
HOT SPRINGS
EDGEMONT
WALL
PHILIP
MIDLAND
MURDO
KADOKA
CHAMBERLAIN
MADISON
MISSOURI RIVER
LAKE OAHE
WIND CAVE NATIONAL PARK
BADLANDS NATIONAL PARK
BUFFALO GAP NATIONAL GRASSLAND

WONDERS IN GOD'S WORLD

A

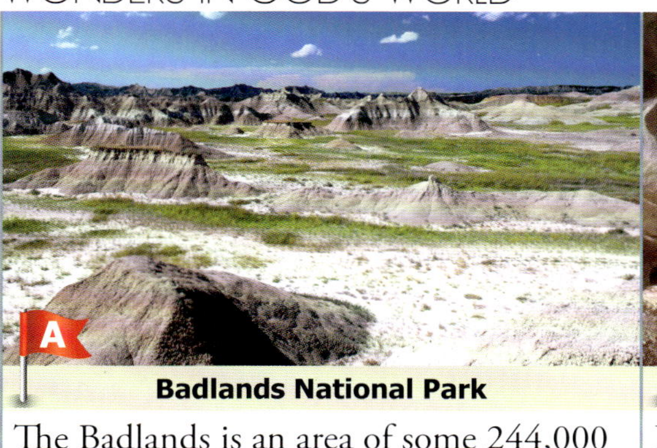

Badlands National Park

The Badlands is an area of some 244,000 acres that helps protect the largest undisturbed mixed-grass prairie in the United States. The park is also home to so much wildlife, including bison, bighorn sheep, and black-footed ferrets.

B

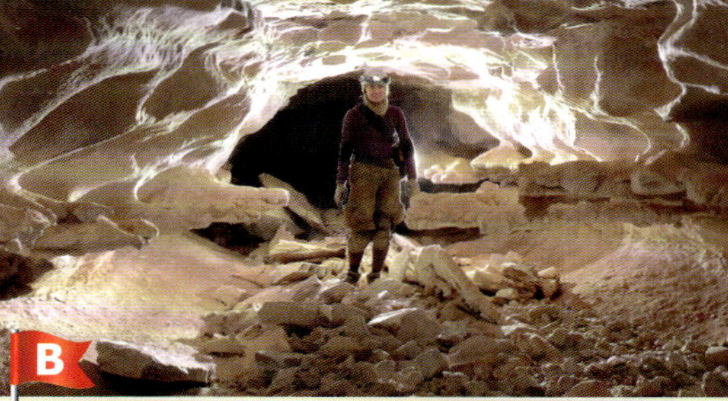

Jewel Cave National Monument

If you enjoy going underground and exploring, this amazing cave has over 195 miles of mapped passages and is considered the third longest cave in the world. See the wondrous formations full of beautiful colors.

C

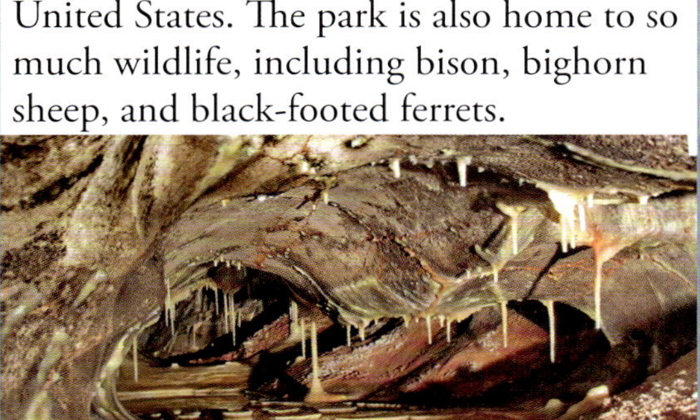

Wind Cave National Park

Established in 1903 by President Theodore Roosevelt, the park has bison, elk, and other wildlife that flourish on the mixed-grass prairie of the Badlands. It was the first cave to be designated a national park anywhere in the world.

D

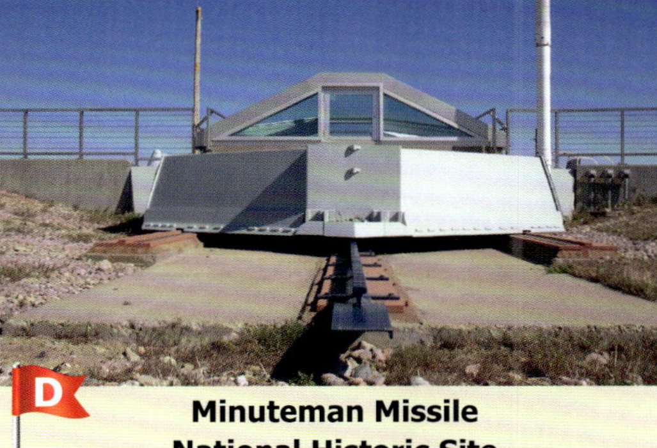

Minuteman Missile National Historic Site

The Cold War (approximately 1946 to 1991) saw an increase in nuclear missiles set up to help protect the U.S. from attack. Some 1,000 of these missiles were kept at the ready. Read the history of this era and the part these missiles played.

E

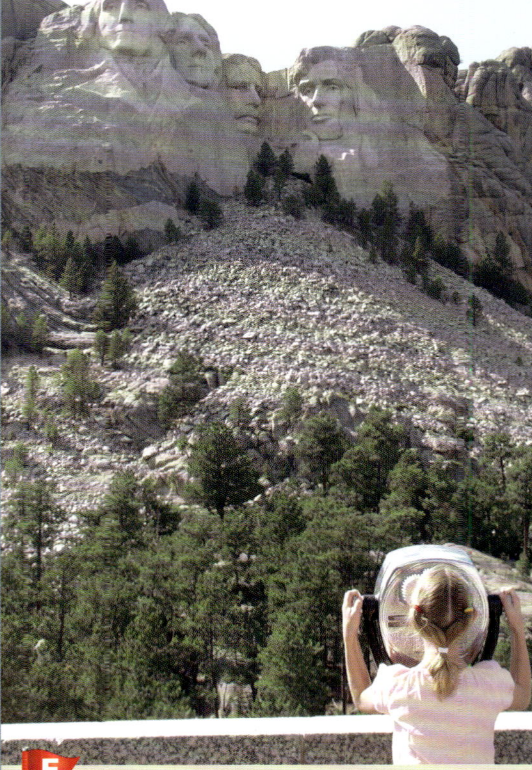

Mount Rushmore National Memorial

This sculpture of the U.S. presidents represents the birth of the nation (George Washington), the growth of the nation (Thomas Jefferson), the development of the nation (Theodore Roosevelt), and the preservation of the nation (Abraham Lincoln).

TENNESSEE

TENNESSEE PREAMBLE

Art. I. Sec. III: That all men have a natural and indefeasible right to worship ***Almighty God*** according to the dictates of their own conscience; that no man can of right be compelled to attend, erect, or support any place of worship, or to maintain any minister against his consent; that no human authority can, in any case whatever, control or interfere with the rights of conscience; and that no preference shall ever be given, by law, to any religious establishment or mode of worship.

Statehood	1796 (16th state)
Population ranking	16th
Capital	Nashville
State flower	Iris
State bird	Mockingbird
Nickname	The Volunteer State
Highest point	Clingmans Dome 6,643 feet

Workers at Norris Dam construction camp site, 1933

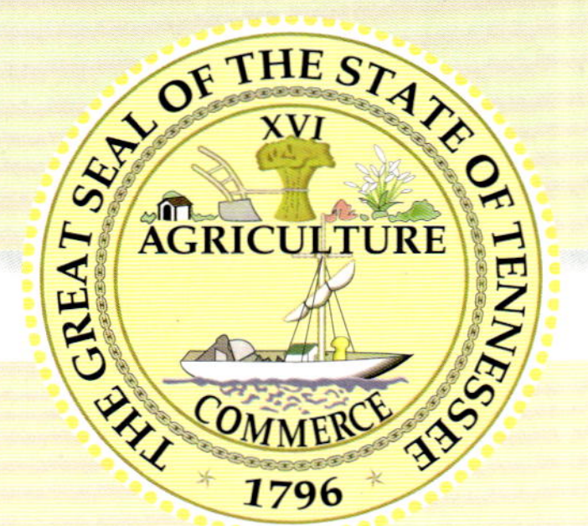

Tennessee is in the South Region of the U.S. It became the 16th state back in 1796. Tennessee has 9 state songs, the most of any state. These include "My Homeland, Tennessee," "When It's Iris Time in Tennessee," "Tennessee Waltz," and "Rocky Top." And the state horse? The Tennessee Walking Horse!

1 The largest earthquake in the 48 contiguous, or adjoining, states was the New Madrid Earthquake. It was actually a series of quakes that started on December 16, 1811, shaking much of northwestern Tennessee and surrounding states. Reelfoot Lake located in Obion was formed during this earthquake.

2 Want to see the most visited national park in America? Come to the Great Smoky Mountains National Park in Tennessee. The park was named for the smoky-looking blue haze that often covers the mountains here.

3 Andrew Johnson held nearly every elective office at the local, state, and federal level over his lifetime. This included becoming president of the United States! He was elected alderman, mayor, state representative, state senator, then served as governor of Tennessee, vice president, and finally president, after Abraham Lincoln was assassinated. Johnson died in Elizabethton, Tennessee.

4 The National Civil Rights Museum is located in Memphis. The museum is at the Lorraine Motel where Dr. Martin Luther King Jr. was assassinated in 1968. If you visit, you'll be able to see the history of the American Civil Rights Movement.

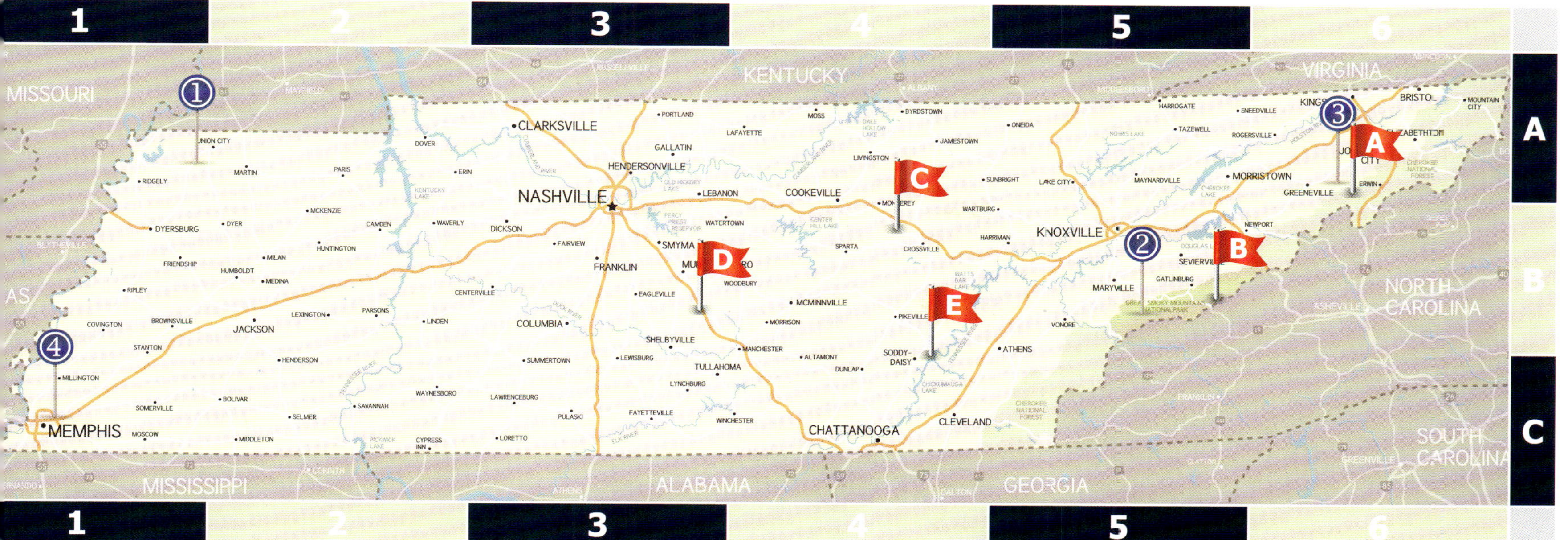

WONDERS IN GOD'S WORLD

Andrew Johnson National Historic Site

Located in Greeneville, The Homestead was Andrew Johnson's home, growing up and after his presidency. Johnson was the 17th president of the United States, and you can see several of the historical homes here as well as his gravesite.

Great Smoky Mountains National Park

This well-loved park runs between the border of Tennessee and North Carolina. Enjoy these beautiful forested mountains and see the diverse plants and animals here, and you'll know why it's the most visited national park in America.

Obed Wild and Scenic River

If you like watching a gentle river flowing or prefer to ride some whitewater rapids, this area is all you could hope for. They say it looks pretty much the same today as it did in the late 1700s when the first European settlers came here.

Stones River National Battlefield

On the last day of 1862, one of the fiercest battles of the Civil War occurred here. The battlefield memorializes the Battle of Stones River, where the Union had a significant victory. This 570-acre park honors their sacrifices.

E

Tennessee Civil War National Heritage Area

This special heritage area covers the whole state and includes eight major corridors. These corridors include the Mississippi River, Cumberland River, Tennessee River, Louisville and Nashville Railroad, and more.

TEXAS

TEXAS PREAMBLE

Humbly invoking the blessings of ***Almighty God***, the people of the State of Texas, do ordain and establish this Constitution.

Statehood	1845 (28th state)
Population ranking	2nd
Capital	Austin
State flower	Bluebonnet
State bird	Mockingbird
Nickname	The Lone Star State
Highest point	Guadalupe Peak, 8,751 feet

America has seen special revival times when the Gospel of Christ has drawn in many to churches and congregations across the country. The First Awakening, as it was called, happened in the 1730s and faded somewhat with the American Revolution. The Second Awakening at the beginning of the 19th century impacted people in the area that eventually became the state of Texas with revivals and camp meetings.

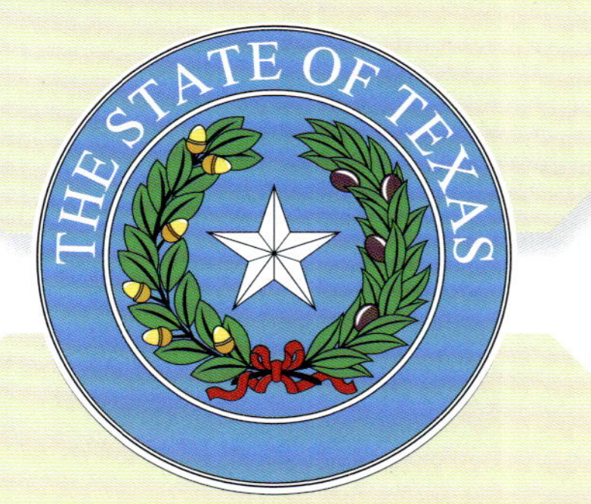

Texas is a state in the South, and Houston is the largest city in this region. It became the 28th state in 1845. "Texas, Our Texas" is the state song. And the state bread? That's Pan de Campo!

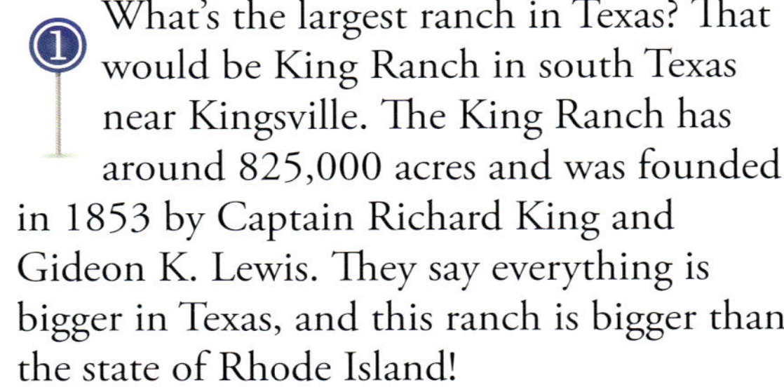

① What's the largest ranch in Texas? That would be King Ranch in south Texas near Kingsville. The King Ranch has around 825,000 acres and was founded in 1853 by Captain Richard King and Gideon K. Lewis. They say everything is bigger in Texas, and this ranch is bigger than the state of Rhode Island!

② The Space Center in Houston has a lot to see about the space program. There are over 400 space artifacts here, which includes spacecraft, moon rocks, and lots of information about the former space shuttle program.

③ If you're searching for the Alamo, come to San Antonio. This is where Texas defenders fell to the army of Mexican General Santa Anna in 1836. It's from that battle that the phrase "Remember the Alamo" originated. This is the state's most popular historic site.

WONDERS IN GOD'S WORLD

A Guadalupe Mountains National Park

The park was established to help protect the four highest peaks in Texas, the diverse plants and wildlife here, and the world's most extensive Permian fossil reef. It also shares the stories of those who traveled through here for hundreds of years.

B Big Bend National Park

Established as a national park in 1935, it helps protect the Chihuahuan (chee-wah-wahn) Desert ecology. There are many diverse plants, birds, and mammals here and some 56 different types of reptiles.

C Lake Meredith National Recreation Area

If you like the great outdoors, this beautiful area offers 11 different campgrounds around the lake or up the river. The lake was created by the Sanford Dam and includes boating, camping, and fishing.

D Padre Island National Seashore

Learn about the rich history of the area, including the Spanish shipwrecks of 1554, or enjoy the 70 miles of coastline. You can see the Laguna Madre, one of the few hypersaline (full of salt) lagoons in the world.

E Rio Grande Wild and Scenic River

This scenic area protects some 260 miles of the Rio Grande ("Big River" in Spanish) in New Mexico and Texas. Established in 1968, there is so much beauty to see and share here.

UTAH

UTAH PREAMBLE

Grateful to ***Almighty God*** for life and liberty, we, the people of Utah, in order to secure and perpetuate the principles of free government, do ordain and establish this CONSTITUTION.

Statehood	1896 (45th state)
Population ranking	30th
Capital	Salt Lake City
State flower	Sego lily
State bird	Seagull
Nickname	The Beehive State
Highest point	Kings Peak, 13,535 feet

Utah can be found in the West Region. In 1896 it became the 45th state. The state song is "Utah, This Is the Place." And the state star cluster? The Beehive Cluster!

Long before wireless phones, messages were often sent across telegraph lines. The First Transcontinental Telegraph opened a communication line between Carson City, Nevada, and Omaha, Nebraska, in 1861. The last portion of the line that had to be finished was near Salt Lake City.

The first Spanish explorers came through Utah in 1776. By the mid-1800s, lots of settlers and miners were coming to Utah looking for land and freedom.

① Kanab is known as Utah's Little Hollywood because of all the television and motion picture companies that come here to make their films.

New Utah flag became official on March 9, 2024.

② The Great Salt Lake is the largest saltwater lake in the Western Hemisphere. It covers more than 1,700 square miles and is about 75 miles long and 28 miles wide. The water in the lake is saltier than the world's oceans.

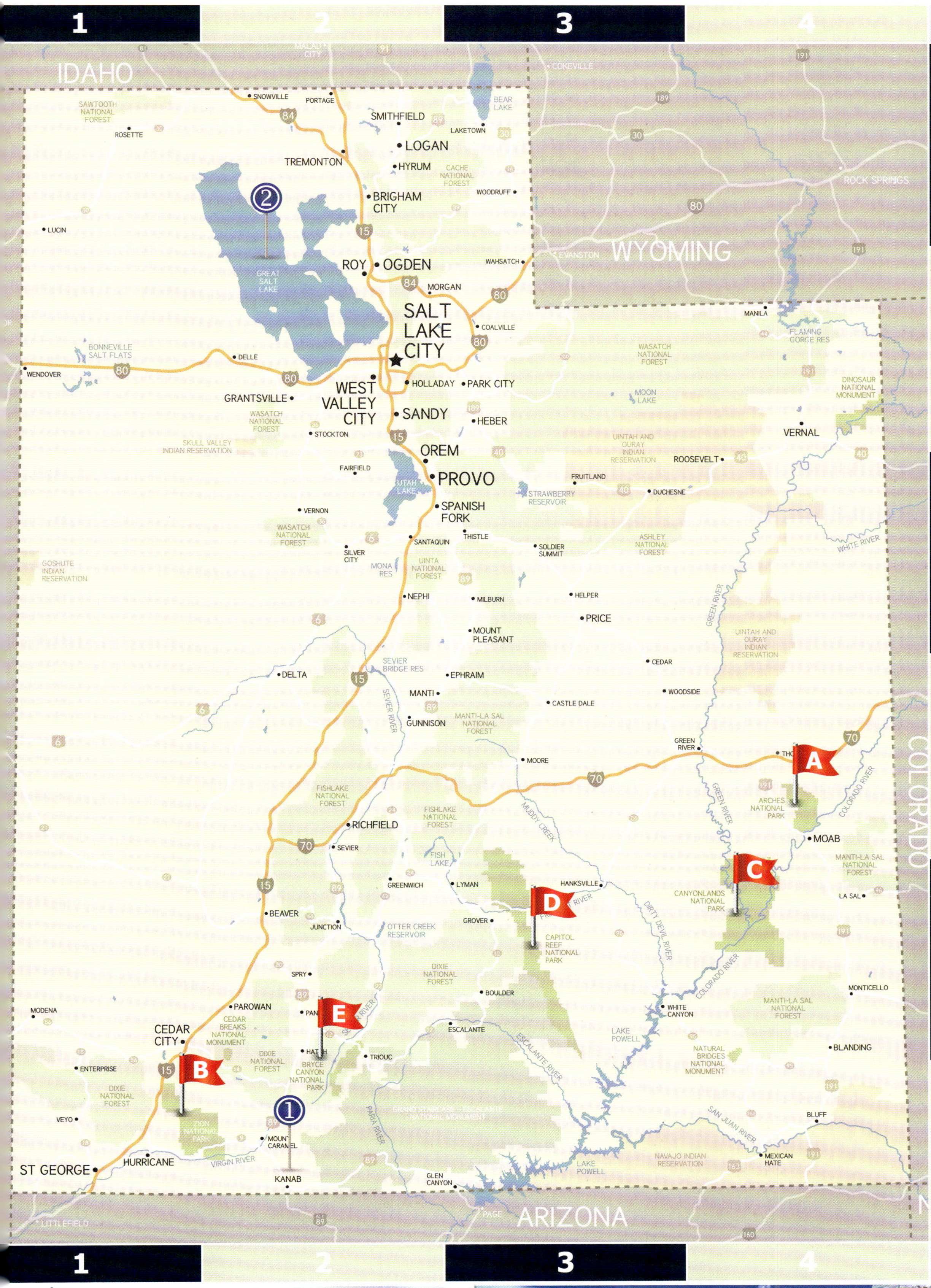
1
2
3
4
A
B
C
D
E
F
IDAHO
WYOMING
COLORADO
ARIZONA
SAWTOOTH NATIONAL FOREST
ROSETTE
SNOWVILLE
PORTAGE
SMITHFIELD
LOGAN
HYRUM
TREMONTON
BRIGHAM CITY
LAKETOWN
BEAR LAKE
COKEVILLE
CACHE NATIONAL FOREST
WOODRUFF
ROCK SPRINGS
LUCIN
GREAT SALT LAKE
ROY
OGDEN
MORGAN
WAHSATCH
EVANSTON
MANILA
FLAMING GORGE RES
SALT LAKE CITY
COALVILLE
BONNEVILLE SALT FLATS
WENDOVER
DELLE
WEST VALLEY CITY
HOLLADAY
PARK CITY
GRANTSVILLE
SANDY
HEBER
WASATCH NATIONAL FOREST
DINOSAUR NATIONAL MONUMENT
MOON LAKE
VERNAL
STOCKTON
SKULL VALLEY INDIAN RESERVATION
OREM
FAIRFIELD
PROVO
UTAH LAKE
UINTAH AND OURAY INDIAN RESERVATION
ROOSEVELT
FRUITLAND
DUCHESNE
STRAWBERRY RESERVOIR
SPANISH FORK
VERNON
THISTLE
SANTAQUIN
SOLDIER SUMMIT
ASHLEY NATIONAL FOREST
WHITE RIVER
SILVER CITY
MONA RES
UINTA NATIONAL FOREST
GOSHUTE INDIAN RESERVATION
NEPHI
MILBURN
HELPER
PRICE
GREEN RIVER
MOUNT PLEASANT
CEDAR
SEVIER BRIDGE RES
DELTA
EPHRAIM
WOODSIDE
MANTI
CASTLE DALE
SEVIER RIVER
GUNNISON
MANTI-LA SAL NATIONAL FOREST
GREEN RIVER
MOORE
FISHLAKE NATIONAL FOREST
ARCHES NATIONAL PARK
MOAB
COLORADO RIVER
RICHFIELD
SEVIER
FISH LAKE
MUDDY CREEK
HANKSVILLE
GREENWICH
LYMAN
CANYONLANDS NATIONAL PARK
LA SAL
BEAVER
JUNCTION
OTTER CREEK RESERVOIR
GROVER
CAPITOL REEF NATIONAL PARK
DIRTY DEVIL RIVER
DIXIE NATIONAL FOREST
SPRY
BOULDER
MONTICELLO
MODENA
PAROWAN
PANGUITCH
CEDAR CITY
CEDAR BREAKS NATIONAL MONUMENT
ESCALANTE
WHITE CANYON
LAKE POWELL
NATURAL BRIDGES NATIONAL MONUMENT
BLANDING
ENTERPRISE
BRYCE CANYON NATIONAL PARK
TROPIC
ESCALANTE RIVER
ZION NATIONAL PARK
VEYO
MOUNT CARMEL
PARIA RIVER
GRAND STAIRCASE - ESCALANTE NATIONAL MONUMENT
SAN JUAN RIVER
BLUFF
MEXICAN HAT
NAVAJO INDIAN RESERVATION
ST GEORGE
HURRICANE
VIRGIN RIVER
KANAB
GLEN CANYON
PAGE
LITTLEFIELD

WONDERS IN GOD'S WORLD

A

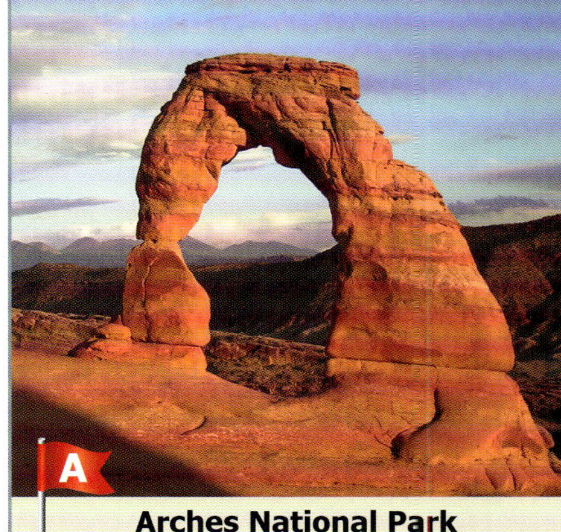

Arches National Park

This area is such a wonderful display of God's glory. It is known for its more than 2,000 natural sandstone arches, the highest density of them in the world. Keep your eyes open for the hundreds of pinnacles, the large fins, and giant balancing rocks all around.

B

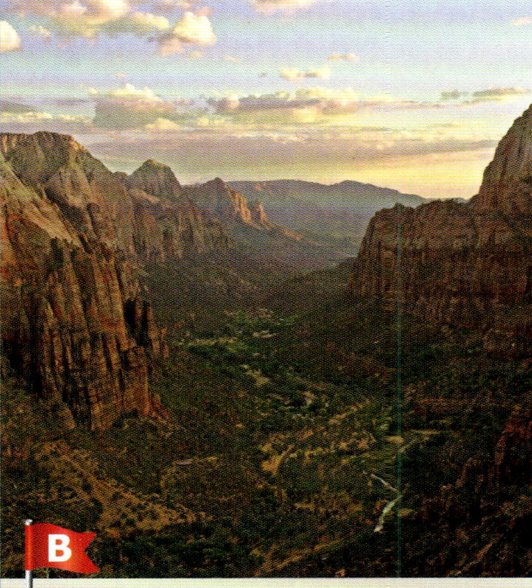

Zion National Park

The brilliance of visiting here is the opportunity to see so much diversity, as the park has various life zones, including desert, woodland, and coniferous forest. In the life zones, you'll also have a chance to see wondrous diversity in wildlife, including 19 types of bats.

C

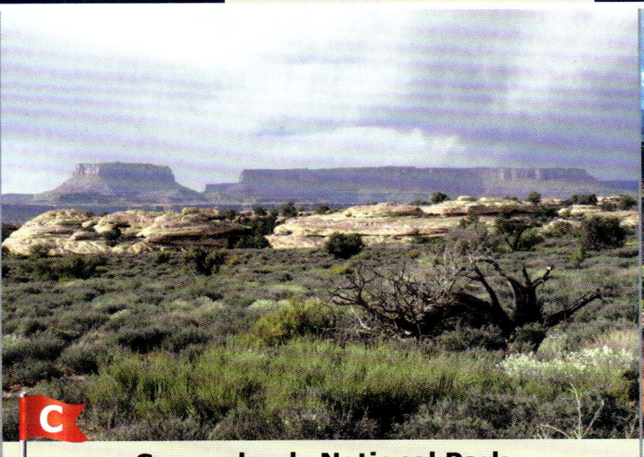

Canyonlands National Park

Explore the countless canyons here, as well as the wondrous diversity of life. The rivers help divide the park into four areas, which are the Island in the Sky, The Needles, The Maze, and the rivers themselves. It has only been a park since 1964.

D

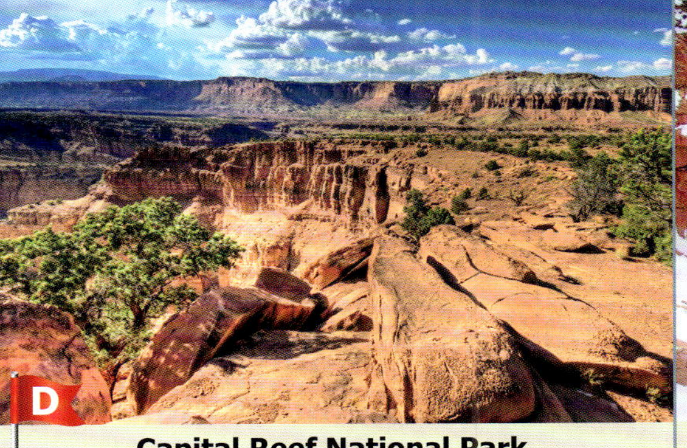

Capital Reef National Park

Established as a national park in 1971 to protect the desert landscape, you'll be amazed to see the colorful canyons, buttes, ridges, and more here. Also, there is a massive wrinkle in the earth here, called a monocline, that is almost 100 miles long.

E

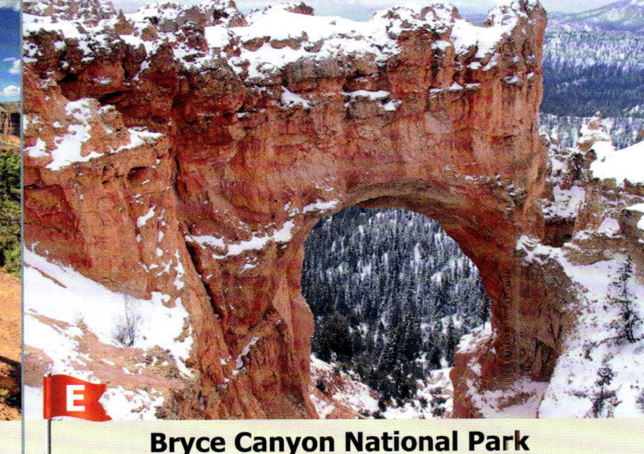

Bryce Canyon National Park

Bryce is another amazing wonder to see in Utah, so keep your eyes out for the hoodoos, which are irregular columns of rock. There are more here than anywhere on earth. Just the vibrant colors of the stones are amazing to see.

VERMONT

VERMONT PREAMBLE

Whereas, all government ought to be instituted and supported for the security and protection of the community as such and to enable the individuals who compose it, to enjoy their natural rights, and the other blessings which ***the Author of existence*** has bestowed upon man; and whenever those great ends of government are not obtained, the people have a right, by common consent, to change it, and take such measures as to them may appear necessary to promote their safety and happiness.

Statehood	1791 (14th state)
Population ranking	49th
Capital	Montpelier
State flower	Red clover
State bird	Hermit thrush
Nickname	The Green Mountain State
Highest point	Mount Mansfield, 4,395 feet

Marlboro Meeting House

Vermont is considered part of the Northeast Region. In 1791, Vermont became the 14th state. Its state song is "These Green Mountains." And the state flavor? Maple!

Jacques Cartier was a French explorer who came across the area of Vermont in 1535. On other voyages to North and South America, he traveled down to Brazil and as far north as Newfoundland.

1 Rudyard Kipling wrote his famous *The Jungle Book* while living in Vermont in the 1890s. He was born in India, where the stories in the book take place, and lived on and off there for some time before he moved to Dummerston, Vermont.

Vermont produces by far the largest amount of maple syrup in the country. About 40 percent of all maple syrup in the United States is produced here.

A **Appalachian National Scenic Trail**

Parts of the trail, which extends more than 2,100 miles through woods and mountain areas, draw some 2 million people every year. The Appalachian (app-uh-LAY-chee [or she] -un) Trail was built by private citizens but is cared for now by several state and federal agencies.

B **Camel's Hump State Park**

The state's most recognized mountain, and featured on the state quarter, Camel's Hump is a beautiful place for camping and hiking. It is a part of the Green Mountain range and is near the Winooski River.

C **Coolidge State Park**

Located in Plymouth, Vermont, the park is named after Calvin Coolidge, who was the 30th president of the United States. This is where Coolidge was born and raised, and it contains the largest state forest in Vermont. Picnic, hike, camp, mountain bike, and more.

D **North Country National Scenic Trail**

This is a 4,600-mile footpath that goes from Vermont to North Dakota. If you like to hike or just love the wilderness, this path allows you to see so much beauty across these states.

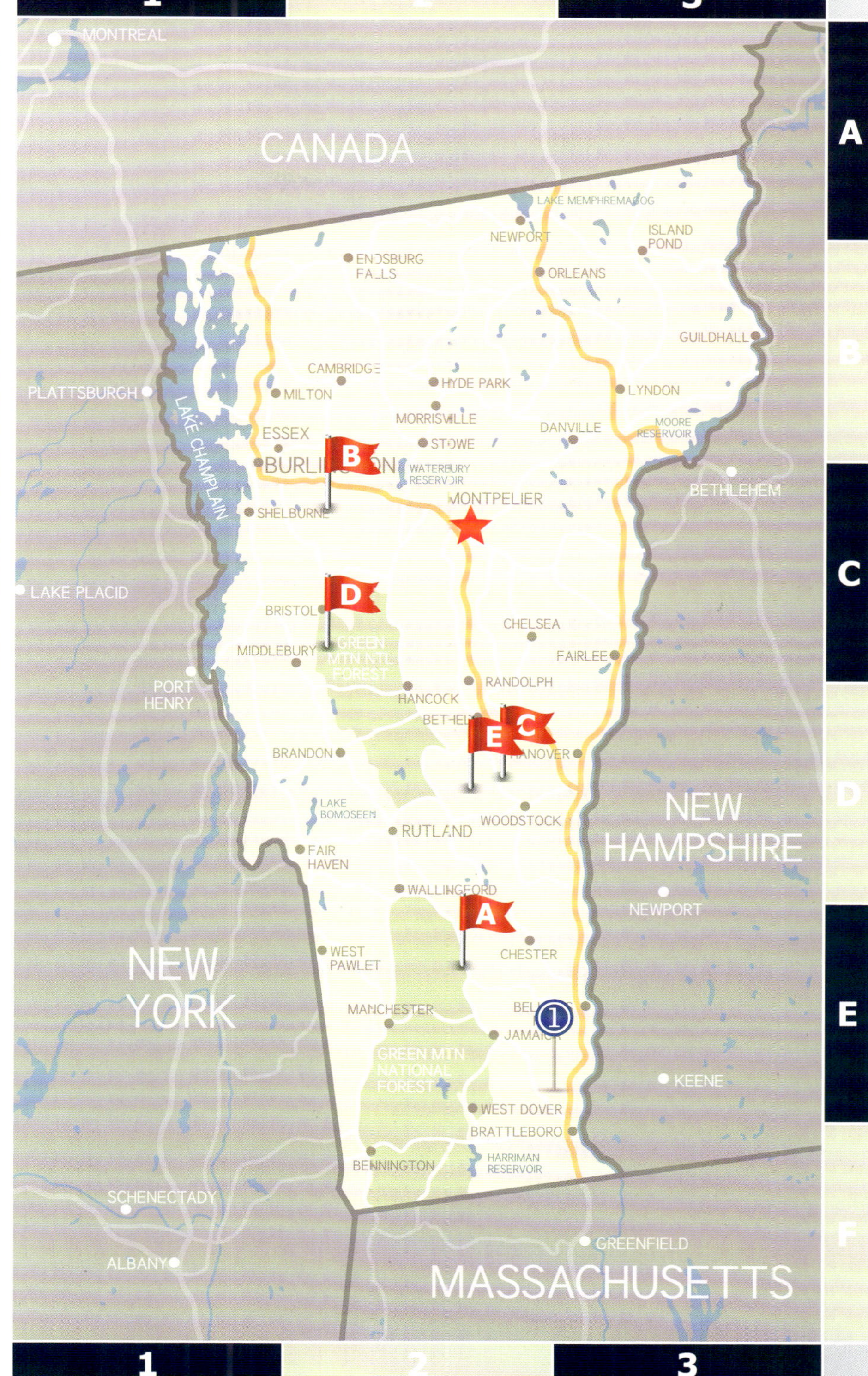

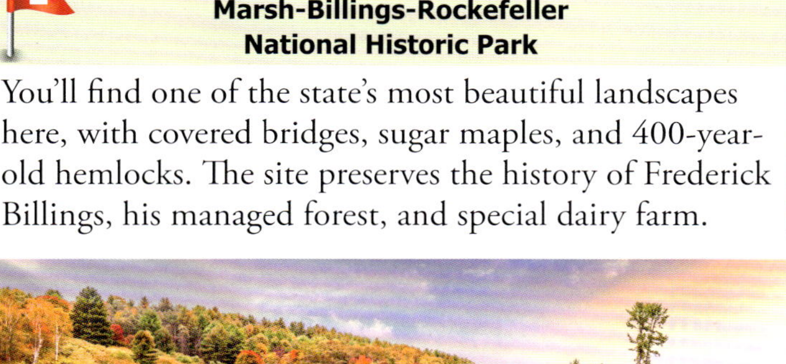

E **Marsh-Billings-Rockefeller National Historic Park**

You'll find one of the state's most beautiful landscapes here, with covered bridges, sugar maples, and 400-year-old hemlocks. The site preserves the history of Frederick Billings, his managed forest, and special dairy farm.

VIRGINIA

VIRGINIA PREAMBLE

That religion or the duty which we owe to our ***Creator***, and the manner of discharging it, can be directed only by reason and conviction, not by force or violence; and, therefore, all men are equally entitled to the free exercise of religion, according to the dictates of conscience; and that it is the mutual duty of all to practice Christian forbearance, love, and charity towards each other. No man shall be compelled to frequent or support any religious worship, place, or ministry whatsoever, nor shall be enforced, restrained, molested, or burthened in his body or goods, nor shall otherwise suffer on account of his religious opinions or belief; but all men shall be free to profess and by argument to maintain their opinions in matters of religion, and the same shall in nowise diminish, enlarge, or affect their civil capacities…

Statehood	1788 (10th state)
Population ranking	12th
Capital	Richmond
State flower	Flowering dogwood
State bird	Cardinal
Nickname	The Old Dominion State
Highest point	Mount Rogers, 5,729 feet

Virginia is in the American South. It became the 10th state in 1788. The state song is "Our Great Virginia." And the state snake? That would be the Eastern Garter Snake.

① The College of William and Mary in Williamsburg is the second-oldest college in the United States. It was founded in 1693. Harvard University was the first, in 1636.

② George Washington's home, Mount Vernon, is located near Alexandria, Virginia. The home you visit today was built in 1758, though the land belonged to Washington's family since 1674.

③ President Thomas Jefferson designed his own home in 1772. He called it Monticello, which is Italian for "little mount," and you can still visit it near Charlottesville, Virginia.

Monticello depicted on the back of the 1953 $2 bill

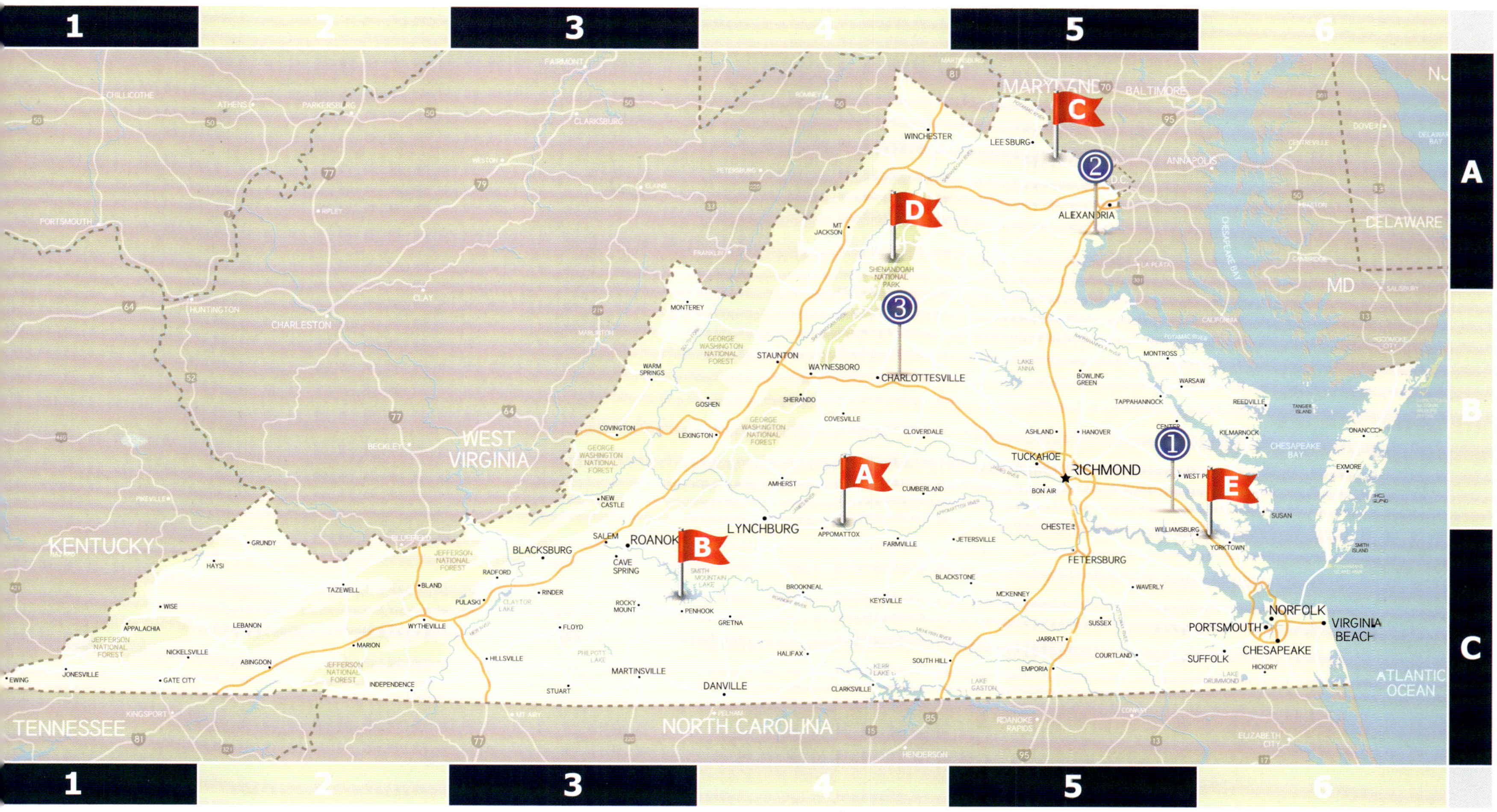

WONDERS IN GOD'S WORLD

A **Appomattox Court House National Historical Park**

This was the site of the surrender of the Confederate army, under Robert E. Lee, to the Union command, under Ulysses S. Grant, which took place on April 9, 1865. The whole Appomattox (app-ah-MAT-ux) area is filled with a deep sense of history.

B **Booker T. Washington National Monument**

Born into slavery on this farm, Booker T. Washington became the first principal of the Tuskegee (tuss-KEY-gey) Normal and Industrial school. He later was an author and orator who helped shape this difficult era of American history.

C **Great Falls Park**

Come and see both the Great Falls of the Potomac (pah-TOW-muck) River, as well as all that remains of the Patowmack Canal, the first canal in the U.S. to use locks to raise and lower boats.

D **Shenandoah National Park**

Explore and enjoy the 200,000-acre forested area of Shenandoah (SHAN-an-dow-uh), with cascading waterfalls, quiet woods, roaming deer, and more. It is part of the Blue Ridge Mountains.

E **Historic Jamestown Colonial National Historical Park**

The account of John Smith and Pocahontas took place in this area. The settlement dates back to 1607.

WASHINGTON

WASHINGTON PREAMBLE

We, the people of the State of Washington, grateful to the ***Supreme Ruler of the Universe*** for our liberties, do ordain this constitution.

Statehood	1889 (42nd state)
Population ranking	13th
Capital	Olympia
State flower	Rhododendron
State bird	Willow goldfinch
Nickname	The Chinook State / Evergreen State
Highest point	Mount Rainier, 14,417 feet

Sonora Smart Dodd, a lady from Spokane, wanted to honor fathers across the state with a special day to celebrate them. Her own father was a Civil War vet who had raised his six children by himself after his wife passed away. This first state celebration happened on June 19, 1910. Though the idea for a national day was supported by two presidents, Woodrow Wilson in 1916 and Calvin Coolidge in 1924, it did not become a national holiday until 1972.

Washington is a part of the West Region. In 1889 it became the 42nd state. "Washington, My Home" is the state song. And the state amphibian? That's the Pacific chorus frog!

1 Want to see the longest floating bridge in the world? You'll need to come to the Governor Albert D. Rosellini Bridge at Evergreen Point in Washington. The bridge helps connect Seattle with its eastern suburbs across Lake Washington, with the floating portion reaching 7,710 feet long.

2 The many islands of Puget Sound are served by the largest ferry fleet in the United States. The 23 ferries cross the waters here, carrying millions of passengers every year.

3 Mount St. Helens is the most active volcano in the lower 48 states. The powerful eruption on May 18, 1980 transformed the whole area, killing 57 people, destroying homes and bridges, and reducing the mountain's summit by 9,677 feet. This showed how dramatically a single catastrophic event could quickly reshape the earth, and it let scientists who had studied facts about Noah's Flood recorded in the Bible see how the Flood waters may have impacted the earth's surface at that time.

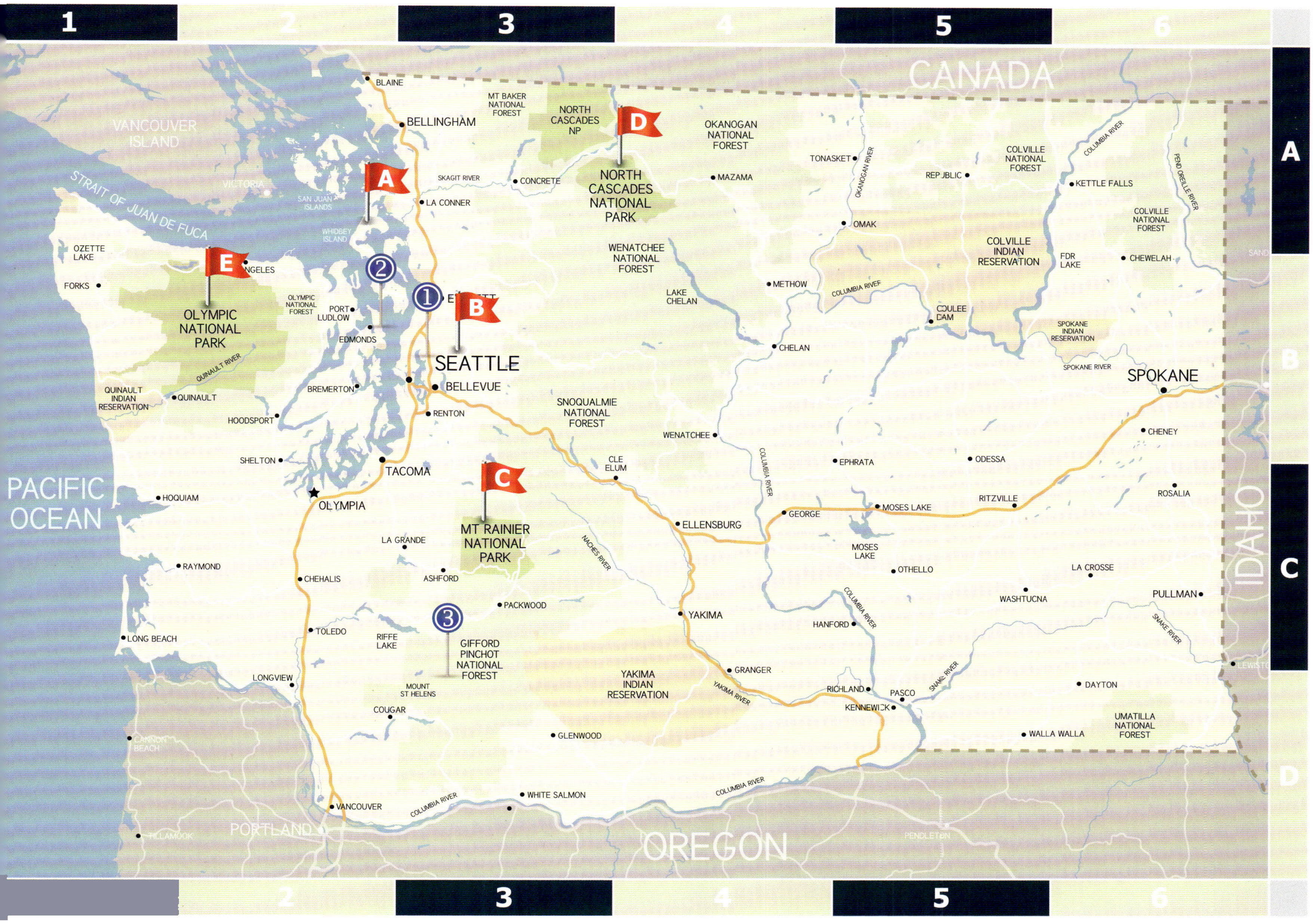

1 2 3 4 5 6

A B C D

CANADA
VANCOUVER ISLAND
VICTORIA
STRAIT OF JUAN DE FUCA
SAN JUAN ISLANDS
WHIDBEY ISLAND
BLAINE
BELLINGHAM
MT BAKER NATIONAL FOREST
NORTH CASCADES NP
NORTH CASCADES NATIONAL PARK
SKAGIT RIVER
CONCRETE
LA CONNER
OKANOGAN NATIONAL FOREST
MAZAMA
TONASKET
OKANOGAN RIVER
OMAK
REPUBLIC
COLVILLE NATIONAL FOREST
KETTLE FALLS
COLUMBIA RIVER
PEND OREILLE RIVER
COLVILLE INDIAN RESERVATION
FDR LAKE
CHEWELAH
OZETTE LAKE
FORKS
OLYMPIC NATIONAL PARK
OLYMPIC NATIONAL FOREST
PORT LUDLOW
EDMONDS
EVERETT
SEATTLE
BELLEVUE
RENTON
BREMERTON
QUINAULT RIVER
QUINAULT INDIAN RESERVATION
QUINAULT
HOODSPORT
SHELTON
WENATCHEE NATIONAL FOREST
LAKE CHELAN
METHOW
CHELAN
COULEE DAM
SPOKANE INDIAN RESERVATION
SPOKANE RIVER
SPOKANE
CHENEY
SNOQUALMIE NATIONAL FOREST
WENATCHEE
CLE ELUM
EPHRATA
ODESSA
PACIFIC OCEAN
HOQUIAM
TACOMA
OLYMPIA
MT RAINIER NATIONAL PARK
LA GRANDE
ASHFORD
NACHES RIVER
ELLENSBURG
COLUMBIA RIVER
GEORGE
MOSES LAKE
RITZVILLE
ROSALIA
IDAHO
RAYMOND
CHEHALIS
PACKWOOD
MOSES LAKE
OTHELLO
LA CROSSE
YAKIMA
WASHTUCNA
PULLMAN
HANFORD
SNAKE RIVER
LONG BEACH
TOLEDO
RIFFE LAKE
GIFFORD PINCHOT NATIONAL FOREST
GRANGER
LONGVIEW
MOUNT ST HELENS
YAKIMA INDIAN RESERVATION
YAKIMA RIVER
RICHLAND
PASCO
KENNEWICK
DAYTON
COUGAR
GLENWOOD
WALLA WALLA
UMATILLA NATIONAL FOREST
VANCOUVER
COLUMBIA RIVER
WHITE SALMON
PORTLAND
OREGON
PENDLETON

WONDERS IN GOD'S WORLD

A Ebey's Landing National Historical Reserve

This reserve is a living historic area on Whidbey Island in Puget Sound. The area preserves and protects the history here, from the initial settlements back in the 19th century to today. Experience farming as it was done in the 1850s.

B Klondike Gold Rush National Historical Park

The gold rush era of Alaska and the Yukon Territory brought thousands through here in the late 1890s. Several areas share the stories and the trails from long ago, including the Pioneer Square National Historic District in Seattle.

C Mount Rainier National Park

Mount Rainier happens to be an active volcano and the most glaciated peak in the lower 48 states. You can see subalpine meadows around the volcano's icy ring, old forests around the lower slopes, and some of the 25 glaciers here.

D North Cascades National Park

It might take a little time to explore the 500,000 acres here. There are beautiful mountains all around that are a part of the North Cascades Range, as well as rivers that start here and flow to the Atlantic Ocean. It is beautiful, wild country.

E Olympic National Park

If you like fishing, get ready to enjoy the char, salmon, and trout that are abundant here. You might also enjoy the mountains, the sandy beaches, and the lush rainforests, all of which make this park a wondrous display of God's diverse creation.

WEST VIRGINIA

WEST VIRGINIA PREAMBLE

Since through Divine Providence we enjoy the blessings of civil, political and religious liberty, we, the people of West Virginia, in and through the provisions of this Constitution, reaffirm our faith in and constant reliance upon ***God*** and seek diligently to promote, preserve and perpetuate good government in the State of West Virginia for the common welfare, freedom and security of ourselves and our posterity.

Statehood	1863 (35th state)
Population ranking	39th
Capital	Charleston
State flower	Big rhododendron
State bird	Cardinal
Nickname	The Mountain State
Highest point	Spruce Knob, 4,863 feet

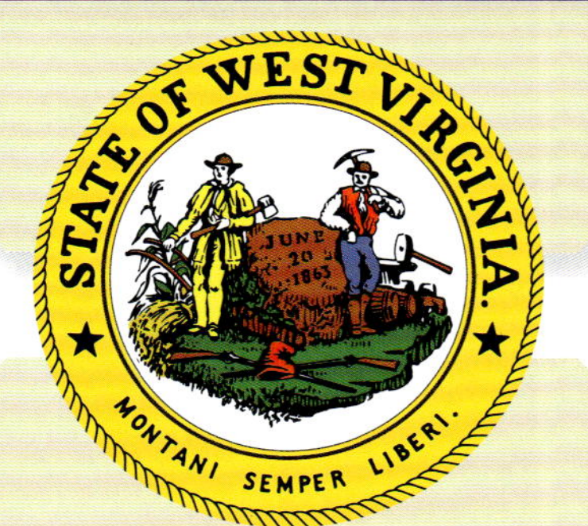

West Virginia can be found in the South. It became the 35th state in 1863. The three state songs are "The West Virginia Hills," "This Is My West Virginia," and "West Virginia, My Home Sweet Home." And the state fruit? The Golden Delicious apple!

West Virginia is the only state in the Union to have separated from a Confederate state. It is unique as well in that President Lincoln issued a proclamation to help those in government accept it as a new state.

1 Grave Creek Mound is the location of one of the largest cone-shaped burial mounds in the United States. The mound is 62 feet high and 240 feet in diameter. Scientists began their first excavations here in 1838.

For many years, coal mining was the leading industry here. Now the tourism industry creates the most jobs and income for the state.

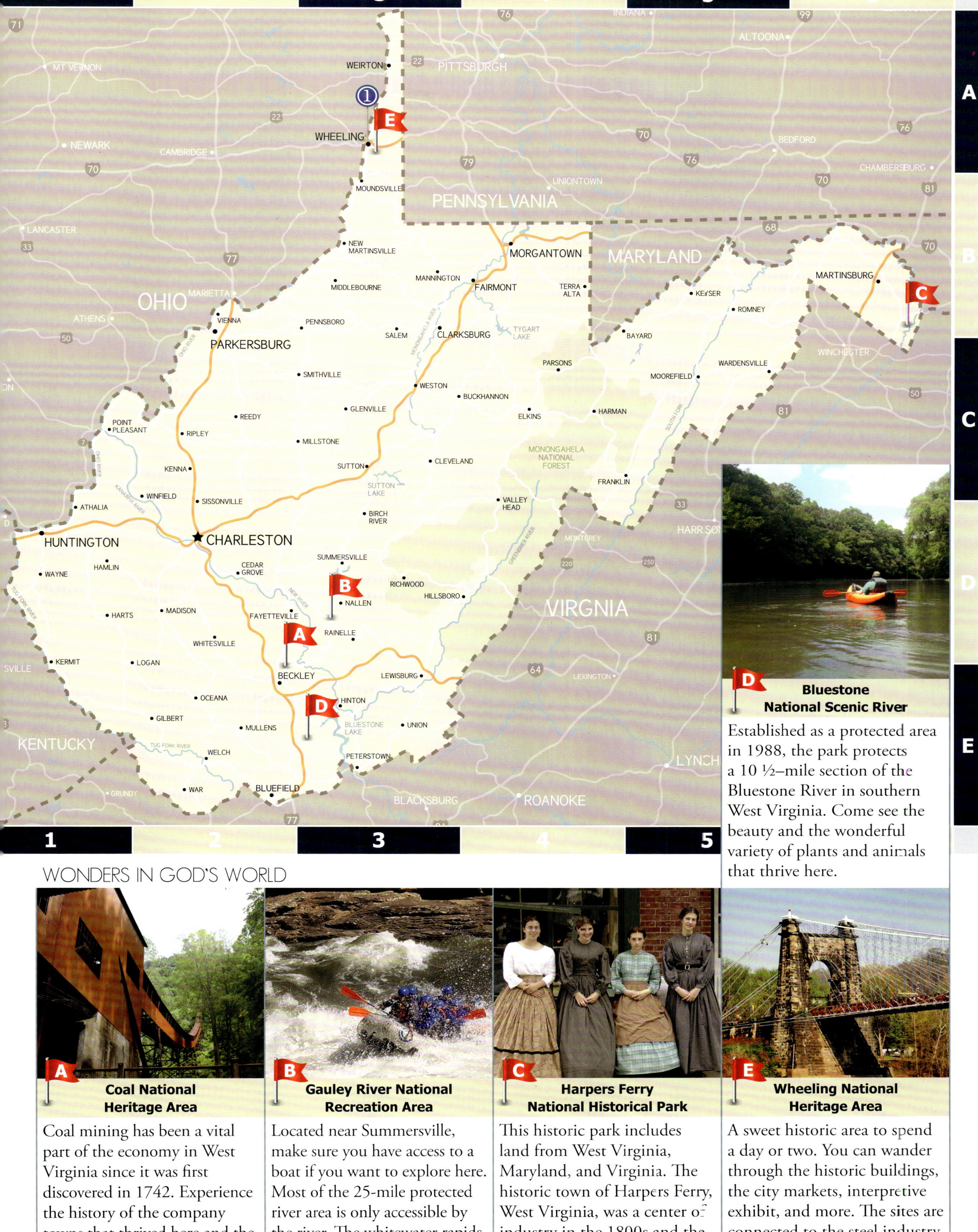

WONDERS IN GOD'S WORLD

Bluestone National Scenic River

Established as a protected area in 1988, the park protects a 10 ½–mile section of the Bluestone River in southern West Virginia. Come see the beauty and the wonderful variety of plants and animals that thrive here.

Coal National Heritage Area

Coal mining has been a vital part of the economy in West Virginia since it was first discovered in 1742. Experience the history of the company towns that thrived here and the stories of those who risked their lives to bring it out of the earth.

Gauley River National Recreation Area

Located near Summersville, make sure you have access to a boat if you want to explore here. Most of the 25-mile protected river area is only accessible by the river. The whitewater rapids will take you through scenic gorges and valleys.

Harpers Ferry National Historical Park

This historic park includes land from West Virginia, Maryland, and Virginia. The historic town of Harpers Ferry, West Virginia, was a center of industry in the 1800s and the place where the abolitionist John Brown's uprising failed.

Wheeling National Heritage Area

A sweet historic area to spend a day or two. You can wander through the historic buildings, the city markets, interpretive exhibit, and more. The sites are connected to the steel industry and other industries created by the Ohio River.

WISCONSIN

WISCONSIN PREAMBLE

We, the people of Wisconsin, grateful to ***Almighty God*** for our freedom, in order to secure its blessings, form a more perfect government, insure domestic tranquility and promote the general welfare, do establish this constitution.

Statehood	1848 (30th state)
Population ranking	20th
Capital	Madison
State flower	Wood violet
State bird	Robin
Nickname	The Badger State
Highest point	Timms Hill, 1,951 feet

① A building known as the Little White Schoolhouse is also called the "Birthplace of the Republican Party." It was built as a schoolhouse in Ripon in 1853, was used by the new Republican Party in 1854, and has been designated a National Historic Landmark.

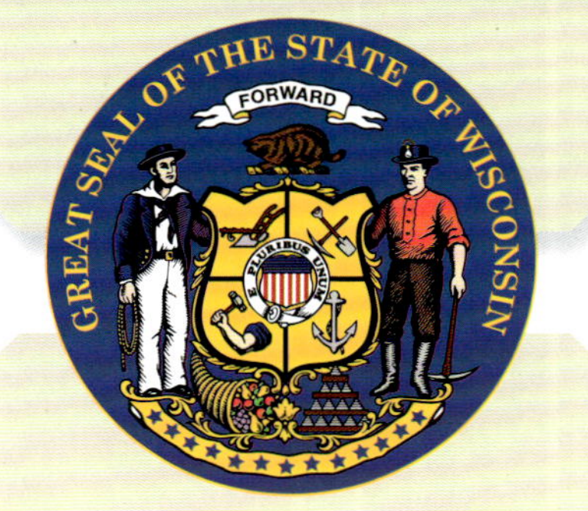

Wisconsin is considered part of the Midwest Region. In 1848, Wisconsin became the 30th state. "On, Wisconsin" is the state song. And the state fruit? That would be the cranberry!

The very first Barbie doll was said to be from Willows, Wisconsin. Barbie's full name is Barbie Millicent Roberts, and she made her debut in 1959 at the toy fair in New York City. Though there is a town called Willow in Wisconsin, Willows is a fictional place.

Wisconsin is known as the Badger State. This is because in the 1820s, people here would sometimes dig their homes into the hillsides . . . like badgers do!

Wisconsin is often called the dairy capital of the United States. In fact, Wisconsin cows produce more milk than any state other than California.

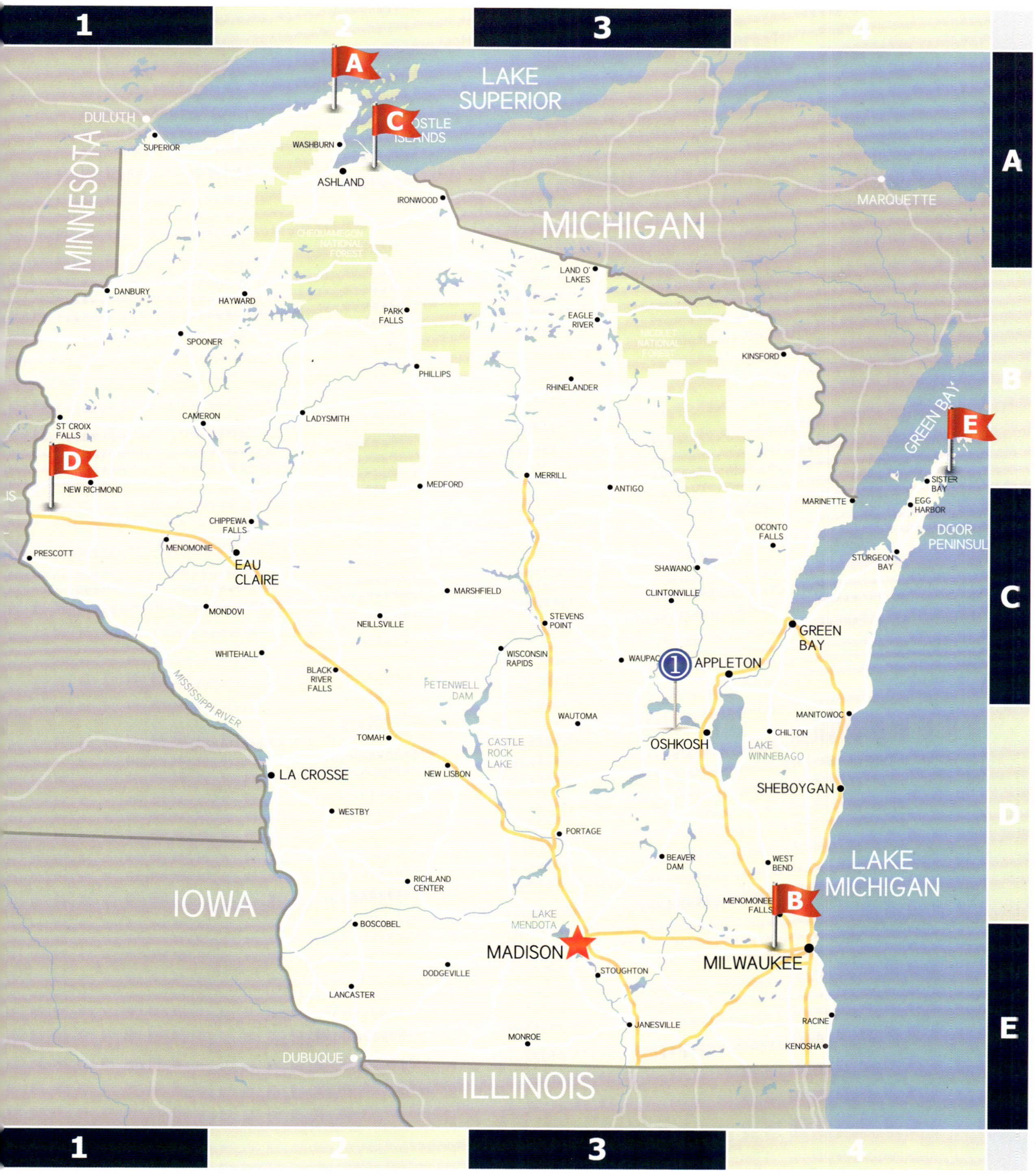

1 2 3 4

A B C D E

LAKE SUPERIOR
MICHIGAN
MINNESOTA
IOWA
ILLINOIS
LAKE MICHIGAN
GREEN BAY
DOOR PENINSULA

DULUTH
SUPERIOR
WASHBURN
ASHLAND
APOSTLE ISLANDS
IRONWOOD
MARQUETTE
DANBURY
HAYWARD
SPOONER
PARK FALLS
LAND O' LAKES
EAGLE RIVER
PHILLIPS
RHINELANDER
KINSFORD
CAMERON
LADYSMITH
ST CROIX FALLS
NEW RICHMOND
MEDFORD
MERRILL
ANTIGO
MARINETTE
SISTER BAY
EGG HARBOR
PRESCOTT
MENOMONIE
CHIPPEWA FALLS
EAU CLAIRE
OCONTO FALLS
STURGEON BAY
SHAWANO
CLINTONVILLE
MONDOVI
MARSHFIELD
NEILLSVILLE
STEVENS POINT
GREEN BAY
WHITEHALL
WISCONSIN RAPIDS
WAUPACA
APPLETON
BLACK RIVER FALLS
PETENWELL DAM
MISSISSIPPI RIVER
WAUTOMA
OSHKOSH
MANITOWOC
CHILTON
LAKE WINNEBAGO
TOMAH
CASTLE ROCK LAKE
LA CROSSE
NEW LISBON
SHEBOYGAN
WESTBY
PORTAGE
BEAVER DAM
WEST BEND
RICHLAND CENTER
MENOMONEE FALLS
LAKE MENDOTA
BOSCOBEL
MADISON
MILWAUKEE
DODGEVILLE
STOUGHTON
LANCASTER
JANESVILLE
RACINE
MONROE
KENOSHA
DUBUQUE

Apostle Islands National Lakeshore

This beautiful area contains 21 of the Apostle Islands and a shoreline that includes some 69,372 acres on the shore of Lake Superior. Come view the historic lighthouses, the sea caves, and the wondrous animal habitats.

Ice Age National Scenic Trail

Established in 1980, this 1,200-mile footpath traces the edge of the glacier. The entire trail is located within Wisconsin and is one of only 11 national scenic trails in the United States.

North Country National Scenic Trail

This 4,600-mile trail passes over eight states, from Vermont to North Dakota. That makes this national scenic trail the longest of all those designated by Congress.

Saint Croix National Scenic Riverway

This system of riverways includes areas in Wisconsin and Minnesota. Over 250 miles of rivers are protected, which includes the St. Croix River and the Namekagon River.

Whitefish Dunes State Park

This 867-acre park was created to protect the fragile dune environments of the peninsula. You can journey over the boardwalk that takes you out to the wetlands, watch waterfowl, or explore the eight Native American villages here.

WYOMING

WYOMING PREAMBLE

We, the people of the State of Wyoming, grateful to ***God*** for our civil, political and religious liberties, and desiring to secure them to ourselves and perpetuate them to our posterity, do ordain and establish this Constitution.

Statehood	1890 (44th state)
Population ranking	50th
Capital	Cheyenne
State flower	Indian paintbrush
State bird	Meadowlark
Nickname	The Equality State
Highest point	Gannett Peak, 13,804 feet

The official state dinosaur of Wyoming is the *Triceratops*, though many other dinosaur fossils have been found here, including *Stegosaurus*, *Allosaurus*, and *Tyrannosaurus rex*. Fossils are formed when a living thing is buried by water that is full of dirt and other minerals. Such fossils are found all over the world, one of the evidences of the global Flood of Noah.

Wyoming is in the West Region of the U.S. It became the 44th state in 1890 and has the lowest population of all the 50 states with fewer than 600,000 people living in the whole state. The state song is called "Wyoming Where I Belong." And the state mammal? That's the American Bison!

FRANK LESLIE'S ILLUSTRATED NEWSPAPER

NEW YORK—FOR THE WEEK ENDING NOVEMBER 24, 1888.

WOMAN SUFFRAGE IN WYOMING TERRITORY.—SCENE AT THE POLLS IN CHEYENNE.

In 1869, Wyoming Territory became the first place connected to the United States that gave women the right to vote.

① President Theodore Roosevelt established the first national monument on September 24, 1906. This was Devils Tower in northeastern Wyoming, which is a butte that rises 867 feet from the base to the summit.

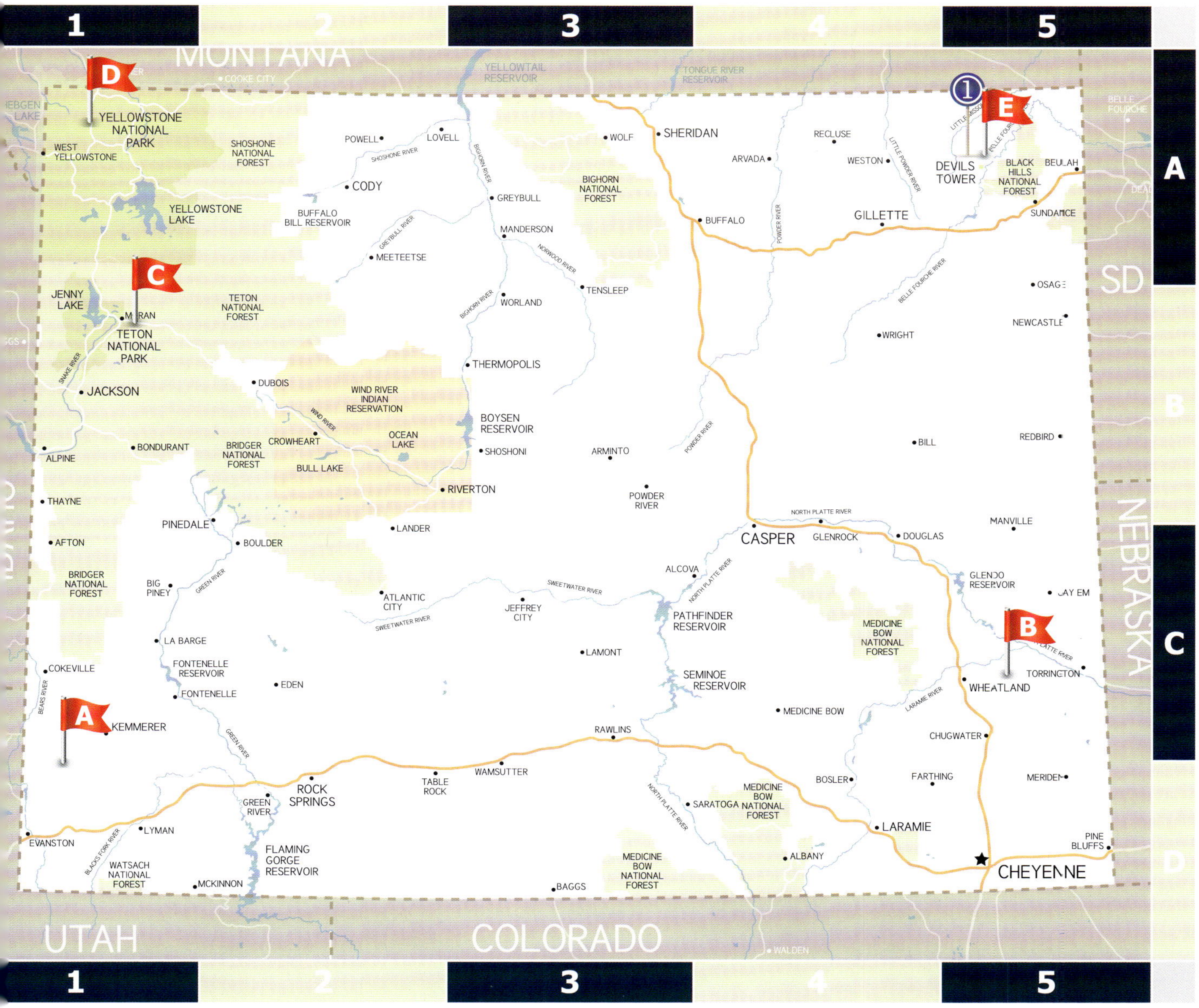

1 2 3 4 5

A B C D

MONTANA
COOKE CITY
YELLOWTAIL RESERVOIR
TONGUE RIVER RESERVOIR
HEBGEN LAKE
D
YELLOWSTONE NATIONAL PARK
WEST YELLOWSTONE
SHOSHONE NATIONAL FOREST
POWELL
LOVELL
WOLF
SHERIDAN
RECLUSE
1
E
CODY
BIGHORN NATIONAL FOREST
ARVADA
WESTON
DEVILS TOWER
BLACK HILLS NATIONAL FOREST
BEULAH
BELLE FOURCHE
GREYBULL
YELLOWSTONE LAKE
BUFFALO BILL RESERVOIR
BUFFALO
GILLETTE
SUNDANCE
MANDERSON
MEETEETSE
C
TENSLEEP
OSAGE
SD
JENNY LAKE
MORAN
TETON NATIONAL FOREST
WORLAND
NEWCASTLE
TETON NATIONAL PARK
WRIGHT
THERMOPOLIS
JACKSON
DUBOIS
WIND RIVER INDIAN RESERVATION
BOYSEN RESERVOIR
ALPINE
BONDURANT
BRIDGER NATIONAL FOREST
CROWHEART
OCEAN LAKE
SHOSHONI
ARMINTO
BILL
REDBIRD
BULL LAKE
THAYNE
RIVERTON
POWDER RIVER
PINEDALE
NEBRASKA
MANVILLE
AFTON
BOULDER
LANDER
CASPER
GLENROCK
DOUGLAS
BRIDGER NATIONAL FOREST
BIG PINEY
ATLANTIC CITY
JEFFREY CITY
ALCOVA
GLENDO RESERVOIR
LAY EM
PATHFINDER RESERVOIR
MEDICINE BOW NATIONAL FOREST
B
LA BARGE
LAMONT
FONTENELLE RESERVOIR
TORRINGTON
COKEVILLE
SEMINOE RESERVOIR
WHEATLAND
FONTENELLE
EDEN
A
KEMMERER
MEDICINE BOW
RAWLINS
CHUGWATER
WAMSUTTER
FARTHING
MERIDEN
ROCK SPRINGS
GREEN RIVER
TABLE ROCK
BOSLER
SARATOGA
MEDICINE BOW NATIONAL FOREST
LARAMIE
LYMAN
EVANSTON
FLAMING GORGE RESERVOIR
WATSACH NATIONAL FOREST
MCKINNON
BAGGS
MEDICINE BOW NATIONAL FOREST
ALBANY
PINE BLUFFS
CHEYENNE
UTAH
COLORADO
WALDEN

A Fossil Butte National Monument

In Wyoming's sagebrush desert, you can find lots of wildlife and lots of wildlife fossils too. This includes fossils of birds, fish, insects, plants, mammals, and more. This amazing site is just 15 miles west of Kemmerer, Wyoming.

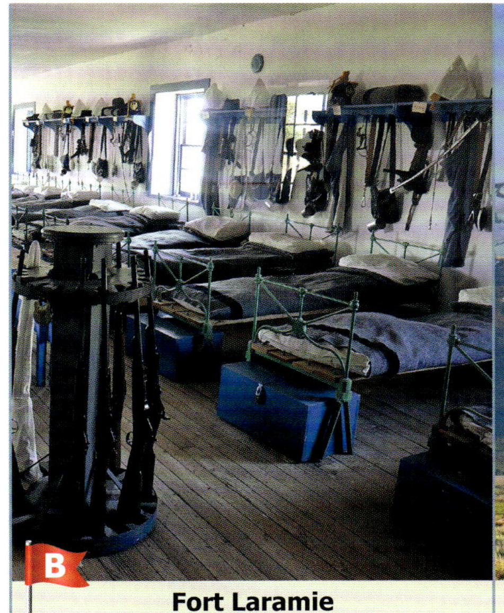

B Fort Laramie National Historic Site

In 1834, Fort Laramie opened as a private fur trading site. It became a vital military post out on the Northern Plains until it was abandoned in 1890. It has been restored so that you can tour the area and sense the history all around you.

C Grand Teton National Park

The park offers some 200 miles of trails, float trips on the Snake River, and the stunning beauty of the Tetons themselves. The area including Grand Teton National Park, Yellowstone National Park, and the national forests here protect some 18,000,000 acres of land.

D Yellowstone National Park

It was on March 1, 1872 when Yellowstone became what many call the first national park in the world. There is so much to explore here, including geysers, rivers, diverse wildlife, and more. Be prepared to be in awe of God's handiwork.

E Devils Tower National Monument

The very visible Devils Tower is called a butte, which is an isolated mountain that rises up from the surrounding area. It is made of igneous rock. Travelers through this area used it as a marker.

DISTRICT OF COLUMBIA

NATIONAL ANTHEM
"The Star-Spangled Banner"

O say can you see, by the dawn's early light,

What so proudly we hailed at the twilight's last gleaming,

Whose broad stripes and bright stars through the perilous fight,

O'er the ramparts we watched, were so gallantly streaming?

And the rockets' red glare, the bombs bursting in air,

Gave proof through the night that our flag was still there;

O say does that star-spangled banner yet wave

O'er the land of the free and the home of the brave?

Established	December 1, 1800
Motto	Justice for all
Capital	United States Capital
Official flower	American Beauty rose
Official bird	Wood thrush

Washington, D.C., is in the South Region of the country and is the capital of the United States. The city's population is actually greater than Vermont or Wyoming. And the official dinosaur fossil of D.C.? That would be the Capitalsaurus, formerly known as *Creosaurus potens*!

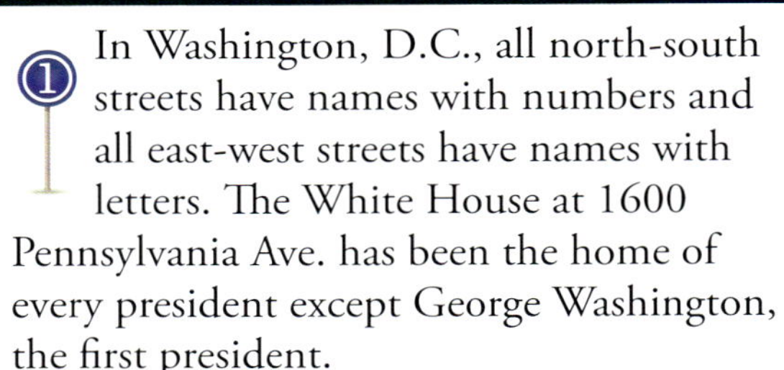

1 In Washington, D.C., all north-south streets have names with numbers and all east-west streets have names with letters. The White House at 1600 Pennsylvania Ave. has been the home of every president except George Washington, the first president.

Each spring, beautiful cherry tree blossoms fill the city with gorgeous pink flowers. The first 3,000 cherry trees were a friendship gift from Tokyo, Japan, in 1912.

2 Established in 1889, the National Zoo is one of the oldest zoos in the United States. Its purpose is to help teach about conservation, helping connect people to animals in order to help save and protect them. There are 2,700 animals here to see and enjoy.

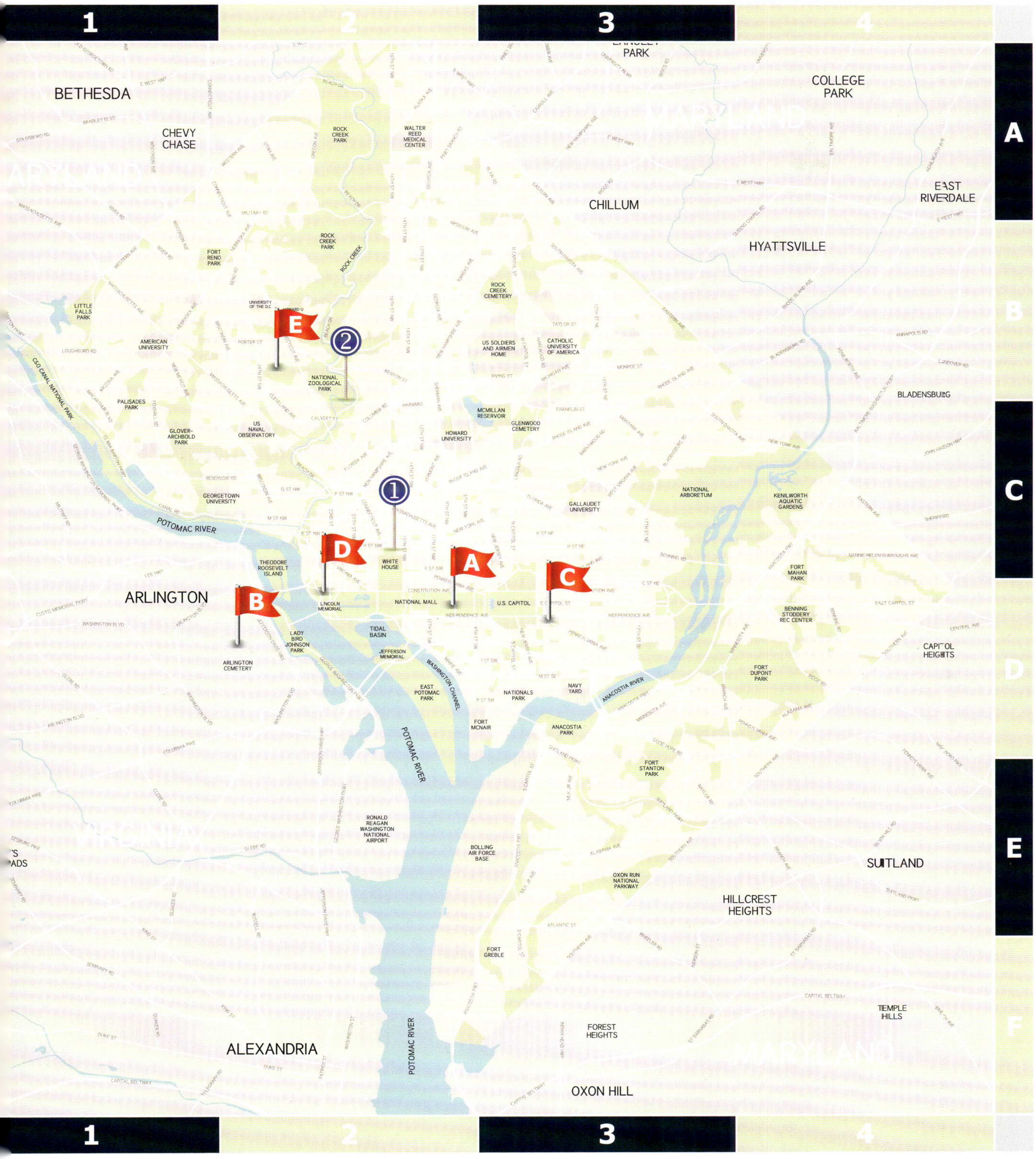

1 2 3 4

A B C D E F

BETHESDA
CHEVY CHASE
COLLEGE PARK
EAST RIVERDALE
CHILLUM
HYATTSVILLE
BLADENSBURG
ARLINGTON
CAPITOL HEIGHTS
SUITLAND
HILLCREST HEIGHTS
TEMPLE HILLS
FOREST HEIGHTS
ALEXANDRIA
OXON HILL
POTOMAC RIVER
WHITE HOUSE
NATIONAL MALL
U.S. CAPITOL
LINCOLN MEMORIAL
ARLINGTON CEMETERY
NATIONAL ZOOLOGICAL PARK
ANACOSTIA RIVER

1 2 3 4

A **Washington Monument**

The Washington Monument was created to honor the nation's first president. At the time it was completed in 1884, it was the tallest building in the world at 555 feet, 5 1/8 inches.

B **Arlington Cemetery**

Across from the Potomac River, you'll find the Arlington National Cemetery. It is a military cemetery that honors the dead from all the nation's conflicts, with reinterred dead from conflicts before the Civil War. It was opened in 1864.

C **Library of Congress**

If you love books, this is the place for you. It is the largest library in the world, with more than 162 million items that include books, sound recordings, photographs, maps, and more. There are materials here in more than 450 languages.

D **Lincoln Memorial**

Built in honor of Abraham Lincoln, the 16th president of the United States, it was dedicated in 1922 and has become a symbolic place to address issues of race relations because of Lincoln's role in ending slavery in America.

E **The National Cathedral**

The official name is The Cathedral Church of Saint Peter and Saint Paul in the City and Diocese of Washington, but most just call it the National Cathedral. It is the second-largest church building in the U.S. and the fourth-tallest building in Washington.

GLOSSARY

archipelago: A group of islands close together in an ocean or sea. Hawaii is an archipelago.

bay: An area of water in a lake or sea that is partially encircled by land. Mount Hope Bay is a bay in Rhode Island.

butte: A rocky mountain like a mesa but with a smaller, flat surface. Shadow Butte in Idaho is an example.

canyon: A gorge or valley with rocky, sloped sides. The Grand Canyon in Arizona is considered one of the most magnificent canyons in the world.

cave: A tunnel or hollowed-out area underground, some with miles of connected caverns. Marvel Cave is an example in Missouri.

coastline (shoreline): The land at the edge of or surrounding a bay or ocean. The Gulf Coast of the United States includes the coastlines of the states of Alabama, Florida, Louisiana, Mississippi, and Texas.

continent: There are seven continents on earth, which are large areas of land with various countries. The United States is part of the North American continent.

deserts: Deserts can be hot or cold, but they are most often dry places that receive less than 10 inches of rain each year. The Mojave Desert that covers parts of Arizona, California, and Nevada is the driest desert in North America.

fjord: Narrow waterways connected to the sea with tall, steep cliffs. Puget Sound in Washington is a fjord system.

forests: Coniferous forests (forests with trees that have cones and needles, like those around the Great Lakes and Minnesota), rainforests (forests with lots of rain and trees that never lose their leaves, like the Hoh Rain Forest in Washington), and deciduous forests (forests with trees that lose their leaves in fall, like a large part of the U.S. from Florida up to New England).

geyser: A hole in the ground that releases hot water and steam into the air from underground. Old Faithful in Wyoming is the most famous in the U.S.

glacier: A river of ice that stays frozen all year and moves very slowly down mountain slopes, like Mills Glacier in Colorado.

grasslands: Grasslands cover about one-fourth of earth's land. They are found where there is too little rain for trees and more rain than a desert receives. In South America, they are known as pampas. If you're in the United States, they are called prairies, and they compose most or all of Kansas, Nebraska, North Dakota, Oklahoma, and South Dakota. In Russia they are called steppes, and in Africa they are called savannas.

gulf: An area of the sea or ocean that is partially surrounded by land but much larger than a bay. The states called the Gulf States are Alabama, Florida, Louisiana, Mississippi, and Texas.

hill: A mound of land raised above the surrounding landscape but smaller than a mountain. Floyd's Bluff is a hill in Iowa.

iceberg: A large portion of floating ice; often 90 percent of it is under water. You can find icebergs in America, many in the Knik Glacier in Alaska.

island: Islands are landforms surrounded by water. They can be created by breaking away from a larger landform or through volcanic activity on the ocean floor. Aquidneck Island is an island that is a part of the state of Rhode Island.

isthmus: A thin area of land with water on two sides and connecting two larger portions of land, like the Madison Isthmus in Wisconsin.

key: Small islands made from sand and coral structures. The Florida Keys are the most well known in the U.S.

knob: Like a hill, but smaller in size. Bald Knob in West Virginia is an example.

lake: A large body of fresh water enclosed by land, like Moores Lake in Delaware.

marsh: A low-lying wetland filled with diverse life and covered in tall grasses. If you're in Michigan, look for Tobico Marsh.

mesa: A rocky mountain like a butte but with a larger, flat top. Big Top Mesa in North Dakota is an example.

mountains: Mountains are raised-up areas of land formed either by volcanic activity or movement in the earth's crust. The higher elevations of a mountain have less oxygen and less rainfall. This makes it more difficult for plants to grow at higher elevations. Wheeler Peak is a mountain in New Mexico.

oceans: Though the waters all cycle together, there are five distinct oceans recognized in the world, listed here in order of size: Pacific Ocean (parts of the Western U.S.), Atlantic Ocean (parts of the Eastern U.S.), Indian Ocean, Southern Ocean, and Arctic Ocean (parts of Alaska). These are filled with salty water that is not drinkable, and much diverse life is designed to thrive here.

peninsula: A large section of land that sticks far out into a large body of water. New Jersey has several, including Barnegat Peninsula and Sandy Hook.

plain: A broad flatland covered mostly with grasses rather than trees. The Great Plains in the U.S. include areas of Colorado, Kansas, Oklahoma, and more.

plateau: A large, flat area of land that is raised above the surrounding area. The Ozarks is a plateau that covers parts of Arkansas, Kansas, Oklahoma, and Missouri.

reef (coral): Made of limestone (calcium carbonate), reefs are formed when various algae, clams, corals, sponges, and other creatures cement themselves together in warm, shallow seas, like areas of Hawaii and Florida.

rivers (brooks, creeks, streams): These water sources are fed by rainfall and snowfall, transporting large amounts of water over hundreds and thousands of miles. Smaller brooks and creeks merge to form streams, which merge to form rivers. These bring water on a continual basis to lakes and eventually to the ocean, moving down sloped mountains and hills. Along the way, many towns and cities have often been built that use the water for drinking, for crops and animals, for fishing, and for transportation by boat. The Missouri River is the longest river in North America, and it crosses through 10 states.

sea: A large inland area of saltwater too small to be considered an ocean. This includes the Beaufort Sea north of Alaska.

tundra: Cold climate lands with very few plants. There are both alpine and arctic tundra areas in Alaska.

valley: The lower areas between hills and mountains. Ash Coulee is a valley that is in South Dakota.

volcano: A break in the ground that releases hot gas, ash, and lava from deep in the earth. Mount St. Helens in Washington State is a volcano that had a massive eruption in 1980.

waterfall: A stream or river that flows over a cliff, either as one drop (a cataract) or in sloped steps down a hill or mountain (a cascade). Multnomah Falls in Oregon is a beautiful example.

AMERICAN HOLIDAYS

Holidays (originally from "holy days") are days of celebration or honor or remembrance for families, people groups, or nations. Here is a calendar of a few of the holy days, federal holidays, and special days celebrated in the United States.

The United States has no official national holidays, but it does have federal holidays. On those days, certain federal facilities and federally regulated businesses close. States can also create statewide holidays. Many people across the country celebrate these federal holidays.

January

*New Year's Day: January 1

*Martin Luther King Day: 3rd Monday in January

February

Black History Month

Groundhog Day: February 2

Valentine's Day: February 14

*President's Day: 3rd Monday in February

March

Easter: Spring Sunday, date varies

St. Patrick's Day: March 17

April

Earth Day: April 22

May

Asian/Pacific American Heritage Month

Cinco de Mayo: May 5

Mother's Day: 2nd Sunday in May

*Memorial Day: last Monday in May

June

Flag Day: June 14

Father's Day: 3rd Sunday in June

July

*Independence Day: July 4

August

Women's Equality Day: August 26

September

*Labor Day: 1st Monday in September

October

*Columbus Day: 2nd Monday in October

Halloween: October 31

November

*Veterans Day: November 11

*Thanksgiving Day: 4th Thursday in November

Native American Heritage Day: the day following Thanksgiving

December

*Christmas Day: December 25

Kwanzaa: December 26–January 1

**Federal holidays*

Photo Credits: T-top, B-bottom, L-left, R-right, C-center

All images istock.com or getty.com unless stated.
Superstock.com: p 10, p 74,
Library of Congress: p 7(4), p 19, p 8, p 19, p 37, p 38, p 46, p 49, p 60, p 64, p 65(3), p 68, p 76, p 82, p 84, p 89, p 104
National Parks Service: p 9, p 13, p 15, p 17, p 21, p 23, p 27, p 29, p 31, p 33, p 35, p 37, p 39, p 41, p 45, p 47, p 49, p 51, p 53, p 59, p 61, p 63, p 69, p 71, p 75, p 77, p 79, p 81, p 85, p 87, p 88, p 89, p 91, p 97, p 99, p 101
flickr.com: p 16 (William Andrus), p 27 (Ken Lund), p 31(Jay Galvin), p 36 (U.S. Army), p 39 (Rich Bowen), p 45 (Maryland GovPics), p 60 (Berlin-Ichthyosaur State Park), p 68 (Carolyn), p 70 (Gerry Dincher), p 72 (Adam Moss), p 102 (RomitaGirl67)
Ark Encounter (AiG): p 38
Tongass National Forest: p 9
US Department of Education: p 6,
Old Log Theatre: p 50
Passion Play: p 12
Bluespring Caverns: p 32
Ag Museum: p 20
Alabama archives: p 6
Publicdomainpictures.net: p 76
Wikimedia Commons: p 6, p 7, p 8, p 10, p 11, p 12, p 13, p 14, p 16, p 17, p 18, p 19, p 20, p 21, p 22, p 23, p 24, p 25, p 26, p 28, p 30, p 31, p 32, p 33, p 34, p 35, p 36, p 37, p 38, p 39, p 40, p 41, p 42, p 43, p 44, p 45, p 46, p 47, p 48, p 49, p 50, p 51, p 52, p 53, p 54, p 55, p 56, p 58, p 59, p 56, p 57, p 60, p 62, p 63, p 64, p 65, p 66, p 67, p 68, p 69, p 70, p 72, p 73, p 74, p 75, p 76, p 77, p 78, p 79, p 80, p 81, p 82, p 83, p 84, p 85, p 86, p 88, p 89, p 90, p 91, p 92, p 93, p 94, p 95, p 96, p 97, p 98, p 99, p 100, p 102, p 103, p 104, p 105, p 106, p 107

INDEX

Within this index you will find page numbers for each entry. Those places found on the maps include a grid reference. Note the following example:

National Cathedral.................. 107, **B2**

The National Cathedral on page 107. Then trace your fingers from the letter B and the number 2 on the grid surrounding the map to find its general location.

INDEX

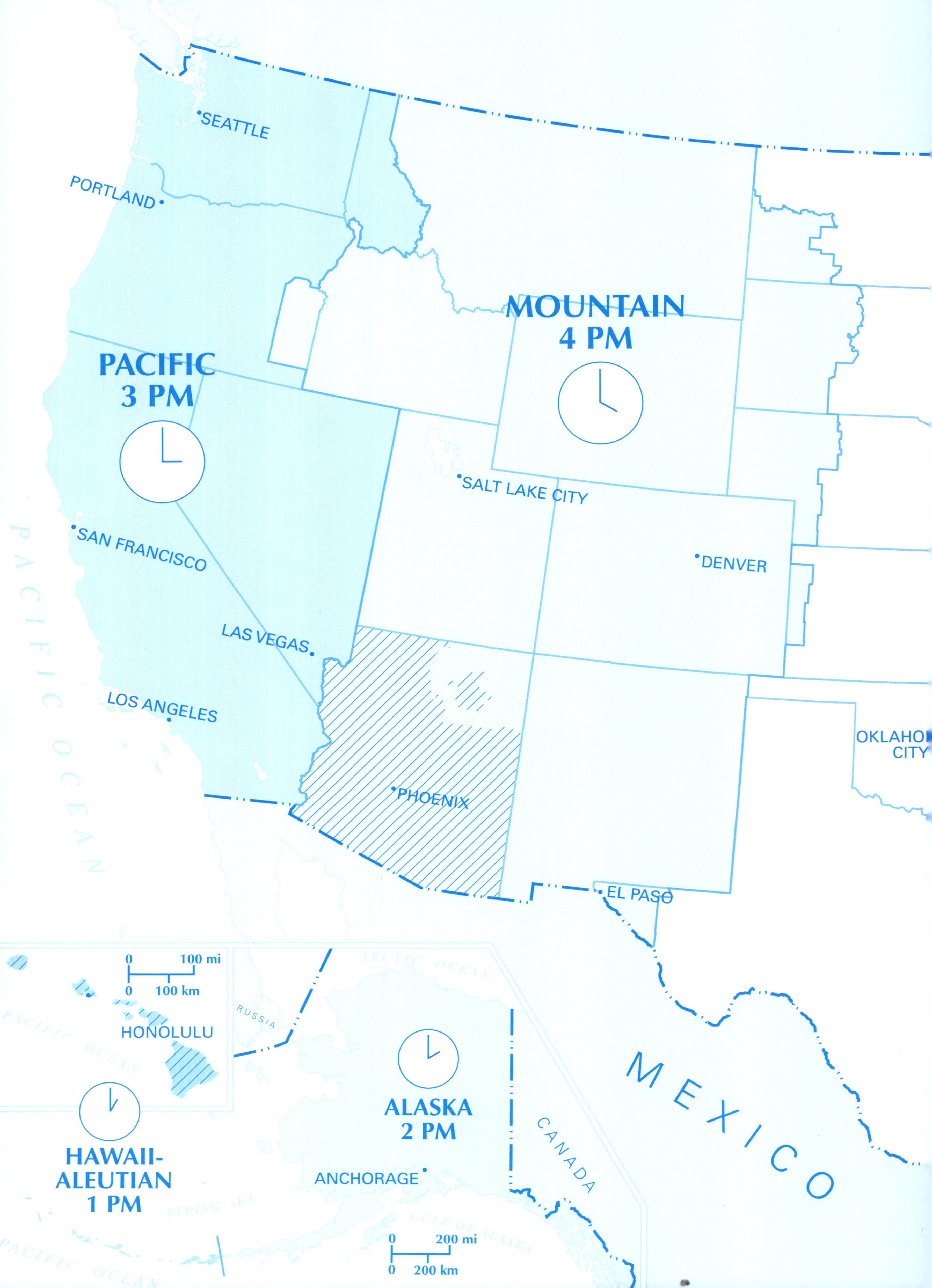

SEATTLE
PORTLAND
MOUNTAIN
4 PM
PACIFIC
3 PM
SALT LAKE CITY
SAN FRANCISCO
DENVER
PACIFIC OCEAN
LAS VEGAS
LOS ANGELES
OKLAHOMA
CITY
PHOENIX
EL PASO
0 100 mi
0 100 km
RUSSIA
ARCTIC OCEAN
PACIFIC OCEAN
HONOLULU
MEXICO
ALASKA
2 PM
CANADA
HAWAII-
ALEUTIAN
1 PM
ANCHORAGE
BERING SEA
GULF OF ALASKA
0 200 mi
0 200 km
PACIFIC OCEAN